The Oxford

GENERAL EDITOR

HENRY VAUGHAN (1621–95) was b⋯⋯⋯⋯⋯⋯⋯⋯⋯⋯
by-Usk, in Breconshire, and may, ⋯⋯⋯ ⋯⋯ twin brother Thomas, have spoken Welsh as his earliest language. After attending Oxford he went to London for the study of law, but this plan was broken off by the outbreak of civil war in 1642. Returning to his home in Wales, he seems to have joined the King's army there in 1645, and may have participated in the battle of Rowton Heath. He deeply resented the overthrow of the monarchy and the established Church in the late 1640s, years which also saw the death of a much-loved younger brother. These events coincided with the development of Vaughan's intense admiration for the poetry of George Herbert, demonstrated in *Silex Scintillans* (1650), where Vaughan transcends his earlier secular poems by creating religious poetry in a manner strongly influenced by Herbert. After the second edition of *Silex Scintillans* (1655) he wrote little poetry, but pursued for his remaining forty years a successful career as a country physician in Breconshire. His poems received little attention until the nineteenth century; today it is generally recognized that his poems at their best can 'match' Herbert's, as he hoped.

LOUIS L. MARTZ is retired Sterling Professor of English at Yale University. He is the author of five books on seventeenth-century poetry: *The Poetry of Meditation*, *The Paradise Within*, *The Wit of Love*, *Milton: Poet of Exile*, and *From Renaissance to Baroque*. He is co-editor of Thomas More's *Dialogue of Comfort* in the Yale edition of More's works. He has also written extensively on twentieth-century poetry, and has edited both the *Collected Poems* and the *Selected Poems* of 'H.D.'.

FRANK KERMODE, retired King Edward VII Professor of English literature at Cambridge, is the author of many books, including *Romantic Image*, *The Sense of an Ending*, *The Classic*, *The Genius of Secrecy*, *Forms of Attention*, and *History and Value*; he is also co-editor with John Hollander of *The Oxford Anthology of English Literature*.

THE OXFORD POETRY LIBRARY

GENERAL EDITOR: FRANK KERMODE

Matthew Arnold	*Miriam Allott*
William Blake	*Michael Mason*
Lord Byron	*Jerome McGann*
Samuel Taylor Coleridge	*Heather Jackson*
John Dryden	*Keith Walker*
Thomas Hardy	*Samuel Hynes*
George Herbert	*Louis Martz*
Gerard Manley Hopkins	*Catherine Phillips*
Ben Jonson	*Ian Donaldson*
John Keats	*Elizabeth Cook*
Andrew Marvell	*Frank Kermode and Keith Walker*
John Milton	*Jonathan Goldberg and Stephen Orgel*
Alexander Pope	*Pat Rogers*
Sir Philip Sidney	*Katherine Duncan-Jones*
Henry Vaughan	*Louis Martz*
William Wordsworth	*Stephen Gill and Duncan Wu*

The Oxford Poetry Library

Henry Vaughan

Edited by
LOUIS L. MARTZ

Oxford   New York
OXFORD UNIVERSITY PRESS
1995

Oxford University Press, Walton Street, Oxford OX2 6DP
Oxford New York
Athens Auckland Bangkok Bombay
Calcutta Cape Town Dar es Salaam Delhi
Florence Hong Kong Istanbul Karachi
Kuala Lumpur Madras Madrid Melbourne
Mexico City Nairobi Paris Singapore
Taipei Tokyo Toronto
and associated companies in
Berlin Ibadan

Oxford is a trade mark of Oxford University Press

© Introduction, edited text, and editorial matter, Louis L. Martz 1995

This selection first published in the Oxford Poetry Library 1995

British Library Cataloguing in Publication Data
Data available

Library of Congress Cataloging in Publication Data
Data available
ISBN 0-19-282302-7

1 3 5 7 9 10 8 6 4 2

Printed in Great Britain by
Biddles Ltd
Guildford and King's Lynn

Contents

Introduction   xi

Acknowledgements   xix

Chronology   xx

Note on the Text   xxii

SILEX SCINTILLANS, OR SACRED POEMS AND PRIVATE
  EJACULATIONS, 1650   1

Authoris (de se) Emblema   2

The Dedication   3

Regeneration   3

Death. A Dialogue   6

Resurrection and Immortality   7

Day of Judgement   9

Religion   11

The Search   13

Isaac's Marriage   15

The British Church   17

The Lamp   18

Man's Fall and Recovery   19

The Shower   20

Distraction   21

The Pursuit   22

Mount of Olives
  I. *'Sweet, sacred hill! on whose fair brow'*   22

The Incarnation and Passion   23

The Call   24

'Thou that know'st for whom I mourn'   25

Vanity of Spirit   26

The Retreat   27

'Come, come, what do I here?'   28

Midnight 29

Content 30

'Joy of my life! while left me here' 31

The Storm 32

The Morning-watch 33

The Evening-watch. A Dialogue 34

'Silence and stealth of days! 'tis now' 34

Church Service 35

Burial 36

Cheerfulness 37

'Sure, there's a tie of bodies! and as they' 38

Peace 39

The Passion 39

Rom. Cap. 8. ver. 19 41

The Relapse 42

The Resolve 43

The Match 44

Rules and Lessons 45

Corruption 49

H. Scriptures 50

Unprofitableness 51

Christ's Nativity 51

The Check 53

Disorder and Frailty 54

Idle Verse 56

Son-days 57

Repentance 58

The Burial of an Infant 60

Faith 61

The Dawning 62

Admission 63

Praise 64

Dressing	66
Easter-day	67
Easter Hymn	68
The Holy Communion	68
Psalm 121	70
Affliction	70
The Tempest	71
Retirement	73
Love and Discipline	75
The Pilgrimage	76
The Law and the Gospel	77
The World	78
The Mutiny	80
The Constellation	81
The Shepherds	83
Misery	85
The Sap	88
Mount of Olives	
II. 'When first I saw true beauty, and thy joys'	89
Man	90
'I walked the other day (to spend my hour)'	91
Begging	
I. 'King of Mercy, King of Love'	93
SILEX SCINTILLANS: POEMS AND PREFATORY MATTER ADDED IN 1655	97
The Author's Preface to the following Hymns	97
The Dedication	102
'Vain wits and eyes'	104
Ascension-day	105
Ascension Hymn	106
'They are all gone into the world of light!'	107
White Sunday	109

The Proffer   111

Cock-crowing   112

The Star   114

The Palm-tree   115

Joy   116

The Favour   117

The Garland   117

Love-sick   118

Trinity Sunday   119

Psalm 104   119

The Bird   122

The Timber   123

The Jews   125

Begging
    II. *'O, do not go! thou know'st, I'll die!'*   126

Palm Sunday   127

Jesus Weeping
    I. *'Blessed, unhappy city! dearly loved'*   129

The Daughter of Herodias   129

Jesus Weeping
    II. *'My dear, Almighty Lord! why dost thou weep?'*   130

Providence   132

The Knot   133

The Ornament   134

St. Mary Magdalen   134

The Rainbow   136

The Seed Growing Secretly   137

'As time one day by me did pass'   139

'Fair and young light! my guide to holy'   140

The Stone   142

The Dwelling-place   143

The Men of War   144

The Ass   145

The Hidden Treasure   147
Child-hood   148
The Night   149
Abel's Blood   151
Righteousness   152
Anguish   154
Tears   154
Jacob's Pillow and Pillar   155
The Agreement   156
The Day of Judgement   159
Psalm 65   160
The Throne   161
Death   162
The Feast   163
The Obsequies   165
The Waterfall   166
Quickness   167
The Wreath   168
The Queer   168
The Book   169
To the Holy Bible   170
L'Envoy   171

Notes   174
Further Reading   226
Index of Titles and First Lines   229

Introduction

The language of Henry Vaughan's poetry derives much of its power from two sources that reverberate throughout his poems: the Bible and the poetry of George Herbert. Indeed Vaughan treats Herbert's poetry as virtually a continuation of sacred scripture, and he echoes Herbert's words almost as much as he echoes the Bible. Vaughan is following here the common Renaissance practice of creative imitation, usually displayed, as with Ben Jonson, in the imitation of classical authors: Martial, Juvenal, Horace. But for Vaughan, Herbert is the prime Christian classic, a 'true saint and a seer', a writer of 'incomparable prophetic poems', and 'the first that with any effectual success attempted a diversion of this foul and overflowing stream' of secular poetry in England.[1] Consequently, the first edition of *Silex Scintillans* (1650) seems designed, even in its physical form and size, as a companion to Herbert's *Temple*—but a companion with its own individual integrity.

These echoes of Herbert and the Bible provide the instruments through which Vaughan can explore and express his own genius: his individual apprehension of the divine presence in external nature and in the self. The older critics who associated Vaughan with Wordsworth were not far wrong, for Vaughan stands almost alone among poets of his era in his appreciation of the vitality of the Creation—an appreciation shared by Milton in the seventh book of *Paradise Lost*. Vaughan's advice in *Rules and Lessons* is enough to distinguish him at once from Herbert, even as he follows here the stanza-form and epigrammatic manner of Herbert's *Church-porch*:

> Walk with thy fellow-creatures: note the *hush*
> And *whispers* amongst them. There's not a *spring*,
> Or *leaf* but hath his *morning-hymn*; Each *bush*
> And *oak* doth know *I AM*; canst thou not sing? . . .
>
> To heighten thy *devotions*, and keep low
> All mutinous thoughts, what business e'er thou hast
> Observe God in his works; here *fountains* flow,
> *Birds* sing, *beasts* feed, *fish* leap, and th' *Earth* stands fast;

[1] *Mount of Olives*, Vaughan's *Works*, ed. L. C. Martin (2nd edn., Oxford, 1957), 186; and the 1655 Preface, below, p. 100.

> Above are restless *motions*, running *lights*,
> Vast circling *azure*, giddy *clouds*, days, nights.
>
> When *seasons* change, then lay before thine eyes
> His wondrous *Method*; mark the various *scenes*
> In heav'n; *hail, thunder, rainbows, snow*, and *ice*,
> *Calms, tempests, light*, and *darkness* by his means;
>   Thou canst not miss his praise; each *tree, herb, flower*
>   Are shadows of his *wisdom* and his *pow'r*.

Vaughan places this advice for daily living exactly in the middle of his book: twenty-four stanzas, one for every hour of the day, whereas Herbert has presented his advice in seventy-seven stanzas (a perfect number) that prepare the reader to enter the fabric of his interior *Church*, with all its ecclesiastical symbolism.

The world of *Silex Scintillans* is utterly different from that of Herbert's *Temple*. Vaughan is writing these poems in the period 1648–54, after the defeat of Charles I and the dissolution of the established Church of England. Vaughan, as a staunch royalist who appears to have fought in Charles's army, and a strong believer in the 'British Church', must find his solace in the three 'Books' cultivated by the ancient Augustinian tradition: the Book of Scripture, the Book of Nature, and the Book of the Soul. Along with this tradition Vaughan's vision of the universe was strongly influenced by the popular occult philosophy in which his twin brother Thomas was deeply learned: the peculiar amalgam of Neoplatonism, magic, alchemy, medicine, and astrology deriving from the writings attributed to the mythical Hermes Trismegistus ('Thrice-great Hermes'), works dating from the first three centuries of the Christian era.[2] The third poem in Vaughan's book, *Resurrection and Immortality*, shows clearly the impact of this philosophy, with its belief in 'that renewing breath | that binds and loosens death' and its view that

> a preserving spirit doth still pass
> Untainted through this mass,
> Which doth resolve, produce, and ripen all
>   That to it fall . . .

It was this philosophy, together with the words of St Paul (Romans 8: 19–22) concerning 'the earnest expectation of the creature', that

[2] See the studies by Elizabeth Holmes and Ross Garner, and Alan Rudrum's edition of Thomas Vaughan's *Works* (listed in Further Reading).

supported Vaughan's no doubt intuitive feeling for the sentient life in nature.

Above all, it is the engraved title-page of *Silex 1650* that dramatizes the immense difference between the works of Vaughan and Herbert. Here the hand of God reaches forth from the cloud to strike with steel the flinty heart, producing the fire of love and the tears (and blood?) of repentance, as through the broken wall of the heart we can discern the features of a man within, while along the edges of the heart (now made flesh) we may also find two (or perhaps three) faces in profile. *Regeneration*, the opening poem, then presents an allegorical version of this experience of 'sudden illumination' (to use Eliot's words). Answering a mysterious call, the pilgrim of this poem is led into a 'fair, fresh field' reserved for 'Prophets, and friends of God'. From there he sees a grove

> Of stately height, whose branches met
> And mixed on every side;
> I entered, and once in
> (Amazed to see't)
> Found all was changed, and a new spring
> Did all my senses greet . . .

The pilgrim has been born again.

We may read the poem as an allegory of Christian conversion— or as a biographical experience. What actually happened we will never know. We do know that some time during the early 1640s, at the outbreak of civil war, Vaughan gave up his study of law in London, during which, as his early secular poetry makes plain, he became well versed in the poetry being produced there by the sons of Ben Jonson. Returning to his native Wales, in the valley of the Usk, he at some point took up or returned to his studies in the 'Hermetic philosophy', and these studies, it seems, led him towards his later, forty-year career as a country physician in Breconshire. He renounced his early secular verse (see *Mount of Olives* (I) and *Idle Verse*) and delayed the publication of his secular volume *Olor Iscanus* until 1651, though the preface is dated 17 December 1647. The death of his brother William in 1648, the destruction of his beloved 'British Church', the execution of his king—all these events no doubt played their part in Vaughan's changing attitude towards life and poetry. His identification of himself as 'Henry Vaughan Silurist' on the title-page of *Silex 1650* shows his determined loyalty to Wales, for *Silures* was the name given by Tacitus to the Welsh tribe of Vaughan's region which fiercely opposed the Roman conquest[3] (does this imply an equal opposition to the powers now victorious in England?).

Whatever the causes, in 1650 Vaughan emerges as a poet significantly different from the poet of his early secular verses, in theme, in style, in quality. He has learnt from Herbert the use of easy colloquial language in poetical conversations with the self, and he uses that language flexibly in variant stanza-forms, as Herbert did. But he does not give up his earlier training in the School of Ben, which also practised a colloquial mode, especially in the couplet form, which Vaughan uses in many of his best poems—a form not often used by Herbert. Indeed this sort of couplet rhetoric invades many of Vaughan's stanzaic poems, which often rhyme in couplets, with lines of varying length. Vaughan is his own man; when he echoes a Herbertian title or phrase, the context is usually quite different; Herbert's words, like the words of the Bible, have become a part of Vaughan's own vocabulary, and so he uses them as he will.

Vaughan's best manner (unlike Herbert's mode of concentrated wit) is diffuse, expansive, earnest, groping, as he seeks to explore or recover the memory of an inner light. His poem *Mount of Olives* (II) is a companion piece to Herbert's *Jordan* (II) and *The Glance*; it is replete with Herbertian echoes, but its floating, associative, incremental movement, done in fluent pentameter couplets, is all Vaughan's own, as its sense of actual landscape is his own:

> So have I known some beauteous *paisage* rise
> In sudden flowers and arbours to my eyes,
> And in the depth and dead of winter bring
> To my cold thoughts a lively sense of spring.

As this whole poem implies, the centre of Vaughan's poetical inspiration lies in such memories of moments of 'light'; moments of a felt, experienced unity with the Creation and with the divine power working through this Creation. The basic drama that runs throughout his poetry has little to do with theological issues or with internal debates: his best poems either enact a search for a light that has disappeared, or break forth in praise of a moment when the vision of a possible unity of all being has been glimpsed, as in *The Morning-watch*:

[3] See Tacitus, *Annals* 12. 32–3, 39–40, and *Agricola* 11, 17.

> O joys! Infinite sweetness! with what flowers,
> And shoots of glory, my soul breaks and buds!
>   All the long hours
>   Of night and rest
>   Through the still shrouds
>   Of sleep and clouds,
>   This dew fell on my breast;
>   O how it *bloods*,
> And *spirits* all my earth! hark! In what rings,
> And *hymning circulations* the quick world
>   Awakes and sings . . .

The outer world of *Man* is a sombre scene:

> He knows he hath a home, but scarce knows where,
>   He says it is so far
> That he hath quite forgot how to go there . . .
> Man is the shuttle, to whose winding quest
>   And passage through these looms
> God ordered motion, but ordained no rest.

But in nature, in herbs and stars, in vivid and sustained reading of
the Bible, and sometimes in the depths of the self, Vaughan can
find the sense of unity with the divine that he is seeking.

Thus in *Religion* Vaughan moves intimately within the 'leaves' of
the Bible:

> My God, when I walk in those groves
> And leaves thy spirit doth still fan,
> I see in each shade that there grows
> An angel talking with a man.
>
> Under a *juniper*, some house,
> Or the cool *myrtle's* canopy,
> Others beneath an *oak's* green boughs,
> Or at some *fountain's* bubbling eye . . .

In *Vanity of Spirit*, pursuing a mode of Augustinian meditation, he
seems to attain a glimpse of the shattered Image of God within the
self. In *Corruption* he imagines the life and landscapes of the earth
not long after the Fall:

> Sure, it was so. Man in those early days
>   Was not all stone and earth,
> He shined a little, and by those weak rays
>   Had some glimpse of his birth. . . .

> He sighed for Eden, and would often say,
> *Ah! what bright days were those!*
> Nor was Heav'n cold unto him; for each day
> The valley, or the mountain
> Afforded visits, and still Paradise lay
> In some green shade, or fountain.

Now all is changed:

> All's in deep sleep and night; thick darkness lies
> And hatcheth o'er thy people;
> But hark! what trumpet's that? what Angel cries
> *Arise! Thrust in thy sickle.*

Maintaining the contrast, *The World* encloses all the dark sins and follies of humankind within that 'great *Ring* of pure and endless light' with which the poem opens and ends.

Mainly Vaughan proceeds by the sort of interior search found in the next-to-last poem of *Silex 1650*, 'I walked the other day (to spend my hour)'. Here the fluent, associative movement of thought begins with the 'gallant flower'—a phrase borrowed from Herbert—but this flower is remembered growing from the 'soil' of a certain 'field'. He recalls how in winter he 'digged about' and finally found 'the warm Recluse'—'Where fresh and green | He lived of us unseen.' This personification of the root, with religious overtones, leads toward a sudden shift into a memory of the deathbed or grave of the dead brother ('I threw the clothes quite o'er his head'), and from here by an easy transition into a prayer that the speaker may 'track' the 'steps' of God in the Creation, 'And by those hid ascents climb to that day | Which breaks from thee | Who art in all things, though invisibly . . . '

> There, hid in thee, show me his life again
> At whose dumb urn
> Thus all the year I mourn.

The quiet conclusion returns the poem to earth and to the memory of the beloved brother, drawing the whole poem together. It is a poem well placed at the close of *Silex 1650*, for it seems, in Vaughan's associative way, to draw the whole volume together with an action of the whole man in meditation. The contrast between the 'day' that breaks from God and the mourner at the 'dumb urn' completes the imagery of light against darkness that runs in many patterns throughout the book: the beams, flames, fires, rays, sunshine, the 'fiery thread' of stars, the 'train of lights' remembered sadly from 'those sunshine days' of Eden, the 'fiery-liquid light' that 'some say' makes up the heavens—all these and many other flashes of light play off against the images of cloud, mist, shadow, veil, dust, and grave[4] that constitute the 'thick darkness' of this life. *Silex Scintillans*: the flashing flint: the search to remember, maintain, or recover the 'ray' thus provides the volume's unifying imagery and central theme.

The large body of new poems added in 1655 creates a subtle shift in the dominant tone and meaning of the book, a change in which some of the causes may perhaps be glimpsed in *Begging (II)*:

> My sins long since have made thee strange,
> A very stranger unto me;
> No morning-meetings since this change,
> Nor evening-walks have I with thee.
>
> Why is my God thus slow and cold,
> When I am most, most sick and sad?
> Well fare those blessèd days of old
> When thou didst hear the *weeping lad*!

Something has happened between 1650 and 1655 to change the dominant tone, as Vaughan suggests in the enigmatic words of the prose preface that he added for the 1655 edition (in which the unsold sheets of 1650 were bound up with new matter): 'By the last poems in the book (were not that mistake here prevented) you would judge all to be fatherless, and the edition posthume; for (indeed) *I was nigh unto death*, and am still at no great distance from it; which was the necessary reason for that solemn and accomplished dress, you will now find this impression in.' What does he mean by the 'solemn and accomplished dress' of this second edition? First of all, perhaps, he refers to the removal of the dramatic title-page of 1650, with its engraved emblem, and its replacement by a sober, even sombre, printed title-page bearing the motto from Job that begins 'Where is God my Maker, who giveth Songs in the night?' The earlier title-page had no need to ask that question. Following the prose preface we have now the solemn series of biblical texts, a chain of verses woven into a personal psalm of prayer and thanksgiving for deliverance from death. And

---

[4] See Frank Kermode, 'The Private Imagery of Henry Vaughan', *Review of English Studies*, NS 1 (1950), 206–25.

then we have the extended verses of dedication, where the new portion begins by saying 'Dear Lord, 'tis finished!' That is, the book of poems (and perhaps the life that wrote them) is finished: the book is truly 'accomplished', done, and the poems of the second part, with all their frequent laments, move towards a faith consolidated, stable, and affirmed—ready for death. Stable and affirmed, yes, but except for eight or nine poems that show the poet at his best, the new poems do not work at the level generally though not always achieved in 1650. They rely more overtly on the Bible than the poems of 1650, and many seem to struggle for utterance, as in *Child-hood* (a poem that one might compare with *The Retreat* of 1650). The 1655 volume has a completeness of its own, but it is not the vital unity of 1650, where, as one looks back, everything seems to radiate from the face within the blazing, weeping heart on the title-page, while the opening allegory of *Regeneration*, with its echoes of Herbert's *Pilgrimage*, its contrast of light and dark, and its garden that is both natural and biblical, foretells the themes and images that run throughout and bind together the whole of *Silex 1650*.

LOUIS L. MARTZ

Yale University

Acknowledgements

I wish to thank the general editor, Frank Kermode, for his careful scrutiny of the introduction and notes, and for a number of helpful suggestions. I am indebted to frequent discussions with my former colleague, Conrad Russell, for a better understanding of the religious situation in seventeenth-century England. For assistance in the preparation of the modernized text and the notes I am grateful to Claire Preston and JoLynn Bennett. The notes are frequently indebted to the annotation provided in earlier editions of Vaughan by Martin, Fogle, and Rudrum, as listed in Further Reading. I also wish to thank the staff of several libraries whose courtesies have helped to advance the work: the Bodleian Library, the Beinecke Rare Book and Manuscript Library of Yale University, and the Sterling Memorial Library of Yale. The Bodleian Library has supplied photographs for the reproductions of title-pages: *Silex Scintillans*, 1650 (Don. f. 208) and *Silex Scintillans*, 1655 (Arch. A f. 106). I am grateful to Martha Achilles for her careful preparation of the typescript. Finally, I wish to thank Hilary O'Shea, Simon Mason, and George Miller for constant advice, and Richard Jeffery for his scrupulous reading of the notes.

L.L.M.

Chronology

1621   Henry and his twin brother Thomas born at Newton-by-Usk, in the parish of Llansantffraed, Breconshire, Wales.

1632–8   Henry and Thomas taught by Matthew Herbert, a schoolmaster and clergyman at Llangattock.

1637   Death of Ben Jonson.

1638   Thomas Vaughan admitted to Jesus College, Oxford, 4 May. No records for Henry, but the assumption is that he also attended Oxford at this time.

1640   Leaves Oxford to study law in London. Here comes under the influence of the poetical sons of Ben Jonson.

1642   Returns to his home in Breconshire at outbreak of civil war.

1643–5?   Serves as secretary to Judge Marmaduke Lloyd, of Brecon.

1645   Appears to have joined the armed forces being raised for King Charles in Wales: evidently took part in battle of Rowton Heath, near Chester (24 September), a disastrous defeat for the King. Archbishop Laud executed (10 January). Book of Common Prayer disestablished (4 January).

1646   *Poems, with the Tenth Satire of Juvenal Englished*. Married to Catherine Wise, perhaps about this time.

1647   Prepares a second volume of secular poetry, with dedication dated 17 December 1647; later issued with changes as *Olor Iscanus*, 1651.

1648   14 July, Vaughan's younger brother William dies. Second Civil War; the King's forces defeated.

1649   30 January, King Charles executed.

1650   *Silex Scintillans*, first edition.
Thomas Vaughan publishes four treatises on 'Hermetic philosophy': *Anthroposophia Theomagica*, *Anima Magica Abscondita*, *Magia Adamica*, and *The Man-Mouse*, the last an answer to an attack by Henry More on the first two treatises.

1651   *Olor Iscanus*. Containing occasional and memorial poems, verse translations from Ovid (poems in exile), Ausonius, Boethius, and Casimir, with translations of four short prose pieces, two by Plutarch, one by Maximus of Tyre, and one by Antonio de Guevara.
Thomas Vaughan publishes another 'Hermetic' treatise, *Lumen*

de Lumine: or A New Magical Light Discovered; and *The Second Wash*, another answer to his opponent Henry More.

1652 *The Mount of Olives: or, Solitary Devotions*, a prose handbook for private meditations, followed by an original prose work, *Man in Darkness, or, A Discourse of Death*, and a translation of a treatise attributed to Anselm, *Man in Glory.*
Thomas Vaughan publishes two more 'Hermetic' treatises, *Aula Lucis, or, The House of Light*, and *The Fame and Confession of the Fraternity . . . of the Rosy Cross.*

1653–4 Suffers serious illness.

1654 *Flores Solitudinis. Certain Rare and Elegant Pieces . . . Collected in his Sickness and Retirement.* Contains the following translations: *Of Temperance and Patience* and *Of Life and Death*, by Johannes Eusebius Nierembergius (a Jesuit); *The World Contemned*, by Eucherius, Bishop of Lyons (5th century); and the *Life of Blessed Paulinus . . . Bishop of Nola* (d.431), largely a translation of a Latin life by the Jesuit Francesco Sacchini.

1655 *Silex Scintillans*, second edition, enlarged.
Translation of *Hermetical Physic*, by Henry Nollius.
About this time (?) begins the practice of medicine. His first wife has died, and he marries, perhaps in this year, her sister Elizabeth. Thomas Vaughan publishes his last 'Hermetic' treatise, *Euphrates, or The Waters of the East; Being a short Discourse of that Secret Fountain, whose Water flows from Fire; and carries in it the Beams of the Sun and Moon.*

1657 Translation of *The Chymist's Key*, by Henry Nollius.

1660 Restoration of Charles II.

1666 Thomas Vaughan dies.

1678 *Thalia Rediviva.* A collection of early and late poems hitherto unpublished.

1695 23 April. Henry Vaughan dies; burial in Llansantffraed churchyard.

Note on the Text

The modernized text here presented is based upon the old-spelling text provided by the edition of Vaughan's *Works* edited by L. C. Martin, in the Oxford English Texts (2nd edn., Oxford, 1957). Here and there old forms and spellings have been retained for special reasons of meaning and sound. The punctuation, in accord with the practice of Martin, generally follows that of 1650 and 1655. In Vaughan's poems the use of italics has been retained, except for proper names, since Vaughan uses the italic to indicate special meanings: biblical echoes, technical terms, multiple meanings, and the like; the typography serves rather as the words 'pray mark' in stanza 8 of *Regeneration*.

Silex Scintillans:
or
SACRED POEMS
and
Private Eiaculations
By
Henry Vaughan Silurist

LONDON, Printed by T.W. for H.Blunden
at ye Castle in Cornehill . 1650

Authoris (de se) Emblema

Tentasti, fateor, sine vulnere saepius, et me
  Consultum voluit Vox, sine voce, frequens;
Ambivit placido divinior aura meatu,
  Et frustra sancto murmure praemonuit.
Surdus eram, mutusque Silex: Tu (quanta tuorum
  Cura tibi est!) alia das renovare via,
Permutas curam: iamque irritatus Amorem
  Posse negas, et vim, Vi, superare paras,
Accedis propior, molemque, et saxea rumpis
  Pectora, fitque Caro, quod fuit ante Lapis.   10
En lacerum! Coelosque tuos ardentia tandem
  Fragmenta, et liquidas ex Adamante genas.
Sic olim undantes Petras, Scopulosque vomentes
  Curasti, O populi providus usque tui!
Quam miranda tibi manus est! Moriendo, revixi;
  Et fractas jam sum ditior inter opes.

[The Author's Emblem (concerning himself)

You have often touched me, I confess, without a wound, and your *Voice*, without a voice, has often sought to counsel me; your diviner breath has encompassed me with its calm motion, and in vain has cautioned me with its sacred murmur. I was deaf and dumb: a *Flint*: You (how great care you take of your own!) try to revive another way, you change the remedy; and now angered you say that *Love* has no power, and you prepare to conquer force with *Force*, you come closer, you break through the *Rocky* barrier of my heart, and it is made *Flesh* that was before a *Stone*. Behold me torn asunder! and at last the *Fragments* burning toward your skies, and the cheeks streaming with tears out of the *Adamant*. Thus once upon a time you made the *Rocks* flow and the *Crags* gush, oh ever provident of your people! How marvellous toward me is your hand! In *Dying*, I have been born again; and in the midst of my *shattered means* I am now *richer*.]

The Dedication

My God, thou that didst die for me,
These thy death's fruits I offer thee.
Death that to me was life and light
But dark and deep pangs to thy sight.
Some drops of thy all-quick'ning blood
Fell on my heart, these made it bud
And put forth thus, though, Lord, before
The ground was cursed, and void of store.
   Indeed, I had some here to hire
Which long resisted thy desire,   10
That stoned thy servants, and did move
To have thee murthered for thy Love,
But, Lord, I have expelled them, and so bent
Beg thou wouldst take thy tenant's rent.

SILEX SCINTILLANS

Regeneration

A ward, and still in bonds, one day
      I stole abroad,
It was high-spring, and all the way
    Primrosed, and hung with shade;
     Yet, was it frost within,
        And surly winds
Blasted my infant buds, and sin
     Like clouds eclipsed my mind.

2

Stormed thus, I straight perceived my spring
      Mere stage and show,   10
My walk a monstrous, mountained thing
     Rough-cast with rocks and snow;
     And as a pilgrim's eye
        Far from relief,
Measures the melancholy sky
     Then drops, and rains for grief,

3

So sighed I upwards still, at last
          'Twixt steps, and falls
I reached the pinnacle, where placed
          I found a pair of scales,   20
          I took them up and laid
               In th' one late pains,
The other smoke, and pleasures weighed
          But proved the heavier grains;

4

With that, some cried, *Away*; straight I
          Obeyed, and led
Full East, a fair, fresh field could spy
          Some called it, *Jacob's Bed*;
          A virgin-soil, which no
               Rude feet e'er trod,   30
Where (since he stepped there) only go
          Prophets, and friends of God.

5

Here, I reposed; but scarce well set,
          A grove descried
Of stately height, whose branches met
          And mixed on every side;
          I entered, and once in
               (Amazed to see't)
Found all was changed, and a new spring
          Did all my senses greet;   40

6

The unthrift sun shot vital gold
          A thousand pieces,
And heaven its azure did unfold
          Chequered with snowy fleeces,
          The air was all in spice
               And every bush
A garland wore; thus fed my eyes
          But all the ear lay hush.

7

Only a little fountain lent
   Some use for ears,   50
And on the dumb shades language spent,
   The music of her tears;
   I drew her near, and found
    The cistern full
Of divers stones, some bright, and round,
   Others ill-shaped, and dull.

8

The first (pray mark) as quick as light
   Danced through the flood,
But, th' last more heavy than the night
   Nailed to the Centre stood;   60
   I wondered much, but tired
    At last with thought,
My restless eye that still desired
   As strange an object brought;

9

It was a bank of flowers, where I descried
   (Though 'twas mid-day)
Some fast asleep, others broad-eyed
   And taking in the Ray,
   Here musing long, I heard
    A rushing wind   70
Which still increased, but whence it stirred
   Nowhere I could not find;

10

I turned me round, and to each shade
   Dispatched an eye,
To see, if any leaf had made
   Least motion or reply,
   But while I list'ning sought
    My mind to ease
By knowing, where 'twas, or where not,
   It whispered: *Where I please.*   80

Lord, then said I, *On me one breath,*
And let me die before my death!

Cant. Cap. 5. ver. 17

Arise O North, and come thou South-wind, and blow upon my garden,
that the spices thereof may flow out.

Death

A Dialogue

Soul. 'Tis a sad land, that in one day
          Hath dulled thee thus, when death shall freeze
          Thy blood to ice, and thou must stay
          Tenant for years, and centuries,
          How wilt thou brook't?——

Body. I cannot tell,——
          But if all sense wings not with thee,
          And something still be left the dead,
          I'll wish my curtains off to free
          Me from so dark and sad a bed;   10

          A nest of nights, a gloomy sphere,
          Where shadows thicken, and the cloud
          Sits on the sun's brow all the year,
          And nothing moves without a shroud;

Soul. 'Tis so: but as thou sawest that night
          We travelled in, our first attempts
          Were dull and blind, but custom straight
          Our fears and falls brought to contempt,

          Then, when the ghastly *twelve* was past
          We breathed still for a blushing *East*,   20
          And bade the lazy sun make haste,
          And on sure hopes, though long, did feast;

But when we saw the clouds to crack
And in those crannies light appeared,
We thought the day then was not slack,
And pleased ourselves with what we feared;

Just so it is in death. But thou
Shalt in thy mother's bosom sleep
Whilst I each minute groan to know
How near Redemption creeps.   30

Then shall we meet to mix again, and met,
'Tis last good-night, our Sun shall never set.

Job. Cap. 10. ver. 21. 22

*Before I go whence I shall not return, even to the land of darkness, and
the shadow of death;*
*A land of darkness, as darkness itself, and of the shadow of death,
without any order, and where the light is as darkness.*

Resurrection and Immortality

Heb. Cap. 10. ver. 20

*By that new and living way, which he hath prepared for us, through the
veil, which is his flesh.°*

Body

I

Oft have I seen, when that renewing breath
            That binds and loosens death
Inspired a quick'ning power through the dead
            Creatures abed,
            Some drowsy silk-worm creep
            From that long sleep
And in weak, infant hummings chime and knell
            About her silent cell
Until at last full with the vital Ray
            She winged away,   10
            And proud with life and sense,
                Heav'n's rich expense,
Esteemed (vain things!) of two whole elements

As mean, and span-extents.
Shall I then think such providence will be
                    Less friend to me?
Or that he can endure to be unjust
Who keeps his Covenant even with our dust?

Soul

2

Poor, querulous handful! was't for this
                    I taught thee all that is?   20
Unbowelled nature, showed thee her recruits,
                    And change of suits,
                    And how of death we make
                    A mere mistake,
For no thing can to *Nothing* fall, but still
                    Incorporates by skill,
And then returns, and from the womb of things
                    Such treasure brings
                    As phoenix-like renew'th
                    Both life and youth;   30
For a preserving spirit doth still pass
                    Untainted through this mass,
Which doth resolve, produce, and ripen all
                    That to it fall;
                    Nor are those births which we
                    Thus suffering see
Destroyed at all; but when time's restless wave
                    Their substance doth deprave
And the more noble *Essence* finds his house
                    Sickly and loose,   40
                    He, ever young, doth wing
                    Unto that spring,
And *source* of spirits, where he takes his lot
                    Till time no more shall rot
His passive cottage; which (though laid aside)
                    Like some spruce bride,
Shall one day rise, and clothed with shining light
                    All pure and bright
                    Re-marry to the soul, for 'tis most plain
                    Thou only fall'st to be refined again.   50

3

Then I that here saw darkly in a glass
           But mists and shadows pass,
And, by their own weak *shine*, did search the springs
           And course of things,
       Shall with enlightened Rays
           Pierce all their ways;
And as thou saw'st, I in a thought could go
           To heav'n, or earth below
To read some *star*, or *min'ral*, and in state
           There often sate,   60
       So shalt thou then with me
           (Both winged and free)
Rove in that mighty and eternal light
           Where no rude shade or night
Shall dare approach us; we shall there no more
           Watch stars, or pore
       Through melancholy clouds, and say,
           Would it were day!
One everlasting *Sabbath* there shall run
Without *succession*, and without a *sun*.   70

Dan. Cap. 12. ver. 13

*But go thou thy way until the end be, for thou shalt rest, and stand up
in thy lot, at the end of the days.*

Day of Judgement

When through the North a fire shall rush
           And roll into the East,
And like a fiery torrent brush
           And sweep up South and West,

When all shall stream, and lighten round
           And with surprising flames
Both stars and elements confound
           And quite blot out their names,

When thou shalt spend thy sacred store
        Of thunders in that heat   10
And low as e'er they lay before
        Thy six-days-buildings beat,

When like a scroll the heavens shall pass
        And vanish clean away,
And nought must stand of that vast space
        Which held up night and day,

When one loud blast shall rend the deep,
        And from the womb of earth
Summon up all that are asleep
        Unto a second birth,   20

When thou shalt make the clouds thy seat,
        And in the open air
The quick and dead, both small and great
        Must to thy bar repair;

O then it will be all too late
        To say, *What shall I do?*
Repentance there is out of date
        And so is *mercy* too;

Prepare, prepare me then, O God!
        And let me now begin   30
To feel my loving father's *rod*
        Killing the man of sin!

Give me, O give me crosses here,
        Still more afflictions lend,
That pill, though bitter, is most dear
        That brings health in the end;

Lord, God! I beg nor friends, nor wealth
        But pray against them both;
Three things I'd have, my soul's chief health!
        And one of these seem loath,   40

A living *FAITH*, a *HEART* of flesh,
　　The *WORLD* an enemy,
This last will keep the first two fresh,
　　And bring me, where I'd be.

1 Pet. 4. 7

Now the end of all things is at hand, be you therefore sober, and watching in prayer.

Religion

My God, when I walk in those groves
And leaves thy spirit doth still fan,
I see in each shade that there grows
An angel talking with a man.

Under a *juniper*, some house,
Or the cool *myrtle's* canopy,
Others beneath an *oak's* green boughs,
Or at some *fountain's* bubbling eye;

Here Jacob dreams, and wrestles; there
Elias by a raven is fed,   10
Another time by th' angel, where
He brings him water with his bread;

In Abr'ham's tent the wingèd guests
(O how familiar then was heaven!)
Eat, drink, discourse, sit down, and rest
Until the cool and shady *even*;

Nay thou thyself, my God, in *fire*,
Whirlwinds, and *clouds*, and the *soft voice*
Speak'st there so much, that I admire
We have no conf'rence in these days;   20

Is the truce broke? or 'cause we have
A mediator now with thee,
Dost thou therefore old treaties waive
And by appeals from him decree?

Or is't so, as some green heads say
That now all miracles must cease?
Though thou hast promised they should stay
The tokens of the Church, and peace;

No, no; Religion is a spring
That from some secret, golden mine   30
Derives her birth, and thence doth bring
Cordials in every drop, and wine;

But in her long and hidden course
Passing through the earth's dark veins,
Grows still from better unto worse,
And both her taste and colour stains,

Then drilling on, learns to increase
False echoes and confusèd sounds,
And unawares doth often seize
On veins of sulphur under ground;   40

So poisoned, breaks forth in some clime,
And at first sight doth many please,
But drunk, is puddle, or mere slime
And 'stead of physic, a disease;

Just such a tainted sink we have
Like that Samaritan's dead *well*,
Nor must we for the kernel crave
Because most voices like the *shell*.

Heal then these waters, Lord; or bring thy flock,
Since these are troubled, to the springing rock,   50
Look down great Master of the feast; O shine,
And turn once more our *water* into *wine*!

Cant. Cap. 4. ver. 12

My sister, my spouse is as a garden inclosed, as a spring shut up, and a fountain sealed up.

The Search

'Tis now clear day: I see a Rose
Bud in the bright East, and disclose
The Pilgrim-Sun; all night have I
Spent in a roving ecstasy
To find my Saviour; I have been
As far as Bethlem, and have seen
His inn and cradle; being there
I met the *Wise-men*, asked them where
He might be found, or what star can
Now point him out, grown up a man?   10
To Egypt hence I fled, ran o'er
All her parched bosom to Nile's shore
Her yearly nurse; came back, enquired
Amongst the *Doctors*, and desired
To see the *Temple*, but was shown
A little dust, and for the town
A heap of ashes, where some said
A small bright sparkle was a bed,
Which would one day (beneath the pole)
Awake, and then refine the whole.   20
    Tired here, I come to Sychar; thence
To Jacob's well, bequeathèd since
Unto his sons (where often they
In those calm, golden evenings lay
Wat'ring their flocks, and having spent
Those white days, drove home to the tent
Their *well-fleeced* train; and here (O fate!)
I sit, where once my Saviour sate;
The angry spring in bubbles swelled
Which broke in sighs still, as they filled,   30
And whispered, *Jesus had been there*
But Jacob's children would not hear.
Loath hence to part, at last I rise
But with the fountain in my eyes,
And here a fresh search is decreed:
He must be found, where he did bleed;
I walk the garden, and there see
Ideas of his Agony,

And moving anguishments that set
His blest face in a bloody sweat;　　　　　　　40
I climbed the Hill, perused the Cross
Hung with my gain, and his great loss,
Never did tree bear fruit like this,
Balsam of souls, the body's bliss;
But, O his grave! where I saw lent
(For he had none) a monument,
An undefiled and new-hewed one,
But there was not the *corner-stone*;
Sure (then said I) my quest is vain,
He'll not be found, where he was slain,　　　50
So mild a Lamb can never be
'Midst so much blood and cruelty;
I'll to the wilderness, and can
Find beasts more merciful than man,
He lived there safe, 'twas his retreat
From the fierce Jew, and Herod's heat,
And forty days withstood the fell
And high temptations of hell;
With Seraphins there talkèd he,
His father's flaming ministry,　　　　　　　60
He heav'ned their walks, and with his eyes
Made those wild shades a Paradise,
Thus was the desert sanctified
To be the refuge of his bride;
I'll thither then; see, it is day,
The Sun's broke through to guide my way.
　　But as I urged thus, and writ down
What pleasures should my journey crown,
What silent paths, what shades, and cells,
Fair, virgin-flowers, and hallow'd *wells*　　　70
I should rove in, and rest my head
Where my dear Lord did often tread,
Sug'ring all dangers with success,
Me thought I heard one singing thus;

I

Leave, leave, thy gadding thoughts;
Who pores
and spies

Still out of doors
descries
Within them nought.   80

2

The skin and shell of things
Though fair,
are not
Thy wish, nor pray'r
but got
By mere despair
of wings.

3

To rack old elements,
or dust
and say   90
Sure here he must
needs stay
Is not the way,
nor just.

Search well another world; who studies this,
Travels in clouds, seeks *Manna*, where none is.

Acts Cap. 17. ver. 27, 28

*That they should seek the Lord, if happily they might feel after him,
and find him, though he be not far off from every one of us, for in him we
live, and move, and have our being.*

Isaac's Marriage

Gen. Cap. 24. ver. 63

*And Isaac went out to pray in the field at the even-tide, and he lift up
his eyes, and saw, and behold, the camels were coming.*

Praying! and to be married? It was rare,
But now 'tis monstrous; and that pious care
Though of ourselves, is so much out of date,
That to renew't were to degenerate.
But thou a chosen sacrifice wert given,

And offered up so early unto heaven
Thy flames could not be out; Religion was
Rayed into thee, like beams into a glass,
Where, as thou grewst, it multiplied and shined,
The sacred constellation of thy mind.   10
But being for a bride, prayer was such
A decried course, sure it prevailed not much.
Had'st ne'er an oath, nor compliment? thou wert
An odd dull suitor; hadst thou but the art
Of these our days, thou couldst have coined thee twenty
New sev'ral oaths, and compliments (too) plenty;
O sad and wild excess! and happy those
White days, that durst no impious mirth expose!
When conscience by lewd use had not lost sense,
Nor bold-faced custom banished innocence;   20
Thou hadst no pompous train, nor *antic* crowd
Of young, gay swearers, with their needless, loud
Retinue; all was here smooth as thy bride
And calm like her, or that mild evening-tide;
Yet, hadst thou nobler guests: angels did wind
And rove about thee, guardians of thy mind,
These fetched thee home thy bride, and all the way
Advised thy servant what to do and say;
These taught him at the *well*, and thither brought
The chaste and lovely object of thy thought;   30
But here was ne'er a compliment, not one
Spruce, supple cringe, or studied look put on,
All was plain, modest truth: nor did she come
In *rolls* and *curls*, mincing and stately dumb,
But in a virgin's native blush and fears
Fresh as those roses, which the day-spring wears.
O sweet, divine simplicity! O grace
Beyond a curlèd lock, or painted face!
A pitcher too she had, nor thought it much
To carry that, which some would scorn to touch;   40
With which in mild, chaste language she did woo
To draw him drink, and for his camels too.
    And now thou knewst her coming, it was time
To get thee wings on, and devoutly climb
Unto thy God, for marriage of all states
Makes most unhappy, or most fortunates;

This brought thee forth, where now thou didst undress
Thy soul, and with new pinions refresh
Her wearied wings, which so restored did fly
Above the stars, a track unknown and high,   50
And in her piercing flight perfumed the air,
Scatt'ring the myrrh and incense of thy pray'r.
So from Lahai-roi's well some spicy cloud
Wooed by the sun swells up to be his shroud,
And from his moist womb weeps a fragrant shower,
Which, scattered in a thousand pearls, each flower
And herb partakes, where having stood awhile
And something cooled the parched and thirsty isle,
The thankful earth unlocks herself, and blends
A thousand odours, which (all mixed) she sends   60
Up in one cloud, and so returns the skies
That dew they lent, a breathing sacrifice.
    Thus soared thy soul, who (though young) didst inherit
Together with his blood, thy father's spirit,
Whose active zeal, and tried faith were to thee
Familiar ever since thy infancy.
Others were timed and trained up to't but thou
Didst thy swift years in piety out-grow,
Age made them rev'rend, and a snowy head,
But thou wert so, ere time his snow could shed;   70
Then, who would truly limn thee out, must paint
First, a *young Patriarch*, then a *married Saint*.

The British Church

Ah! he is fled!
And while these here their *mists* and *shadows* hatch,
My glorious head
Doth on those hills of myrrh and incense watch.
Haste, haste my dear,
The soldiers here
Cast in their lots again,
That seamless coat
The Jews touched not,
These dare divide and stain.   10

2

O get thee wings!
Or if as yet (until these clouds depart,
And the day springs)
Thou think'st it good to tarry where thou art,
Write in thy books
My ravished looks,
Slain flock, and pillaged fleeces,
And haste thee so
As a young roe
Upon the mounts of spices.   20

O rosa campi! O lilium convallium! quomodo nunc facta es pabulum aprorum!

The Lamp

'Tis dead night round about: horror doth creep
And move on with the shades; stars nod and sleep,
And through the dark air spin a fiery thread
Such as doth gild the lazy glow-worm's bed.
 Yet, burn'st thou here, a full day; while I spend
My rest in cares, and to the dark world lend
These flames, as thou dost thine to me; I watch
That hour, which must thy life and mine dispatch;
But still thou dost out-go me, I can see
Met in thy flames, all acts of piety;   10
Thy light, is *Charity*; thy heat, is *Zeal*;
And thy aspiring, active fires reveal
Devotion still on wing; then, thou dost weep
Still as thou burn'st, and the warm droppings creep
To measure out thy length, as if thou'dst know
What stock, and how much time were left thee now;
Nor dost thou spend one tear in vain, for still
As thou dissolv'st to them, and they distil,
They're stored up in the socket, where they lie,
When all is spent, thy last, and sure supply, 20
And such is true repentance, ev'ry breath
We spend in sighs, is treasure after death;

Only, one point escapes thee; that thy oil
Is still out with thy flame, and so both fail;
But whensoe'er I'm out, both shall be in,
And where thou mad'st an end, there I'll begin.

Mark Cap. 13. ver. 35

*Watch you therefore, for you know not when the master of the house
cometh, at even, or at midnight, or at the cock-crowing, or in the morning.*

Man's Fall and Recovery

Farewell you everlasting hills! I'm cast
Here under clouds, where storms and tempests blast
    This sullied flower
Robbed of your calm, nor can I ever make
Transplanted thus, one leaf of his t'awake,
    But ev'ry hour
He sleeps and droops, and in this drowsy state
Leaves me a slave to passions, and my fate;
    Besides I've lost
A train of lights, which in those sunshine days   10
Were my sure guides, and only with me stays
    (Unto my cost)
One sullen beam, whose charge is to dispense
More punishment, than knowledge to my sense;
    Two thousand years
I sojourned thus; at last Jeshurun's king
Those famous tables did from Sinai bring;
    These swelled my fears,
Guilts, trespasses, and all this inward awe,
For sin took strength, and vigour from the Law.   20
    Yet have I found
A plenteous way (thanks to that holy one!)
To cancel all that e'er was writ in stone,
    His saving wound
Wept blood, that broke this adamant, and gave
To sinners confidence, life to the grave;
    This makes me span
My father's journeys, and in one fair step

O'er all their pilgrimage and labours leap,
      For God (made man)   30
Reduced th' extent of works of faith; so made
Of their *Red Sea*, a *Spring*; I wash, they wade.

Rom. Cap. 5. ver. 18

As by the offence of one, the fault came on all men to condemnation; so by the righteousness of one, the benefit abounded towards all men to the justification of life.

The Shower

'Twas so, I saw thy birth: that drowsy lake
From her faint bosom breathed thee, the disease
Of her sick waters, and infectious ease.
      But, now at even
      Too gross for heaven,
Thou fall'st in tears, and weep'st for thy mistake.

2

Ah! it is so with me; oft have I pressed
Heaven with a lazy breath, but fruitless this
Pierced not; Love only can with quick access
      Unlock the way,   10
      When all else stray,
The smoke and exhalations of the breast.

3

Yet, if as thou dost melt, and with thy train
Of drops make soft the earth, my eyes could weep
O'er my hard heart, that's bound up and asleep,
      Perhaps at last
      (Some such shower past)
My God would give a sunshine after rain.

Distraction

O knit me, that am crumbled dust! the heap
      Is all dispersed and cheap;
    Give for a handful, but a thought
      And it is bought;
        Hadst thou
Made me a star, a pearl, or a rainbow,
      The beams I then had shot
      My light had lessened not,
        But now
I find myself the less, the more I grow;   10
        The world
Is full of voices; Man is called and hurled
      By each, he answers all,
      Knows ev'ry note and call,
        Hence, still
Fresh dotage tempts, or old usurps his will.
Yet, hadst thou clipped my wings, when coffined in
      This quickened mass of sin,
    And saved that light, which freely thou
      Didst then bestow,   20
        I fear
I should have spurned, and said thou didst forbear;
      Or that thy store was less,
      But now since thou didst bless
        So much,
I grieve, my God! that thou hast made me such.
        I grieve?
O, yes! thou know'st I do; come, and relieve
      And tame, and keep down with thy light
      Dust that would rise, and dim my sight,   30
      Lest left alone too long
      Amidst the noise and throng,
        Oppressèd I
Striving to save the whole, by parcels die.

The Pursuit

Lord! what a busy, restless thing
          Hast thou made man!
Each day and hour he is on wing,
          Rests not a span;
Then having lost the Sun and light
          By clouds surprised
He keeps a commerce in the night
          With air disguised;
Hadst thou given to this active dust
          A state untired,   10
The lost son had not left the husk
          Nor home desired;
That was thy secret, and it is
          Thy mercy too,
For when all fails to bring to bliss,
          Then, this must do.
Ah! Lord! and what a purchase will that be
To take us sick, that sound would not take thee!

Mount of Olives (I)

Sweet, sacred hill! on whose fair brow
My Saviour sate, shall I allow
          Language to love
And idolize some shade, or grove,
Neglecting thee? such ill-placed wit,
Conceit, or call it what you please
          Is the brain's fit,
          And mere disease;

2

Cotswold and Cooper's both have met
With learned swains, and echo yet   10
          Their pipes and wit;
But thou sleep'st in a deep neglect
Untouched by any; and what need

The sheep bleat thee a silly lay
  That heard'st both reed
  And sheepward play?

   3
Yet, if poets mind thee well
They shall find thou art their hill,
  And fountain too,
Their Lord with thee, had most to do;   20
He wept once, walked whole nights on thee,
And from thence (his suff'rings ended)
   Unto glory
   Was attended;

   4
Being there, this spacious ball
Is but his narrow footstool all,
  And what we think
Unsearchable, now with one wink
He doth comprise; but in this air
When he did stay to bear our ill   30
   And sin, this hill
   Was then his chair.

The Incarnation and Passion

Lord! when thou didst thyself undress
Laying by thy robes of glory,
To make us more, thou wouldst be less,
And becam'st a woeful story.

To put on clouds instead of light,
And clothe the morning-star with dust,
Was a translation of such height
As, but in thee, was ne'er expressed;

Brave worms and earth! that thus could have
A God enclosed within your cell,   10
Your maker pent up in a grave,
Life locked in death, heav'n in a shell;

Ah, my dear Lord! what couldst thou spy
In this impure, rebellious clay,
That made thee thus resolve to die
For those that kill thee every day?

O what strange wonders could thee move
To slight thy precious blood and breath!
Sure it was *Love*, my Lord; for *Love*
Is only stronger far than death.   20

The Call

Come my heart! come my head
          In sighs and tears!
'Tis now, since you have lain thus dead
          Some twenty years;
          Awake, awake,
          Some pity take
          Upon yourselves—
Who never wake to groan, nor weep,
Shall be sentenced for their sleep.

2

Do but see your sad estate,   10
          How many sands
Have left us, while we careless sate
          With folded hands;
          What stock of nights,
          Of days and years
          In silent flights
          Stole by our ears,
How ill have we ourselves bestowed
Whose suns are all set in a cloud?

3

Yet, come, and let's peruse them all;   20
          And as we pass,
What sins on every minute fall
          Score on the glass;

Then weigh and rate
Their heavy state
Until
The glass with tears you fill;
That done, we shall be safe and good,
Those beasts were clean, that chewed the cud.

¶

Thou that know'st for whom I mourn,
    And why these tears appear,
That keep'st account, till he return
    Of all his dust left here;
As easily thou mightst prevent
    As now produce these tears,
And add unto that day he went
    A fair supply of years.
But 'twas my sin that forced thy hand
    To cull this *primrose* out,   10
That by thy early choice forewarned
    My soul might look about.
O what a vanity is man!
    How like the eye's quick wink
His cottage fails; whose narrow span
    Begins even at the brink!
Nine months thy hands are fashioning us,
    And many years (alas!)
Ere we can lisp, or ought discuss
    Concerning thee, must pass;   20
Yet have I known thy slightest things,
    A *feather*, or a *shell*,
A *stick*, or *rod* which some chance brings,
    The best of us excel,
Yea, I have known these shreds outlast
    A fair-compacted frame
And for one *twenty* we have past
    Almost outlive our name.
Thus hast thou placed in man's outside
    Death to the common eye,   30
That heaven within him might abide,

And close eternity;
Hence, youth and folly (man's first shame)
 Are put unto the slaughter,
And serious thoughts begin to tame
 The wise-man's madness, *laughter*;
Dull, wretched worms! that would not keep
 Within our first fair bed,
But out of Paradise must creep
 For ev'ry foot to tread;   40
Yet, had our pilgrimage been free,
 And smooth without a thorn,
Pleasures had foiled Eternity,
 And *tares* had choked the *corn*.
Thus by the Cross Salvation runs,
 Affliction is a mother,
Whose painful throes yield many sons,
 Each fairer than the other;
A silent tear can pierce thy throne,
 When loud joys want a wing,   50
And sweeter airs stream from a groan,
 Than any arted string;
Thus, Lord, I see my gain is great,
 My loss but little to it,
Yet something more I must entreat
 And only thou canst do it.
O let me (like him) know my end!
 And be as glad to find it,
And whatsoe'er thou shalt commend,
 Still let thy servant mind it!   60
Then make my soul white as his own,
 My faith as pure and steady,
And deck me, Lord, with the same crown
 Thou hast crowned him already!

Vanity of Spirit

Quite spent with thoughts I left my cell, and lay
Where a shrill spring tuned to the early day.
 I begged here long, and groaned to know

Who gave the clouds so brave a bow,
Who bent the spheres, and circled in
Corruption with this glorious ring,
What is his name, and how I might
Descry some part of his great light.
I summoned nature: pierced through all her store,
Broke up some seals, which none had touched before,   10
 Her womb, her bosom, and her head
 Where all her secrets lay abed
 I rifled quite, and having passed
 Through all the Creatures, came at last
 To search myself, where I did find
 Traces, and sounds of a strange kind.
Here of this mighty spring, I found some drills,
With echoes beaten from th' eternal hills;
 Weak beams, and fires flashed to my sight,
 Like a young East, or moonshine night,   20
 Which showed me in a nook cast by
 A piece of much antiquity,
 With hieroglyphics quite dismembered,
 And broken letters scarce remembered.
I took them up, and (much joyed) went about
T' unite those pieces, hoping to find out
 The mystery; but this near done,
 That little light I had was gone:
 It grieved me much. At last, said I,
 Since in these veils my eclipsed eye   30
 May not approach thee (for at night
 Who can have commerce with the light?),
 I'll disapparel, and to buy
 But one half glance, most gladly die.

The Retreat

Happy those early days! when I
Shined in my angel-infancy.
Before I understood this place
Appointed for my second race,
Or taught my soul to fancy ought

But a white, celestial thought,
When yet I had not walked above
A mile or two, from my first love,
And looking back (at that short space)
Could see a glimpse of his bright face;   10
When on some *gilded cloud*, or *flower*
My gazing soul would dwell an hour,
And in those weaker glories spy
Some shadows of eternity;
Before I taught my tongue to wound
My conscience with a sinful sound,
Or had the black art to dispense
A sev'ral sin to ev'ry sense,
But felt through all this fleshly dress
Bright *shoots* of everlastingness.   20
  O how I long to travel back
And tread again that ancient track!
That I might once more reach that plain,
Where first I left my glorious train,
From whence th' inlightened spirit sees
That shady city of palm trees;
But (ah!) my soul with too much stay
Is drunk, and staggers in the way.
Some men a forward motion love,
But I by backward steps would move,   30
And when this dust falls to the urn
In that state I came return.

¶

Come, come, what do I here?
    Since he is gone
Each day is grown a dozen year,
    And each hour, one;
    Come, come!
   Cut off the sum,
  By these soiled tears!
  (Which only thou
  Know'st to be true)
Days are my fears.   10

2

There's not a wind can stir,
        Or beam pass by,
But straight I think (though far)
        Thy hand is nigh;
        Come, come!
    Strike these lips dumb:
    This restless breath
    That soils thy name,
    Will ne'er be tame
    Until in death.   20

3

Perhaps some think a tomb
        No house of store,
But a dark and sealed up womb,
        Which ne'er breeds more.
        Come, come!
    Such thoughts benumb;
    But I would be
    With him I weep
    Abed, and sleep
    To wake in thee.   30

Midnight

        When to my eyes
(Whilst deep sleep others catches)
        Thine host of spies
The stars shine in their watches,
        I do survey
        Each busy ray,
And how they work and wind,
        And wish each beam
        My soul doth stream,
With the like ardour shined;   10
        What emanations,
        Quick vibrations
And bright stirs are there!

What thin ejections,
Cold affections,
And slow motions here!

2

Thy heav'ns (some say)
Are a fiery-liquid light,
Which mingling aye
Streams, and flames thus to the sight.   20
Come then, my God!
Shine on this blood
And water in one beam
And thou shalt see
Kindled by thee
Both liquors burn and stream.
O what bright quickness,
Active brightness,
And celestial flows
Will follow after   30
On that water,
Which thy spirit blows!

Math. Cap. 3. ver. xi
I indeed baptize you with water unto repentance, but he that cometh
after me, is mightier than I, whose shoes I am not worthy to bear, he shall
baptize you with the holy Ghost, and with fire.

Content

Peace, peace! I know 'twas brave,
But this coarse fleece
I shelter in, is slave
To no such piece.
When I am gone,
I shall no wardrobes leave
To friend, or son
But what their own homes weave,

2

Such, though not proud, nor full,
    May make them weep,   10
And mourn to see the wool
    Outlast the sheep;
    Poor, pious wear!
Hadst thou been rich, or fine
    Perhaps that tear
Had mourned thy loss, not mine.

3

Why then these curled, puffed points,
    Or a laced story?
Death sets all out of joint
    And scorns their glory;   20
    Some love a *Rose*
In hand, some in the skin;
    But cross to those,
I would have mine *within*.

¶

Joy of my life! while left me here,
    And still my love!
How in thy absence thou dost steer
    Me from above!
    A life well led
    This truth commends,
    With quick or dead
    It never ends.

2

Stars are of mighty use: the night
    Is dark and long;   10
The road foul, and where one goes right,
    Six may go wrong.
    One twinkling ray
    Shot o'er some cloud,
    May clear much way
    And guide a crowd.

3

God's Saints are shining lights; who stays
   Here long must pass
O'er dark hills, swift streams, and steep ways
   As smooth as glass;   20
   But these all night
   Like candles, shed
   Their beams, and light
   Us into bed.

4

They are (indeed) our pillar-fires
   Seen as we go,
They are that City's shining spires
   We travel to;
   A swordlike gleam
   Kept man for sin   30
   First *Out*; this beam
   Will guide him *In*.

The Storm

I see the use: and know my blood
   Is not a sea,
But a shallow, bounded flood
   Though red as he;
Yet have I flows, as strong as his,
   And boiling streams that rave
With the same curling force and hiss,
   As doth the mountained wave.

2

But when his waters billow thus,
   Dark storms and wind   10
Incite them to that fierce discuss,
   Else not inclined,
Thus the enlarged, enragèd air
   Uncalms these to a flood,
But still the weather that's most fair
   Breeds tempests in my blood;

3

Lord, then round me with weeping clouds,
   And let my mind
In quick blasts sigh beneath those shrouds
   A spirit-wind,   20
So shall that storm purge this *Recluse*
   Which sinful ease made foul,
And *wind* and *water* to thy use
   Both *wash* and *wing* my soul.

The Morning-watch

O joys! Infinite sweetness! with what flowers,
And shoots of glory, my soul breaks and buds!
   All the long hours
   Of night and rest
   Through the still shrouds
   Of sleep and clouds,
  This dew fell on my breast;
   O how it *bloods*,
And *spirits* all my earth! hark! In what rings,
And *hymning circulations* the quick world   10
   Awakes and sings;
   The rising winds,
   And falling springs,
   Birds, beasts, all things
  Adore him in their kinds.
   Thus all is hurled
In sacred *hymns* and *order*, the great *chime*
And *symphony* of nature. Prayer is
   The world in tune,
   A spirit-voice,   20
   And vocal joys
  Whose echo is heav'n's bliss.
   O let me climb
When I lie down! The pious soul by night
Is like a clouded star, whose beams though said
   To shed their light
   Under some cloud
   Yet are above,

And shine and move   30
Beyond that misty shroud.
So in my bed,
That curtained grave, though sleep, like ashes, hide
My lamp and life, both shall in thee abide.

The Evening-watch

A Dialogue

Farewell! I go to sleep; but when   *Body.*
The day-star springs, I'll wake again.
Go, sleep in peace; and when thou liest   *Soul.*
Unnumbered in thy dust, when all this frame
Is but one dram, and what thou now descriest
In sev'ral parts shall want a name,
Then may his peace be with thee, and each dust
Writ in his book, who ne'er betrayed man's trust!
Amen! but hark, ere we two stray,   *Body.*
How many hours dost think till day?   10
Ah! go; th'art weak and sleepy. Heav'n   *Soul.*
Is a plain watch, and without figures winds
All ages up; who drew this circle even
He fills it; days and hours are *blinds*.
Yet, this take with thee; the last gasp of time
Is thy first breath, and man's *eternal prime*.

¶

Silence and stealth of days! 'tis now
          Since thou art gone,
Twelve hundred hours, and not a brow
          But clouds hang on.
As he that in some cave's thick damp
          Locked from the light,
Fixeth a solitary lamp,
          To brave the night
And walking from his sun, when past

That glimm'ring ray   10
Cuts through the heavy mists in haste
Back to his day,
So o'er fled minutes I retreat
Unto that hour
Which showed thee last, but did defeat
Thy light and pow'r.
I search and rack my soul to see
Those beams again,
But nothing but the snuff to me
Appeareth plain;   20
That dark and dead sleeps in its known
And common urn,
But those fled to their Maker's throne,
There shine and burn;
O could I track them! but souls must
Track one the other,
And now the spirit, not the dust
Must be thy brother.
Yet I have one *Pearl* by whose light
All things I see,   30
And in the heart of earth and night
Find Heaven and thee.

Church Service

Blest be the God of Harmony and Love!
The God above!
And holy dove!
Whose interceding, spiritual groans
Make restless moans
For dust and stones,
For dust in every part,
But a hard, stony heart.

2

O how in this thy choir of souls I stand
(Propped by thy hand)   10
A heap of sand!

Which busy thoughts (like winds) would scatter quite
And put to flight,
But for thy might;
Thy hand alone doth tame
Those blasts, and knit my frame,

3

So that both stones and dust, and all of me
Jointly agree
To cry to thee,
And in this music by thy Martyr's blood   20
Sealed and made good
Present, O God!
The echo of these stones
—My sighs and groans.

Burial

O thou! the first fruits of the dead
And their dark bed,
When I am cast into that deep
And senseless sleep
The wages of my sin,
O then,
Thou great Preserver of all men!
Watch o'er that loose
And empty house,
Which I sometimes lived in.   10

2

It is (in truth!) a ruined piece
Not worth thy eyes,
And scarce a room but wind and rain
Beat through and stain
The seats and cells within;
Yet thou
Led by thy Love wouldst stoop thus low,
And in this cot
All filth and spot,
Didst with thy servant inn.   20

3

And nothing can, I hourly see,
         Drive thee from me,
Thou art the same, faithful and just
         In life, or dust;
     Though then (thus crumbed) I stray
         In blasts,
Or exhalations, and wastes
         Beyond all eyes
         Yet thy love spies
     That change, and knows thy clay.   30

4

The world's thy box: how then (there tossed)
         Can I be lost?
But the delay is all; Time now
         Is old and slow,
     His wings are dull and sickly;
         Yet he
Thy servant is, and waits on thee;
         Cut then the sum,
         Lord haste, Lord come,
     O come Lord Jesus quickly!   40

Rom. Cap. 8. ver. 23

And not only they, but ourselves also, which have the first fruits of the spirit, even we ourselves groan within ourselves, waiting for the adoption, to wit, the redemption of our body.

Cheerfulness

Lord, with what courage and delight
         I do each thing
When thy least breath sustains my wing!
         I shine and move
         Like those above,
         And (with much gladness
         Quitting sadness)
Make me fair days of every night.

2

Affliction thus, mere pleasure is,
      And hap what will,   10
If thou be in't, 'tis welcome still;
      But since thy rays
      In sunny days
      Thou dost thus lend
      And freely spend,
Ah! what shall I return for this?

3

O that I were all Soul! that thou
      Wouldst make each part
Of this poor, sinful frame pure heart!
      Then would I drown   20
      My single one,
      And to thy praise
      A consort raise
Of *Hallelujahs* here below.

¶

Sure, there's a tie of bodies! and as they
      Dissolve (with it) to clay,
Love languisheth, and memory doth rust
      O'er-cast with that cold dust;
For things thus *centred*, without *beams*, or *action*
      Nor give, nor take *contaction*,
And man is such a marigold, these fled,
      That shuts, and hangs the head.

2

Absents within the line conspire, and *sense*
      Things distant doth unite,   10
Herbs sleep unto the East, and some fowls thence
      Watch the returns of light;
But hearts are not so kind: false, short delights
      Tell us the world is brave,
And wrap us in imaginary flights
      Wide of a faithful grave;

Thus Lazarus was carried out of town;
  For 'tis our foe's chief art
By distance all good objects first to drown,
  And then besiege the heart.   20
But I will be my own *Death's-head*; and though
  The flatt'rer say, *I live*,
Because incertainties we cannot know
  Be sure, not to believe.

Peace

My soul, there is a country
  Far beyond the stars,
Where stands a wingèd sentry
  All skilful in the wars,
There above noise and danger
  Sweet peace sits crowned with smiles,
And one born in a manger
  Commands the beauteous files,
He is thy gracious friend,
  And (O my soul awake!)   10
Did in pure love descend
  To die here for thy sake,
If thou canst get but thither,
  There grows the flower of peace,
The Rose that cannot wither,
  Thy fortress and thy ease;
Leave then thy foolish ranges;
  For none can thee secure,
But one, who never changes,
  Thy God, thy life, thy cure.   20

The Passion

  O my chief good!
  My dear, dear God!
  When thy blest blood
Did issue forth forced by the rod,

What pain didst thou
Feel in each blow!
How didst thou weep,
And thyself steep
In thy own precious, saving tears!
What cruel smart   10
Did tear thy heart!
How didst thou groan it
In the spirit,
O thou, whom my soul loves and fears!

2

Most blessèd Vine!
Whose juice so good
I feel as wine,
But thy fair branches felt as blood,
How wert thou pressed
To be my feast!   20
In what deep anguish
Didst thou languish,
What springs of sweat and blood did drown thee!
How in one path
Did the full wrath
Of thy great Father
Crowd and gather,
Doubling thy griefs, when none would own thee!

3

How did the weight
Of all our sins,   30
And death unite
To wrench and rack thy blessed limbs!
How pale and bloody
Looked thy body!
How bruised and broke
With every stroke!
How meek and patient was thy spirit!
How didst thou cry,
And groan on high
Father forgive,   40
And let them live,
I die to make my foes inherit!

4

O blessèd Lamb!
That took'st my sin,
That took'st my shame
How shall thy dust thy praises sing!
I would I were
One hearty tear!
One constant spring!
Then would I bring   50
Thee two small mites, and be at strife
Which should most vie,
My heart, or eye,
Teaching my years
In smiles and tears
To weep, to sing, thy *Death*, my *Life*.

Rom. Cap. 8. ver. 19

Etenim res creatae exerto capite observantes expectant revelationem
Filiorum Dei.

And do they so? have they a sense
Of ought but influence?
Can they their heads lift, and expect,
And groan too? why th' Elect
Can do no more: my volumes said
They were all dull and dead,
They judged them senseless, and their state
Wholly inanimate.
Go, go; seal up thy looks,
And burn thy books.   10

2

I would I were a stone, or tree,
Or flower by pedigree,
Or some poor highway herb, or spring
To flow, or bird to sing!
Then should I (tied to one sure state)
All day expect my date;
But I am sadly loose, and stray
A giddy blast each way;
O let me not thus range!
Thou canst not change.   20

3

Sometimes I sit with thee, and tarry
    An hour, or so, then vary.
Thy other creatures in this scene
    Thee only aim, and mean;
Some rise to seek thee, and with heads
    Erect peep from their beds;
Others, whose birth is in the tomb,
    And cannot quit the womb,
      Sigh there, and groan for thee,
        Their liberty.   30

4

O let not me do less! shall they
    Watch, while I sleep, or play?
Shall I thy mercies still abuse
    With fancies, friends, or news?
O brook it not! thy blood is mine,
    And my soul should be thine;
O brook it not! why wilt thou stop
    After whole showers one drop?
      Sure, thou wilt joy to see
        Thy sheep with thee.   40

The Relapse

My God, how gracious art thou! I had slipped
    Almost to hell,
And on the verge of that dark, dreadful pit
    Did hear them yell,
But O thy love! thy rich, almighty love
    That saved my soul,
And checked their fury, when I saw them move,
    And heard them howl;
O my sole Comfort, take no more these ways,
    This hideous path,   10
And I will mend my own without delays,
    Cease thou thy wrath!
I have deserved a thick, Egyptian damp,

Dark as my deeds,
Should *mist* within me, and put out that lamp
Thy spirit feeds;
A darting conscience full of stabs and fears;
No shade but *yew*,
Sullen and sad eclipses, cloudy spheres,
These are my due.   20
But he that with his blood (a price too dear)
My scores did pay,
Bid me, by virtue from him, challenge here
The brightest day;
Sweet, downy thoughts; soft *lily*-shades; calm streams;
Joys full and true;
Fresh, spicy mornings; and eternal beams:
These are his due.

The Resolve

I have considered it; and find
A longer stay
Is but excused neglect. To mind
One path, and stray
Into another, or to none,
Cannot be love;
When shall that traveller come home,
That will not move?
If thou wouldst thither, linger not,
Catch at the place,   10
Tell youth and beauty they must rot,
They're but a *case*;
Loose, parcelled hearts will freeze: the sun
With scattered locks
Scarce warms, but by contraction
Can heat rocks;
Call in thy *powers*; run and reach
Home with the light,
Be there, before the shadows stretch,
And *span* up night;   20
Follow the *cry* no more: there is

An ancient way
All strewed with flowers and happiness
And fresh as May;
There turn, and turn no more; let wits
Smile at fair eyes,
Or lips; but who there weeping sits,
Hath got the *Prize*.

The Match

Dear friend! whose holy, ever-living lines
Have done much good
To many, and have checked my blood,
My fierce, wild blood that still heaves and inclines,
But is still tamed
By those bright fires which thee inflamed;
Here I join hands, and thrust my stubborn heart
Into thy *Deed*,
There from no *duties* to be freed,
And if hereafter *youth*, or *folly* thwart   10
And claim their share,
Here I renounce the pois'nous ware.

ii

Accept, dread Lord, the poor oblation,
It is but poor,
Yet through thy mercies may be more.
O thou! that canst not wish my soul's damnation,
Afford me life,
And save me from all inward strife!
Two *lifes* I hold from thee, my gracious Lord,
Both cost thee dear,   20
For one, I am thy tenant here;
The other, the true life, in the next world
And endless is,
O let me still mind *that* in *this*!
To thee therefore my *Thoughts*, *Words*, *Actions*
I do resign,
Thy will in all be done, not mine.

Settle my *house*, and shut out all distractions
                That may unknit
       My heart, and thee planted in it;   30
Lord Jesu! thou didst bow thy blessèd head
                Upon a tree,
       O do as much, now unto me!
O hear and heal thy servant! Lord, strike dead
                All lusts in me,
       Who only wish life to serve thee!
Suffer no more this dust to overflow
                And drown my eyes,
       But seal, or pin them to thy skies.
And let this *grain* which here in tears I sow   40
                Though *dead* and *sick*,
       Through thy *increase* grow *new* and *quick*.

Rules and Lessons

When first thy eyes unveil, give thy soul leave
To do the like; our bodies but forerun
The spirit's duty; true hearts spread and heave
Unto their God, as flow'rs do to the sun.
      Give him thy first thoughts then; so shalt thou keep
      Him company all day, and in him sleep.

Yet, never sleep the sun up; prayer should
Dawn with the day; there are set, awful hours
'Twixt heaven and us; the *manna* was not good
After sun-rising, far-day sullies flowers.   10
      Rise to prevent the sun; sleep doth sins glut,
      And heav'ns gate opens, when this world's is shut.

Walk with thy fellow-creatures: note the *hush*
And *whispers* amongst them. There's not a *spring*,
Or *leaf* but hath his *morning-hymn*; Each *bush*
And *oak* doth know *I AM*; canst thou not sing?
      O leave thy cares and follies! go this way
      And thou art sure to prosper all the day.

Serve God before the world; let him not go
Until thou hast a blessing, then resign   20
The whole unto him; and remember who
Prevailed by *wrestling* ere the *sun* did *shine*.
     Pour *oil* upon the *stones*, weep for thy sin,
     Then journey on, and have an eye to heav'n.

Mornings are *mysteries*; the first world's *youth*,
Man's *Resurrection*, and the future's *bud*
Shroud in their births: the Crown of life, light, truth
Is styled their *star*, the *stone*, and *hidden food*.
     Three *blessings* wait upon them, two of which
     Should move; they make us *holy*, *happy*, rich.   30

When the world's up, and ev'ry swarm abroad,
Keep thou thy temper, mix not with each clay;
Dispatch necessities, life hath a load
Which must be carried on, and safely may.
     Yet keep those cares without thee, let the heart
     Be God's alone, and choose the better part.

Through all thy *actions*, *counsels*, and *discourse*,
Let *mildness* and *Religion* guide thee out,
If truth be thine, what needs a brutish force?
But what's not *good* and *just* ne'er go about.   40
     Wrong not thy conscience for a rotten stick,
     That gain is dreadful, which makes spirits sick.

To God, thy Country, and thy friend be true,
If *priest*, and *people* change, keep thou thy ground.
Who sells Religion, is a Judas Jew,
And, oaths once broke, the soul cannot be sound.
     The perjurer's a devil let loose: what can
     Tie up his hands, that dares mock God and man?

Seek not the same steps with the *crowd*; stick thou
To thy sure trot; a constant, humble mind   50
Is both his own joy, and his Maker's too;
Let folly dust it on, or lag behind.
     A sweet *self-privacy* in a right soul
     Out-runs the Earth, and lines the utmost pole.

To all that seek thee, bear an open heart;
Make not thy breast a *Labyrinth*, or *trap*;
If trials come, this will make good thy part,
For honesty is safe, come what can hap;
  It is the good man's *feast*; the prince of flowers
  Which thrives in *storms*, and smells best after *showers*. 60

Seal not thy eyes up from the poor, but give
Proportion to their *merits*, and thy *purse*;
Thou may'st in rags a mighty Prince relieve
Who, when thy sins call for't, can fence a Curse.
  Thou shalt not lose one *mite*. Though waters stray,
  The bread we cast returns in fraughts one day.

Spend not an hour so, as to weep another,
For tears are not thine own; if thou giv'st words
Dash not thy *friend*, nor *Heav'n*; O smother
A vip'rous thought; some *syllables* are *swords*. 70
  Unbitted tongues are in their penance double,
  They shame their *owners*, and the *hearers* trouble.

Injure not modest blood, whose *spirits* rise
In judgement against *lewdness*; that's base wit
That voids but *filth and stench*. Hast thou no prize
But *sickness* or *infection*? stifle it.
  Who makes his jests of sins, must be at least
  If not a very *devil*, worse than a *beast*.

Yet, fly no friend, if he be such indeed,
But meet to quench his *longings*, and thy *thirst*; 80
Allow your joys *Religion*; that done, speed
And bring the same man back, thou wert at first.
  Who so returns not, cannot pray aright,
  But shuts his door, and leaves God out all night.

To heighten thy *devotions*, and keep low
All mutinous thoughts, what busines e'er thou hast
Observe God in his works; here *fountains* flow,
Birds sing, *beasts* feed, *fish* leap, and th' *Earth* stands fast;
  Above are restless *motions*, running *lights*,
  Vast circling *azure*, giddy *clouds*, days, nights. 90

When *seasons* change, then lay before thine eyes
His wondrous *Method*; mark the various *scenes*
In heav'n; *hail, thunder, rainbows, snow,* and *ice,*
Calms, tempests, light, and *darkness* by his means;
  Thou canst not miss his praise; each *tree, herb, flower*
  Are shadows of his *wisdom* and his pow'r.

To *meals* when thou dost come, give him the praise
Whose *Arm* supplied thee; take what may suffice,
And then be thankful; O admire his ways
Who fills the world's unemptied granaries!   100
  A thankless feeder is a *thief*, his feast
  A very *robbery*, and himself no *guest*.

High-noon thus past, thy time decays; provide
Thee other thoughts; away with friends and mirth;
The sun now stoops, and hastes his beams to hide
Under the dark and melancholy Earth.
  All but preludes thy End. Thou art the man
  Whose *rise, height,* and *descent* is but a span.

Yet, set as he doth, and 'tis well. Have all
Thy beams home with thee: trim thy *lamp*, buy *oil*, 110
And then set forth; who is thus dressed, the *Fall*
Furthers his glory, and gives death the foil.
  Man is a *summer's day*; whose *youth* and *fire*
  Cool to a glorious *evening*, and expire.

When night comes, list thy deeds; make plain the way
'Twixt Heaven and thee; block it not with delays,
But perfect all before thou sleep'st; then say
There's one sun more strung on my bead of days.
  What's good score up for joy; the bad well scanned
  Wash off with tears, and get thy *Master's* hand. 120

Thy accounts thus made, spend in the grave one hour
Before thy time; be not a stranger there
Where thou may'st sleep whole ages; life's poor flow'r
Lasts not a night sometimes. Bad spirits fear
  This conversation; but the good man lies
  Intombèd many days before he dies.

Being laid and dressed for sleep, close not thy eyes
Up with thy curtains; give thy soul the wing
In some good thoughts; so when the day shall rise
And thou *unrak'st* thy *fire*, those *sparks* will bring   130
    New *flames*; besides where these lodge vain *heats* mourn
    And die; that *bush* where God is, shall not burn.

When thy *nap's* over, stir thy fire, unrake
In that *dead age*; one beam i' th' dark outvies
Two in the day; then from the *damps* and *ache*
Of night shut up thy *leaves*, be chaste; God pries
    Through thickest nights; though then the sun be far
    Do thou the works of *day*, and rise a *star*.

Briefly, *Do as thou would'st be done unto*,
Love God, and love thy neighbour; watch, and pray.   140
These are the *Words* and *Works* of life; this do,
And live; who doth not thus, hath lost *Heav'ns* way.
    O lose it not! look up, wilt change those *lights*
    For *chains* of *darkness* and *eternal nights*?

Corruption

    Sure, it was so. Man in those early days
        Was not all stone and earth,
He shined a little, and by those weak rays
        Had some glimpse of his birth.
He saw Heaven o'er his head, and knew from whence
        He came (condemnèd) hither,
And, as first love draws strongest, so from hence
        His mind sure progressed thither.
Things here were strange unto him: sweat and till,
        All was a thorn, or weed,   10
Nor did those last, but (like himself) died still
        As soon as they did *seed*;
They seemed to quarrel with him; for that Act
        That felled him, foiled them all,
He drew the Curse upon the world, and cracked
        The whole frame with his fall.

This made him long for *home*, as loath to stay
    With murmurers and foes;
He sighed for Eden, and would often say
    Ah! what bright days were those!   20
Nor was Heav'n cold unto him; for each day
    The valley, or the mountain
Afforded visits, and still Paradise lay
    In some green shade, or fountain.
Angels lay *leiger* here; each bush and cell,
    Each oak and highway knew them,
Walk but the fields, or sit down at some *well*,
    And he was sure to view them.
Almighty *Love*! where art thou now? mad man
    Sits down, and freezeth on,   30
He raves, and swears to stir nor fire, nor fan,
    But bids the thread be spun.
I see, thy curtains are close-drawn; thy bow
    Looks dim too in the cloud,
Sin triumphs still, and man is sunk below
    The Centre and his shroud;
All's in deep sleep and night; thick darkness lies
    And hatcheth o'er thy people;
But hark! what trumpet's that? what Angel cries
    Arise! Thrust in thy sickle.   40

H. Scriptures

Welcome dear book, soul's joy and food! The feast
    Of spirits, Heav'n extracted lies in thee;
    Thou art life's charter, the Dove's spotless nest
Where souls are hatched unto Eternity.

In thee the hidden stone, the *manna* lies,
    Thou art the great *elixir*, rare and choice;
    The key that opens to all mysteries,
The *Word* in characters, God in the *Voice*.

O that I had deep cut in my hard heart
    Each line in thee! Then would I plead in groans   10
    Of my Lord's penning, and by sweetest Art
Return upon himself the *Law*, and *stones*.
    Read here, my faults are thine. This Book and I
    Will tell thee so; *Sweet Saviour thou didst die!*

Unprofitableness

How rich, O Lord! how fresh thy visits are!
'Twas but just now my bleak leaves hopeless hung
    Sullied with dust and mud;
Each snarling blast shot through me, and did share
Their youth and beauty, cold showers nipped and wrung
    Their spiciness and blood;
But since thou didst in one sweet glance survey
Their sad decays, I flourish, and once more
    Breathe all perfumes and spice;
I smell a dew like *myrrh*, and all the day   10
Wear in my bosom a full Sun; such store
    Hath one beam from thy eyes.
But, ah, my God! what fruit hast thou of this?
What one poor leaf did ever I yet fall
    To wait upon thy wreath?
Thus thou all day a thankless weed dost dress,
And when th' hast done, a stench, or fog is all
    The odour I bequeath.

Christ's Nativity

    Awake, glad heart! get up, and sing,
    It is the birthday of thy King,
        Awake! awake!
        The Sun doth shake
    Light from his locks, and all the way
    Breathing perfumes, doth spice the day.

2

Awake, awake! hark, how th' *wood* rings,
Winds whisper, and the busy *springs*
    A consort make;
    Awake, awake!   10
Man is their high-priest, and should rise
To offer up the sacrifice.

3

I would I were some *bird*, or star,
Flutt'ring in woods, or lifted far
    Above this *inn*
    And road of sin!
Then either star, or *bird*, should be
Shining, or singing still to thee.

4

I would I had in my best part
Fit rooms for thee! or that my heart   20
    Were so clean as
    Thy manger was!
But I am all filth, and obscene,
Yet, if thou wilt, thou canst make clean.

5

Sweet Jesu! will then; let no more
This leper haunt and soil thy door,
    Cure him, ease him,
    O release him!
And let once more by mystic birth
The Lord of life be born in earth.   30

II

How kind is heav'n to man! If here
    One sinner doth amend
Straight there is joy, and ev'ry sphere
    In music doth contend;
And shall we then no voices lift?
    Are mercy and salvation
Not worth our thanks? Is life a gift

Of no more acceptation?
Shall he that did come down from thence,
And here for us was slain, 40
Shall he be now cast off? no sense
Of all his woes remain?
Can neither love, nor suff'rings bind?
Are we all stone and earth?
Neither his bloody passions mind,
Nor one day bless his birth?
Alas, my God! Thy birth now here
Must not be numbered in the year.

The Check

Peace, peace! I blush to hear thee; when thou art
A dusty story,
A speechless heap, and in the midst my heart
In the same livery dressed
Lies tame as all the rest;
When six years thence digged up, some youthful eye
Seeks there for symmetry
But finding none, shall leave thee to the wind,
Or the next foot to crush,
Scatt'ring thy kind 10
And humble dust, tell then dear flesh
Where is thy glory?

2

As he that in the midst of day expects
The hideous night,
Sleeps not, but shaking off sloth and neglects,
Works with the sun, and sets,
Paying the day its debts;
That (for repose and darkness bound) he might
Rest from the fears i' th' night;
So should we too. All things teach us to die 20
And point us out the way
While we pass by
And mind it not; play not away
Thy glimpse of light.

3

View thy fore-runners: creatures giv'n to be
    Thy youth's companions,
Take their leave, and die; birds, beasts, each tree,
      All that have growth, or breath
      Have one large language, *Death*.
O then play not! but strive to him, who can   30
    Make these sad shades pure sun,
Turning their mists to beams, their damps to day,
      Whose pow'r doth so excel
        As to make clay
    A spirit, and true glory dwell
      In dust and stones.

4

Hark, how he doth invite thee! with what voice
    Of love and sorrow
He begs and calls; *O that in these thy days*
    Thou knew'st but thy own good!   40
      Shall not the cries of blood,
Of God's own blood awake thee? He bids beware
      Of drunkness, surfeits, care,
But thou sleep'st on; where's now thy protestation,
    Thy lines, thy love? Away,
      Redeem the day,
    The day that gives no observation,
      Perhaps tomorrow.

Disorder and Frailty

When first thou didst even from the grave
And womb of darkness beckon out
My brutish soul, and to thy slave
Becam'st thyself, both guide and scout;
    Even from that hour
Thou gotst my heart; and though here tossed
    By winds, and bit with frost
      I pine, and shrink
      Breaking the link
'Twixt thee and me; and oft-times creep   10

Into th' old silence and dead sleep,
     Quitting thy way
     All the long day,
Yet, sure, my God! I love thee most.
    Alas, thy love!

2

I threaten heaven, and from my cell
Of clay and frailty break and bud
Touched by thy fire and breath; thy blood
Too, is my dew, and springing well.
    But while I grow   20
And stretch to thee, aiming at all
    Thy stars and spangled hall,
     Each fly doth taste,
     Poison, and blast
My yielding leaves; sometimes a show'r
Beats them quite off, and in an hour
     Not one poor shoot
     But the bare root
Hid under ground survives the fall.
    Alas, frail weed!   30

3

Thus like some sleeping exhalation
(Which waked by heat and beams, makes up
Unto that comforter, the sun,
And soars and shines; but ere we sup
    And walk two steps,
Cooled by the damps of night, descends,
   And, whence it sprung, there ends)
     Doth my weak fire
     Pine and retire,
And (after all my height of flames)   40
In sickly expirations tames
     Leaving me dead
     On my first bed
Until thy Sun again ascends.
    Poor, falling star!

4

O, yes! but give wings to my fire,
And hatch my soul, until it fly
Up where thou art, amongst thy tire
Of stars, above infirmity;
      Let not perverse   50
And foolish thoughts add to my bill
    Of forward sins, and kill
      That seed, which thou
      In me didst sow,
But dress and water with thy grace,
Together with the seed, the place;
    And for his sake
    Who died to stake
His life for mine, tune to thy will
    My heart, my verse.   60

Hosea Cap. 6. ver. 4

O Ephraim what shall I do unto thee? O Judah how shall I intreat thee? for thy goodness is as a morning cloud, and as the early dew it goeth away.

Idle Verse

Go, go, quaint follies, sugared sin,
    Shadow no more my door;
I will no longer cobwebs spin,
    I'm too much on the score.

For since amidst my youth and night,
    My great preserver smiles,
We'll make a match, my only light,
    And join against their wiles;

Blind, desp'rate *fits*, that study how
    To dress and trim our shame,
That gild rank poison, and allow   10
    Vice in a fairer name;

The *purls* of youthful blood and bowls,
    Lust in the robes of love,
The idle talk of fev'rish souls
    Sick with a scarf, or glove;

Let it suffice my warmer days
    Simpered and shined on you,
Twist not my cypress with your bays,
    Or roses with my yew;   20

Go, go, seek out some greener thing,
    It snows, and freezeth here;
Let nightingales attend the spring,
    Winter is all my year.

Son-days

Bright shadows of true rest! some shoots of bliss,
                Heaven once a week;
The next world's gladness prepossessed in this;
                A day to seek
Eternity in time; the steps by which
We climb above all ages; lamps that light
Man through his heap of dark days; and the rich
And full redemption of the whole week's flight.

2

The pulleys unto headlong man; time's bower;
                The narrow way;   10
Transplanted Paradise; God's walking hour;
                The cool o' th' day;
The Creatures' *jubilee*; God's parle with dust;
Heaven here; man on those hills of myrrh and flowers;
Angels descending; the returns of trust;
A gleam of glory, after six-days-showers.

3

The Church's love-feasts; time's prerogative
          And interest
Deducted from the whole; the combs and hive,
          And home of rest.   20
The milky way chalked out with suns; a clue
That guides through erring hours; and in full story
A taste of Heav'n on earth; the pledge and cue
Of a full feast; and the out-courts of glory.

Repentance

Lord, since thou didst in this vile clay
    That sacred ray
Thy spirit plant, quick'ning the whole
With that one grain's infusèd wealth,
My forward flesh creeped on, and subtly stole
Both growth and power; checking the health
And heat of thine: that little gate
And narrow way, by which to thee
The passage is, he termed a grate
And entrance to captivity;   10
Thy laws but nets, where some small birds
(And those but seldom too) were caught,
Thy Promises but empty words
Which none but children heard, or taught.
This I believed: and though a friend
Came oft from far, and whispered, *No*;
Yet that not sorting to my end
I wholly listened to my foe.
Wherefore, pierced through with grief, my sad
Seducèd soul sighs up to thee,   20
To thee who with true light art clad
And seest all things just as they be.
Look from thy throne upon this roll
Of heavy sins, my high transgressions,
Which I confess with all my soul,
My God, accept of my confession.
        It was last day

(Touched with the guilt of my own way)
I sate alone, and taking up
    The bitter cup,   30
Through all thy fair and various store
Sought out what might outvie my score.
    The blades of grass, thy Creatures feeding,
    The trees, their leafs; the flowers, their seeding;
    The dust, of which I am a part,
    The stones much softer than my heart,
    The drops of rain, the sighs of wind,
    The stars to which I am stark blind,
    The dew thy herbs drink up by night,
    The beams they warm them at i' th' light,   40
    All that have signature or life,
    I summoned to decide this strife,
    And lest I should lack for arrears,
    A spring ran by, I told her tears,
    But when these came unto the scale,
    My sins alone outweighed them all.
O my dear God! my life, my love!
Most blessèd lamb! and mildest dove!
Forgive your penitent offender,
And no more his sins remember,   50
Scatter these shades of death, and give
Light to my soul, that it may live;
Cut me not off for my transgressions,
Wilful rebellions, and suppressions,
But give them in those streams a part
Whose spring is in my Saviour's heart.
Lord, I confess the heinous score,
And pray, I may do so no more;
Though then all sinners I exceed
O think on this; *Thy Son did bleed*;   60
O call to mind his wounds, his woes,
His Agony, and bloody throes;
Then look on all that thou hast made,
And mark how they do fail and fade,
The heavens themselves, though fair and bright,
Are dark and unclean in thy sight,
How then, with thee, can man be holy
Who dost thine angels charge with folly?

O what am I, that I should breed
Figs on a thorn, flowers on a weed!   70
I am the gourd of sin and sorrow
Growing o'er night, and gone tomorrow;
In all this *round* of life and death
Nothing's more vile than is my breath,
Profaneness on my tongue doth rest,
Defects and darkness in my breast,
Pollutions all my body wed,
And even my soul to thee is dead,
Only in him, on whom I feast,
Both soul and body are well dressed,   80
  His pure perfection quits all score,
  And fills the boxes of his poor;
He is the Centre of long life and light,
I am but finite, He is Infinite.
O let thy *Justice* then in him confine,
And through his merits, make thy mercy mine!

The Burial of an Infant

Blest infant bud, whose blossom-life
Did only look about, and fall,
Wearied out in a harmless strife
Of tears and milk, the food of all;

Sweetly didst thou expire: thy soul
Flew home unstained by his new kin,
For ere thou knew'st how to be foul,
Death *weaned* thee from the world and sin.

Softly rest all thy virgin-crumbs!
Lapped in the sweets of thy young breath,   10
Expecting till thy Saviour comes
To *dress* them, and *unswaddle* death.

Faith

Bright and blest beam! whose strong projection
    Equal to all,
Reacheth as well things of dejection
    As th' high and tall;
How hath my God by raying thee
    Inlarged his spouse,
And of a private family
    Made open house!
All may be now co-heirs; no noise
    Of *bond*, or *free*   10
Can interdict us from those joys
    That wait on thee,
The Law and Ceremonies made
    A glorious night,
Where stars and clouds, both light and shade
    Had equal right;
But, as in nature, when the day
    Breaks, night adjourns,
Stars shut up shop, mists pack away,
    And the moon mourns;   20
So when the Sun of righteousness
    Did once appear,
That scene was changed, and a new dress
    Left for us here;
Veils became useless, altars fell,
    Fires smoking die;
And all that sacred pomp and shell
    Of things did fly;
Then did he shine forth, whose sad fall
    And bitter fights   30
Were figured in those mystical
    And cloudy rites;
And as i' th' natural sun, these three,
    Light, motion, heat,
So are now *Faith, Hope, Charity*
    Through him complete;
Faith spans up bliss; what sin and death
    Put us quite from,

Lest we should run for't out of breath,
                Faith brings us home;   40
So that I need no more, but say
                I do believe,
And my most loving Lord straightway
                Doth answer, *Live.*

The Dawning

Ah! what time wilt thou come? when shall that cry
                The Bridegroom's coming! fill the sky?
Shall it in the evening run
When our words and works are done?
Or will thy all-surprising light
                Break at midnight?
When either sleep, or some dark pleasure
Possesseth mad man without measure;
Or shall these early, fragrant hours
                Unlock thy bowers?   10
And with their blush of light descry
Thy locks crowned with eternity;
Indeed, it is the only time
That with thy glory doth best chime,
All now are stirring, ev'ry field
                Full hymns doth yield,
The whole Creation shakes off night,
And for thy shadow looks the light,
Stars now vanish without number,
Sleepy planets set and slumber,   20
The pursy clouds disband and scatter,
All expect some sudden matter,
Not one beam triumphs, but from far
                That morning-star;

O at what time soever thou
(Unknown to us) the heavens wilt bow,
And, with thy angels in the *van,*
Descend to judge poor careless man,
Grant, I may not like puddle lie

In a corrupt security,
Where, if a traveller water crave,
He finds it dead, and in a grave;
But as this restless, vocal *spring*
All day and night doth run and sing,
And though here born, yet is acquainted
Elsewhere, and flowing keeps untainted;
So let me all my busy age
In thy free services engage,
And though (while here) of force I must
Have commerce sometimes with poor dust,   40
And in my flesh, though vile and low,
As this doth in her channel flow,
Yet let my course, my aim, my love,
And chief acquaintance be above;
So when that day and hour shall come
In which thyself will be the Sun,
Thou'lt find me dressed and on my way,
Watching the break of thy great day.

Admission

How shrill are silent tears! when sin got head
 And all my bowels turned
To brass and iron; when my stock lay dead,
 And all my powers mourned;
 Then did these drops (for marble sweats,
  And rocks have tears)
 As rain here at our windows beats,
  Chide in thine ears;

2

No quiet couldst thou have: nor didst thou wink,
 And let thy beggar lie,   10
But ere my eyes could overflow their brink
 Didst to each drop reply;
 Bowels of love! at what low rate,
  And slight a price
 Dost thou relieve us at thy gate,
  And still our cries!

3

We are thy infants, and suck thee; if thou
　　But hide, or turn thy face,
Because where thou art, yet, we cannot go,
　　We send tears to the place,　　　　　　　　20
　　These find thee out, and though our sins
　　　　Drove thee away,
　　Yet with thy love that absence wins
　　　　Us double pay.

4

O give me then a thankful heart! a heart
　　After thy own, not mine;
So after thine, that all and ev'ry part
　　Of mine, may wait on thine;
　　O hear! yet not my tears alone,
　　　　Hear now a flood,　　　　　　　　　30
　　A flood that drowns both tears and groans,
　　　　My Saviour's blood.

Praise

King of comforts! King of life!
　　Thou hast cheered me,
And when fears and doubts were rife,
　　Thou hast cleared me!

Not a nook in all my breast
　　But thou fill'st it,
Not a thought, that breaks my rest,
　　But thou kill'st it;

Wherefore with my utmost strength
　　I will praise thee,　　　　　　　　　10
And as thou giv'st line and length,
　　I will raise thee;

Day and night, not once a day
　　I will bless thee,
And my soul in new array
　　I will dress thee;

Not one minute in the year
        But I'll mind thee,
As my seal and bracelet here
        I will bind thee;   20

In thy word, as if in heaven
        I will rest me,
And thy promise till made even
        There shall feast me.

Then, thy sayings all my life
        They shall please me,
And thy bloody wounds and strife
        They will ease me;

With thy groans my daily breath
        I will measure,   30
And my life hid in thy death
        I will treasure.

            Though then thou art
            Past thought of heart
All perfect fullness,
            And canst no whit
            Access admit
From dust and dullness;

            Yet to thy name
            (As not the same   40
With thy bright Essence)
            Our foul, clay hands
            At thy commands
Bring praise and incense;

            If then, dread Lord,
            When to thy board
Thy wretch comes begging,
            He hath a flower
            Or (to his pow'r)
Some such poor off'ring;   50

When thou hast made
   Thy beggar glad,
And filled his bosom,
   Let him (though poor)
   Strow at thy door
That one poor blossom.

Dressing

O thou that lovest a pure and whitened soul!
That feed'st among the lilies, till the day
Break, and the shadows flee; touch with one coal
My frozen heart; and with thy secret key

Open my desolate rooms; my gloomy breast
With thy clear fire refine, burning to dust
These dark confusions, that within me nest,
And soil thy Temple with a sinful rust.

Thou holy, harmless, undefiled high-priest!
The perfect, full oblation for all sin,   10
Whose glorious conquest nothing can resist,
But even in babes dost triumph still and win;

    Give to thy wretched one
  Thy mystical *Communion*,
      That, absent, he may see,
      Live, die, and rise with thee;
Let him so follow here, that in the end
He may take thee, as thou dost him intend.
      Give him thy private seal,
  Earnest, and sign; thy gifts so deal   20
      That these forerunners here
      May make the future clear;
Whatever thou dost bid, let faith make good,
Bread for thy body, and wine for thy blood.
      Give him (with pity) love,
  Two flowers that grew with thee above;
      Love that shall not admit

Anger for one short fit,
And pity of such a divine extent
That may thy members, more than mine, resent.   30

Give me, my God! thy grace,
The beams and brightness of thy face,
That never like a beast
I take thy sacred feast,
Or the dread mysteries of thy blest blood
Use, with like custom, as my kitchen food.
Some sit to thee, and eat
Thy body as their common meat,
O let not me do so!
Poor dust should lie still low,   40
Then kneel my soul and body; kneel and bow;
If *Saints* and *Angels* fall down, much more thou.

Easter-day

Thou, whose sad heart and weeping head lies low,
Whose cloudy breast cold damps invade,
Who never feel'st the Sun, nor smooth'st thy brow,
But sitt'st oppressèd in the shade,
Awake, awake,
And in his Resurrection partake,
Who on this day (that thou might'st rise as he)
Rose up, and cancelled two deaths due to thee.

Awake, awake; and, like the Sun, disperse
All mists that would usurp this day;   10
Where are thy palms, thy branches, and thy verse?
Hosanna! hark, why dost thou stay?
Arise, arise,
And with his healing blood anoint thine eyes,
Thy inward eyes; his blood will cure thy mind,
Whose spittle only could restore the blind.

Easter Hymn

Death and darkness get you packing,
Nothing now to man is lacking,
All your triumphs now are ended,
And what Adam marred is mended;
Graves are beds now for the weary,
Death a nap, to wake more merry;
Youth now, full of pious duty,
Seeks in thee for perfect beauty,
The weak and agèd, tired with length
Of days, from thee look for new strength,   10
And infants with thy pangs contest
As pleasant, as if with the breast;
    Then, unto him, who thus hath thrown
Even to contempt thy kingdom down,
And by his blood did us advance
Unto his own inheritance,
To him be glory, power, praise,
From this, unto the last of days.

The Holy Communion

Welcome sweet and sacred feast; welcome life!
    Dead I was, and deep in trouble;
But grace and blessings came with thee so rife,
That they have quickened even dry stubble;
    Thus souls their bodies animate,
        And thus, at first, when things were rude,
            Dark, void, and crude,
They, by thy Word, their beauty had, and date;
            All were by thee,
            And still must be,   10
        Nothing that is, or lives,
    But hath his quick'nings and reprieves
        As thy hand opes, or shuts;
            Healings and cuts,
Darkness and daylight, life and death

Are but mere leaves turned by thy breath.
       Spirits without thee die,
           And blackness sits
           On the divinest wits,
       As on the sun eclipses lie.
But that great darkness at thy death
When the veil broke with thy last breath,
           Did make us see
           The way to thee;
And now by these sure, sacred ties,
           After thy blood
           (Our sov'reign good)
           Had cleared our eyes,
           And given us sight;
Thou dost unto thyself betroth
           Our souls and bodies both
           In everlasting light.

Was't not enough that thou hadst paid the price
           And given us eyes
When we had none, but thou must also take
           Us by the hand
           And keep us still awake,
           When we would sleep,
           Or from thee creep,
Who without thee cannot stand?

Was't not enough to lose thy breath
And blood by an accursèd death,
           But thou must also leave
           To us that did bereave
Thee of them both, these seals the means
           That should both cleanse
           And keep us so,
           Who wrought thy woe?
O rose of Sharon! O the lily
           Of the valley!
How art thou now, thy flock to keep,
Become both *food* and *Shepherd* to thy sheep.

Psalm 121

Up to those bright and gladsome hills
    Whence flows my weal and mirth,
I look and sigh for him, who fills
    (Unseen) both heaven and earth.

He is alone my help and hope,
    That I shall not be moved,
His watchful eye is ever ope,
    And guardeth his beloved;

The glorious God is my sole stay,
    He is my sun and shade,   10
The cold by night, the heat by day,
    Neither shall me invade.

He keeps me from the spite of foes,
    Doth all their plots control,
And is a shield (not reckoning those)
    Unto my very soul.

Whether abroad, amidst the crowd,
    Or else within my door,
He is my pillar and my cloud,
    Now, and for evermore.   20

Affliction

Peace, peace; it is not so. Thou dost miscall
    Thy physic; pills that change
Thy sick accessions into settled health,
This is the great *Elixir* that turns gall
To wine and sweetness; poverty to wealth,
  And brings man home, when he doth range.
  Did not he, who ordained the day,
    Ordain night too?
  And in the greater world display

What in the lesser he would do?   10
All flesh is clay, thou know'st; and but that God
      Doth use his rod,
And by a fruitful change of frosts and showers
    Cherish and bind thy *pow'rs*,
Thou wouldst to weeds and thistles quite disperse,
    And be more wild than is thy verse;
Sickness is wholesome, and crosses are but curbs
    To check the mule, unruly man,
They are heaven's husbandry, the famous fan
    Purging the floor which chaff disturbs.   20
Were all the year one constant sunshine, we
      Should have no flowers,
All would be drought and leanness; not a tree
      Would make us bowers;
Beauty consists in colours; and that's best
    Which is not fixed, but flies and flows;
The settled *red* is dull, and *whites* that rest
    Something of sickness would disclose.
    Vicissitude plays all the game,
        Nothing that stirs,   30
        Or hath a name,
    But waits upon this wheel,
Kingdoms too have their physic, and for steel,
    Exchange their peace and furs.
    Thus doth God *key* disordered man
      (Which none else can)
    Tuning his breast to rise or fall;
And by a sacred, needful art,
Like strings, stretch ev'ry part
Making the whole most musical.   40

The Tempest

How is man parcelled out! how ev'ry hour
    Shows him himself, or something he should see!
    This late, long heat may his instruction be,
And tempests have more in them than a shower.

When nature on her bosom saw
    Her infants die,
And all her flowers withered to straw,
    Her breasts grown dry;
She made the Earth, their nurse and tomb,
    Sigh to the sky,   10
Till to those sighs fetched from her womb
    Rain did reply,
So in the midst of all her fears
    And faint requests
Her earnest sighs procured her tears
    And filled her breasts.

O that man could do so! that he would hear
    The world read to him! all the vast expense
    In the Creation shed and slaved to sense
Makes up but lectures for his eye and ear.   20

Sure, mighty love foreseeing the descent
    Of this poor Creature, by a gracious art
    Hid in these low things snares to gain his heart,
And laid surprises in each element.

All things here show him heaven; *waters* that fall
    Chide and fly up; *mists* of corruptest foam
    Quit their first beds and mount; trees, herbs, flowers, all
Strive upwards still, and point him the way home.

How do they cast off grossness? only *earth*
    And *man* (like Issachar) in loads delight,   30
    Water's refined to *motion*, air to *light*,
Fire to all three, but man hath no such mirth.

Plants in the *root* with earth do most comply,
    Their *leafs* with water and humidity,
    The *flowers* to air draw near, and subtlety,
And *seeds* a kinred fire have with the sky.

All have their *keys* and set *ascents*; but man
    Though he knows these, and hath more of his own,
    Sleeps at the ladder's foot; alas! what can
These new discoveries do, except they drown?   40

Thus grovelling in the shade and darkness, he
    Sinks to a dead oblivion; and though all
    He sees (like *Pyramids*) shoot from this ball
And less'ning still grow up invisibly,

Yet hugs he still his dirt; the *stuff* he wears
    And painted trimming takes down both his eyes,
    Heaven hath less beauty than the dust he spies,
And money better music than the *spheres*.

Life's but a blast, he knows it; what? shall straw
    And bulrush-fetters temper his short hour?   50
    Must he nor sip, nor sing? grows ne'er a flower
To crown his temples? shall dreams be his law?

O foolish man! how hast thou lost thy sight?
    How is it that the sun to thee alone
    Is grown thick darkness, and thy bread, a stone?
Hath flesh no softness now? mid-day no light?

Lord! thou didst put a soul here; if I must
    Be broke again, for flints will give no fire
    Without a steel, O let thy power clear
Thy gift once more, and grind this flint to dust!   60

Retirement

Who on yon throne of azure sits,
    Keeping close house
Above the morning-star,
    Whose meaner shows,
And outward utensils these glories are
    That shine and share
Part of his mansion; he one day
    When I went quite astray
    Out of mere love
    By his mild Dove   10
Did show me home, and put me in the way.

2

Let it suffice at length thy fits
    And lusts (said he)
    Have had their wish and way;
    Press not to be
Still thy own foe and mine; for to this day
    I did delay,
And would not see, but chose to wink,
    Nay, at the very brink
    And edge of all   20
    When thou wouldst fall
My *love-twist* held thee up, my *unseen link*.

3

I know thee well; for I have framed
    And hate thee not,
    Thy spirit too is mine;
    I know thy lot,
Extent, and end, for my hands drew the line
    Assignèd thine;
If then thou would'st unto my seat,
    'Tis not th' applause and feat   30
    Of dust and clay
    Leads to that way,
But from those follies a resolved Retreat.

4

Now here below where yet untamed
    Thou dost thus rove
    I have a house as well
    As there above,
In it my *Name* and *honour* both do dwell
    And shall until
I make all new; there nothing gay   40
    In perfumes or array,
    Dust lies with dust
    And hath but just
The same respect and room, with ev'ry clay.

5

A faithful school where thou mayst see
    In heraldry
  Of stones and speechless earth
    Thy true descent;
Where dead men preach, who can turn feasts and mirth
    To funerals and *Lent*.   50
  There dust that out of doors might fill
    Thy eyes, and blind thee still,
      Is fast asleep;
      Up then, and keep
Within those doors (my doors), dost hear? *I will*.

Love and Discipline

Since in a land not barren still
(Because thou dost thy grace distil)
My lot is fall'n, blest be thy will!

And since these biting frosts but kill
Some tares in me which choke, or spill
That seed thou sow'st, blest be thy skill!

Blest be thy dew, and blest thy frost,
And happy I to be so crossed,
And cured by crosses at thy cost.

The dew doth cheer what is distressed,   10
The frosts ill weeds nip and molest,
In both thou work'st unto the best.

Thus while thy sev'ral mercies plot,
And work on me now cold, now hot,
The work goes on, and slacketh not,

For as thy hand the weather steers,
So thrive I best, 'twixt joys and tears,
And all the year have some green ears.

The Pilgrimage

As travellers when the twilight's come,
And in the sky the stars appear,
The past day's accidents do sum
With, *Thus we saw there, and thus here*;

Then Jacob-like lodge in a place
(A place, and no more, is set down)
Where till the day restore the race
They rest and dream homes of their own:

So for this night I linger here,
And full of tossings to and fro,   10
Expect still when thou wilt appear
That I may get me up, and go.

I long, and groan, and grieve for thee,
For thee my words, my tears do gush,
O that I were but where I see!
Is all the note within my bush.

As birds robbed of their native wood,
Although their diet may be fine,
Yet neither sing, nor like their food,
But with the thought of home do pine: 20

So do I mourn, and hang my head,
And though thou dost me fullness give,
Yet look I for far better bread
Because by this man cannot live.

O feed me then! and since I may
Have yet more days, more nights to count,
So strengthen me, Lord, all the way,
That I may travel to thy Mount.

Heb. Cap. xi. ver. 13
And they confessed, that they were strangers and pilgrims on the earth.

The Law and the Gospel

Lord, when thou didst on Sinai pitch
And shine from Paran, when a fiery Law
Pronounced with thunder, and thy threats did thaw
Thy people's hearts, when all thy weeds were rich
　　　　And inaccessible for light,
　　　　　　Terror and might,
How did poor flesh (which after thou didst wear)
　　　　　Then faint and fear!
Thy chosen flock, like leafs in a high wind,
Whispered obedience, and their heads inclined.　　　　10

2

But now since we to Sion came,
And through thy blood thy glory see,
With filial confidence we touch ev'n thee;
And where the other mount all clad in flame
　　　　And threat'ning clouds would not so much
　　　　　　As bide the touch,
We climb up this, and have too all the way
　　　　　Thy hand our stay,
Nay, thou tak'st ours, and (which full comfort brings)
Thy Dove too bears us on her sacred wings.　　　　20

3

Yet since man is a very brute
And after all thy Acts of grace doth kick,
Slighting that health thou gav'st, when he was sick,
Be not displeased, if I, who have a suit
　　　　To thee each hour, beg at thy door
　　　　　　For this one more;
O plant in me thy *Gospel* and thy *Law*,
　　　　　Both *Faith* and *Awe*;
So twist them in my heart, that ever there
I may as well as *love*, find too thy *fear*!　　　　30

4

Let me not spill, but drink thy blood,
Not break thy fence, and by a black excess
Force down a just curse, when thy hands would bless;
Let me not scatter and despise my food,
    Or nail those blessèd limbs again
      Which bore my pain;
So shall thy mercies flow: for while I fear,
      I know, thou'lt bear,
But should thy mild injunction nothing move me,
I would both think and judge I did not love thee.   40

John Cap. 14. ver. 15
If ye love me, keep my commandments.

The World

I saw Eternity the other night
Like a great *Ring* of pure and endless light,
    All calm, as it was bright,
And round beneath it, Time in hours, days, years
      Driv'n by the spheres
Like a vast shadow moved, in which the world
      And all her train were hurled;
The doting lover in his quaintest strain
      Did there complain,
Near him, his lute, his fancy, and his flights,   10
      Wit's sour delights,
With gloves and knots, the silly snares of pleasure,
      Yet his dear treasure
All scattered lay, while he his eyes did pore
      Upon a flower.

2

The darksome statesman hung with weights and woe
Like a thick midnight-fog moved there so slow
    He did not stay, nor go;
Condemning thoughts (like sad eclipses) scowl
      Upon his soul,   20

And clouds of crying witnesses without
          Pursued him with one shout.
Yet digged the mole, and lest his ways be found
          Worked under ground,
Where he did clutch his prey, but one did see
          That policy,
Churches and altars fed him, perjuries
          Were gnats and flies,
It rained about him blood and tears, but he
          Drank them as free.   30

3

The fearful miser on a heap of rust
Sate pining all his life there, did scarce trust
          His own hands with the dust,
Yet would not place one piece above, but lives
          In fear of thieves.
Thousands there were as frantic as himself
          And hugged each one his pelf,
The downright epicure placed heav'n in sense
          And scorned pretence
While others slipped into a wide excess   40
          Said little less;
The weaker sort slight, trivial wares inslave
          Who think them brave,
And poor, despisèd truth sate counting by
          Their victory.

4

Yet some, who all this while did weep and sing,
And sing and weep, soared up into the *Ring*,
          But most would use no wing.
O fools (said I) thus to prefer dark night
          Before true light,   50
To live in grots and caves, and hate the day
          Because it shows the way,
The way which from this dead and dark abode
          Leads up to God,
A way where you might tread the sun, and be
          More bright than he.

But as I did their madness so discuss
   One whispered thus,
This Ring the Bridegroom did for none provide
   But for his bride.   60

[I] John Cap. 2. ver. 16, 17

All that is in the world, the lust of the flesh, the lust of the eyes, and the
pride of life, is not of the father, but is of the world.

And the world passeth away, and the lusts thereof, but he that doth the
will of God abideth for ever.

The Mutiny

Weary of this same clay and straw, I laid
Me down to breathe, and casting in my heart
The after-burthens and griefs yet to come,
      The heavy sum
So shook my breast, that (sick and sore dismayed)
My thoughts, like water which some stone doth start,
Did quit their troubled channel, and retire
Unto the banks, where, storming at those bounds,
They murmured sore; but I, who felt them boil
      And knew their coil,   10
Turning to him, who made poor sand to tire
And tame proud waves, If yet these barren grounds
      And thirsty brick must be (said I)
         My task and destiny,

                        2

Let me so strive and struggle with thy foes
(Not thine alone, but mine too) that when all
Their arts and force are built unto the height
      That Babel-weight
May prove thy glory and their shame; so close
And knit me to thee, that though in this vale   20
Of sin and death I sojourn, yet one eye
May look to thee, to thee the finisher
And Author of my faith; so show me home
      That all this foam

And frothy noise which up and down doth fly
May find no lodging in mine eye or ear,
     O seal them up! that these may fly
         Like other tempests by.

                    3

Not but I know thou hast a shorter cut
To bring me home, than through a wilderness,   30
A sea, or sands and serpents; yet since thou
         (As thy words show)
Though in this desert I were wholly shut,
Canst light and lead me there with such redress
That no decay shall touch me; O be pleased
To fix my steps, and whatsoever path
Thy sacred and eternal will decreed
         For thy bruised reed
O give it full obedience, that so seized
Of all I have, I may nor move thy wrath   40
     Nor grieve thy *Dove*, but soft and mild
         Both live and die thy Child.

              Revel. Cap. 2. ver. 17
   To him that overcometh will I give to eat of the hidden manna, and I
will give him a white stone, and in the stone a new name written, which
no man knoweth, saving he that receiveth it.

                The Constellation

Fair, ordered lights (whose motion without noise
         Resembles those true joys
Whose spring is on that hill where you do grow
         And we here taste sometimes below)

With what exact obedience do you move
         Now beneath and now above,
And in your vast progressions overlook
         The darkest night and closest nook!

Some nights I see you in the gladsome East,
    Some others near the West,   10
And when I cannot see, yet do you shine
    And beat about your endless line.

Silence, and light, and watchfulness with you
    Attend and wind the clue,
No sleep, nor sloth assails you, but poor man
    Still either sleeps, or slips his span.

He gropes beneath here, and with restless care
    First makes, then hugs a snare,
Adores dead dust, sets heart on corn and grass,
    But seldom doth make heav'n his glass.   20

Music and mirth (if there be music here)
    Take up and tune his year,
These things are kin to him, and must be had,
    Who kneels, or sighs a life is mad.

Perhaps some nights he'll watch with you, and peep
    When it were best to sleep,
Dares know effects, and judge them long before,
    When th' herb he treads knows much, much more.

But seeks he your *obedience, order, light,*
    Your calm and well-trained flight,   30
Where, though the glory differ in each star,
    Yet is there peace still, and no war?

Since placed by him who calls you by your names
    And fixed there all your flames,
Without command you never acted ought
    And then you in your courses fought.

But here commissioned by a black self-will
    The sons the father kill,
The children chase the mother, and would heal
    The wounds they give, by crying, zeal;   40

Then cast her blood and tears upon thy book
    Where they for fashion look,
And like that lamb which had the dragon's voice
    Seem mild, but are known by their noise.

Thus by our lusts disordered into wars
    Our guides prove wand'ring stars,
Which for these mists and black days were reserved,
    What time we from our first love swerved.

Yet O for his sake who sits now by thee
    All crowned with victory,   50
So guide us through this darkness, that we may
    Be more and more in love with day;

Settle and fix our hearts, that we may move
    In order, peace, and love,
And taught obedience by thy whole Creation,
    Become an humble, holy nation.

Give to thy spouse her perfect and pure dress,
    Beauty and *holiness*,
And so repair these rents, that men may see
    And say, *Where God is*, *all agree*.   60

The Shepherds

Sweet, harmless lives! (on whose holy leisure
    Waits innocence and pleasure)
Whose leaders to those pastures and clear springs,
    Were Patriarchs, Saints, and Kings,
How happened it that in the dead of night
    You only saw true light,
While Palestine was fast asleep, and lay
    Without one thought of day?
Was it because those first and blessed swains
    Were pilgrims on those plains   10
When they received the promise, for which now
    'Twas there first shown to you?
'Tis true, he loves that dust whereon they go
    That serve him here below,

And therefore might for memory of those
    His love there first disclose;
But wretched Salem, once his love, must now
    No voice, nor vision know,
Her stately piles with all their height and pride
    Now languishèd and died,   20
And Bethlem's humble cots above them stept
    While all her seers slept;
Her cedar, fir, hewed stones and gold were all
    Polluted through their fall,
And those once sacred mansions were now
    Mere emptiness and show;
This made the Angel call at reeds and thatch,
    Yet where the shepherds watch,
And God's own lodging (though he could not lack)
    To be a common *rack*;   30
No costly pride, no soft-clothed luxury
    In those thin cells could lie,
Each stirring wind and storm blew through their cots
    Which never harboured plots,
Only content, and love, and humble joys
    Lived there without all noise,
Perhaps some harmless cares for the next day
    Did in their bosoms play,
As where to lead their sheep, what silent nook,
    What springs or shades to look,   40
But that was all; and now with gladsome care
    They for the town prepare,
They leave their flock, and in a busy talk
    All towards Bethlem walk
To see their souls' great shepherd, who was come
    To bring all stragglers home,
Where now they find him out, and taught before
    That Lamb of God adore,
That Lamb whose days great Kings and Prophets wished
    And longed to see, but missed.   50
The first light they beheld was bright and gay
    And turned their night to day,
But to this later light they saw in him,
    Their day was dark and dim.

Misery

Lord, bind me up, and let me lie
A pris'ner to my liberty,
If such a state at all can be
As an impris'ment serving thee;
The wind, though gathered in thy fist,
Yet doth it blow still where it list,
And yet shouldst thou let go thy hold
Those gusts might quarrel and grow bold.
  As waters here, headlong and loose
The lower grounds still chase and choose,   10
Where spreading all the way they seek
And search out ev'ry hole and creek;
So my spilt thoughts winding from thee
Take the down-road to vanity,
Where they all stray and strive, which shall
Find out the first and steepest fall;
I cheer their flow, giving supply
To what's already grown too high,
And having thus performed that part
Feed on those vomits of my heart.   20
I break the fence my own hands made
Then lay that trespass in the shade,
Some fig-leafs still I do devise
As if thou hadst nor ears nor eyes.
Excess of friends, of words, and wine
Take up my day, while thou dost shine
All unregarded, and thy book
Hath not so much as one poor look.
If thou steal in amidst the mirth
And kindly tell me, *I am earth*,   30
I shut thee out, and let that slip,
Such music spoils good fellowship.
Thus wretched I, and most unkind,
Exclude my dear God from my mind,
Exclude him thence, who of that cell
Would make a court, should he there dwell.
He goes, he yields; and troubled sore
His holy spirit grieves therefore,

The mighty God, th' eternal King
Doth grieve for dust, and dust doth sing.   40
But I go on, haste to devest
Myself of reason, till oppressed
And buried in my surfeits I
Prove my own shame and misery.
Next day I call and cry for thee
Who shouldst not then come near to me,
But now it is thy servant's pleasure
Thou must (and dost) give him his measure.
Thou dost, thou com'st, and in a shower
Of healing sweets thyself dost pour   50
Into my wounds, and now thy grace
(I know it well) fills all the place;
I sit with thee by this new light,
And for that hour th'art my delight,
No man can more the world despise
Or thy great mercies better prize.
I school my eyes, and strictly dwell
Within the circle of my cell,
That calm and silence are my joys
Which to thy peace are but mere noise.   60
At length I feel my head to ache,
My fingers itch and burn to take
Some new employment, I begin
To swell and foam and fret within.
> '*The Age, the present times, are not*
> *To snudge in, and embrace a cot,*
> *Action and blood now get the game,*
> *Disdain treads on the peaceful name,*
> *Who sits at home too bears a load*
> *Greater than those that gad abroad.*'   70
Thus do I make thy gifts giv'n me
The only quarrellers with thee,
I'd loose those knots thy hands did tie,
Then would go travel, fight or die.
Thousands of wild and waste infusions
Like waves beat on my resolutions,
As flames about their fuel run
And work and wind till all be done,
So my fierce soul bustles about

And never rests till all be out.   80
Thus wilded by a peevish heart
Which in thy music bears no part
I storm at thee, calling my peace
A lethargy and mere disease,
Nay, those bright beams shot from thy eyes
To calm me in these mutinies
I style mere tempers, which take place
At some set times, but are thy grace.

   Such is man's life, and such is mine,
The worst of men, and yet still thine,   90
Still thine thou know'st, and if not so
Then give me over to my foe.
Yet since as easy 'tis for thee
To make man good, as bid him be,
And with one glance (could he that gain)
To look him out of all his pain,
O send me from thy holy hill
So much of strength, as may fulfil
All thy delight (whate'er they be)
And sacred institutes in me;   100
Open my rocky heart, and fill
It with obedience to thy will,
Then seal it up, that as none see,
So none may enter there but thee.

   O hear my God! hear him, whose blood
Speaks more and better for my good!
O let my cry come to thy throne!
My cry not poured with tears alone,
(For tears alone are often foul)
But with the blood of all my soul,   110
With spirit-sighs and earnest groans,
Faithful and most repenting moans,
With these I cry, and crying pine
Till thou both mend and make me thine.

The Sap

Come sapless blossom, creep not still on Earth
    Forgetting thy first birth;
'Tis not from dust, or if so, why dost thou
    Thus call and thirst for dew?
It tends not thither, if it doth, why then
    This growth and stretch for heav'n?
Thy root sucks but diseases, worms there seat
    And claim it for their meat.
Who placed thee here, did something then infuse
    Which now can tell thee news.   10
There is beyond the stars an hill of myrrh
    From which some drops fall here,
On it the Prince of Salem sits, who deals
    To thee thy secret meals,
There is thy country, and he is the way
    And hath withal the key.
Yet lived he here sometimes, and bore for thee
    A world of misery,
For thee, who in the first man's loins didst fall
    From that hill to this vale,   20
And had not he so done, it is most true
    Two deaths had been thy due;
But going hence, and knowing well what woes
    Might his friends discompose,
To show what strange love he had to our good
    He gave his sacred blood
By will our sap and cordial; now in this
    Lies such a heav'n of bliss,
That, who but truly tastes it, no decay
    Can touch him any way,   30
Such secret life and virtue in it lies
    It will exalt and rise
And actuate such spirits as are shed
    Or ready to be dead,
And bring new too. Get then this sap, and get
    Good store of it, but let
The vessel where you put it be for sure
    To all your pow'r most pure;

There is at all times (though shut up) in you
    A powerful, rare dew,   40
Which only grief and love extract; with this
    Be sure, and never miss,
To wash your vessel well: then humbly take
    This balm for souls that ache,
And one who drank it thus, assures that you
    Shall find a joy so true,
Such perfect ease, and such a lively sense
    Of grace against all sins,
That you'll confess the comfort such, as even
    Brings to, and comes from Heaven.   50

Mount of Olives (II)

When first I saw true beauty, and thy joys
Active as light, and calm without all noise
Shined on my soul, I felt through all my powers
Such a rich air of sweets, as evening showers
Fanned by a gentle gale convey and breathe
On some parched bank, crowned with a flow'ry wreath;
Odours, and myrrh, and balm in one rich flood
O'er-ran my heart, and spirited my blood,
My thoughts did swim in comforts, and mine eye
Confessed, *The world did only paint and lie.*   10
And where before I did no safe course steer
But wandered under tempests all the year,
Went bleak and bare in body as in mind,
And was blown through by ev'ry storm and wind,
I am so warmed now by this glance on me,
That, midst all storms I feel a ray of thee;
So have I known some beauteous *paisage* rise
In sudden flowers and arbours to my eyes,
And in the depth and dead of winter bring
To my cold thoughts a lively sense of spring.   20
    Thus fed by thee, who dost all beings nourish,
My withered leafs again look green and flourish,
I shine and shelter underneath thy wing
Where sick with love I strive thy name to sing,
Thy glorious name! which grant I may so do
That these may be thy *praise*, and my *joy* too.

Man

Weighing the steadfastness and state
Of some mean things which here below reside,
Where birds like watchful clocks the noiseless date
  And intercourse of times divide,
Where bees at night get home and hive, and flowers
   Early, as well as late,
Rise with the sun, and set in the same bowers;

2

I would (said I) my God would give
The staidness of these things to man! for these
To his divine appointments ever cleave,   10
  And no new business breaks their peace;
The birds nor sow, nor reap, yet sup and dine,
   The flowers without clothes live,
Yet Solomon was never dressed so fine.

3

Man hath still either toys or care,
He hath no root, nor to one place is tied,
But ever restless and irregular
  About this Earth doth run and ride,
He knows he hath a home, but scarce knows where,
   He says it is so far   20
That he hath quite forgot how to go there.

4

He knocks at all doors, strays and roams,
Nay hath not so much wit as some stones have
Which in the darkest nights point to their homes,
  By some hid sense their Maker gave;
Man is the shuttle, to whose winding quest
   And passage through these looms
God ordered motion, but ordained no rest.

¶

I walked the other day (to spend my hour)
      Into a field
Where I sometimes had seen the soil to yield
      A gallant flower,
But winter now had ruffled all the bower
      And curious store
    I knew there heretofore.

2

Yet I whose search loved not to peep and peer
      I' th' face of things
Thought with myself, there might be other springs   10
      Besides this here
Which, like cold friends, sees us but once a year,
      And so the flower
    Might have some other bower.

3

Then taking up what I could nearest spy
      I digged about
That place where I had seen him to grow out,
      And by and by
I saw the warm Recluse alone to lie
      Where fresh and green   20
    He lived of us unseen.

4

Many a question intricate and rare
      Did I there strow,
But all I could extort was, that he now
      Did there repair
Such losses as befell him in this air
      And would ere long
    Come forth most fair and young.

5

This past, I threw the clothes quite o'er his head,
          And stung with fear   30
Of my own frailty dropped down many a tear
          Upon his bed,
Then sighing whispered, *Happy are the dead!*
          What peace doth now
          Rock him asleep below!

6

And yet, how few believe such doctrine springs
          From a poor root
Which all the winter sleeps here under foot
          And hath no wings
To raise it to the truth and light of things,   40
          But is still trod
          By ev'ry wand'ring clod.

7

O thou! whose spirit did at first inflame
          And warm the dead,
And by a sacred incubation fed
          With life this frame
Which once had neither being, form, nor name,
          Grant I may so
          Thy steps track here below,

8

That in these masques and shadows I may see   50
          Thy sacred way,
And by those hid ascents climb to that day
          Which breaks from thee
Who art in all things, though invisibly;
          Show me thy peace,
          Thy mercy, love, and ease,

9

And from this care, where dreams and sorrows reign,
   Lead me above
Where light, joy, leisure, and true comforts move
   Without all pain,   60
There, hid in thee, show me his life again
   At whose dumb urn
  Thus all the year I mourn.

Begging (I)

King of Mercy, King of Love,
In whom I live, in whom I move,
Perfect what thou hast begun,
Let no night put out this Sun;
Grant I may, my chief desire!
Long for thee, to thee aspire,
Let my youth, my bloom of days
Be my comfort and thy praise,
That hereafter, when I look
O'er the sullied, sinful book,   10
I may find thy hand therein
Wiping out my shame and sin.
O it is thy only Art
To reduce a stubborn heart,
And since thine is victory,
Strongholds should belong to thee;
Lord then take it, leave it not
Unto my dispose or lot,
But since I would not have it mine,
O my God, let it be thine!   20

Jude ver. 24, 25

Now unto him that is able to keep us from falling, and to present us
 faultless before the presence of his glory with exceeding joy,
To the only wise God, our Saviour, be glory and majesty, dominion and
 power, now and ever, Amen.

FINIS

Silex Scintillans:

SACRED
POEMS
And private
EJACULATIONS.

The second Edition, In two Books;
By *Henry Vaughan*, Silurist.

Job chap 35. ver. 10, 11.

Where is God my Maker, who giveth Songs in
the night ?
Who teacheth us more then the beasts of the
earth, and maketh us wiser then the fowls
of heaven ?

London, Printed for *Henry Crips*, and *Lodo*
wick Lloyd, next to the Castle in *Cornhil*,
and in *Popes-head Alley.* 1655.

SILEX SCINTILLANS

The Author's Preface to the Following Hymns

THAT this Kingdom hath abounded with those ingenious persons, which in the late notion are termed *Wits*, is too well known. Many of them having cast away all their fair portion of time in no better employments than a deliberate search, or excogitation of *idle words*, and a most vain, insatiable desire to be reputed *Poets*; leaving behind them no other monuments of those excellent abilities conferred upon them, but such as they may (with a predecessor of theirs) term *parricides*, and a soul-killing issue; for that is the *Brabeion*, and laureate crown, which idle poems will certainly bring to their unrelenting authors.

And well it were for them, if those willingly-studied and wilfully-published vanities could defile no spirits, but their own; but the case is far worse. These vipers survive their parents, and for many ages after (like epidemic diseases) infect whole generations, corrupting always and unhallowing the best-gifted souls, and the most capable vessels; for whose sanctification and welfare, the glorious Son of God laid down his life, and suffered the precious blood of his blessed and innocent heart to be poured out. In the mean time it cannot be denied, but these men are had in remembrance, though we cannot say with any comfort, *Their memorial is blessed*; for, that I may speak no more than the truth (let their passionate worshippers say what they please) all the commendations that can be justly given them, will amount to no more, than what Prudentius the Christian-sacred poet bestowed upon Symmachus:

> Os dignum aeterno tinctum quod fulgeat auro
> Si mallet laudare deum: cui sordida monstra
> Praetulit, et liquidam temeravit crimine vocem;
> Haud aliter, quam cum rastris qui tentat eburnis
> Caenosum versare solum, etc.

10

20

In English thus,

> A wit most worthy in tried gold to shine,
> Immortal gold! had he sung the divine
> Praise of his Maker: to whom he preferred
> Obscene, vile fancies, and profanely marred
> A rich, rare style with sinful, lewd contents;
> No otherwise, than if with instruments
> Of polished ivory, some drudge should stir
> A dirty sink, etc.

This comparison is nothing odious, and it is as true as it is apposite; for a good wit in a bad subject, is (as Solomon said of the *fair* and *foolish woman*) *Like a jewel of gold in a swine's snout*, Prov. 11: 22. Nay, the more acute the author is, there is so much the more danger and death in the work. Where the sun is busy upon a dung-hill, the issue is always some unclean vermin. Divers persons of eminent piety and learning (I meddle not with the seditious and schismatical) have, long before my time, taken notice of this malady; for the complaint against vicious verse, even by peaceful and obedient spirits, is of some antiquity in this Kingdom. And yet, as if the evil consequence attending this inveterate error were but a small thing, there is sprung very lately another prosperous device to assist it in the subversion of souls. Those that want the genius of verse, fall to translating; and the people are (every term) plentifully furnished with various foreign vanities; so that the most lascivious compositions of France and Italy are here naturalized and made English: and this (as it is sadly observed) with so much favour and success, that nothing *takes* (as they rightly phrase it) like a Romance. And very frequently (if that character be not an ivy-bush) the buyer receives this lewd ware from persons of honour: who want not reason to forbear, much private misfortune having sprung from no other seed at first, than some infectious and dissolving legend.

To continue (after years of discretion) in this vanity is an inexcusable desertion of pious sobriety: and to persist so to the end is a wilful despising of God's sacred exhortations, by a constant, sensual volutation or wallowing in impure thoughts and scurrilous conceits, which both defile their authors, and as many more, as they are communicated to. If *every idle word shall be accounted for*, and if *no corrupt communication should proceed out of our mouths*, how desperate (I beseech you) is their condition, who all their lifetime, and out of mere design, study lascivious fictions; then carefully record and publish them, that instead of *grace* and *life*, they *may minister sin and death* unto their readers? It was wisely considered, and piously said by one, *That he would read no idle books; both in regard of love to his own soul, and pity unto his that made them, for* (said he) *if I be corrupted by them, their composer is immediately a cause of my ill: and at the day of reckoning (though now dead) must give an account for it, because I am corrupted by his bad example, which he left behind him. I will write none, lest I hurt them that come after me; I will read none, lest I augment his punishment that is gone before me. I will neither write, nor read, lest I prove a foe to my own soul: while I live, I sin too much; let me not continue longer in wickedness, than I do in life.* It is a sentence of sacred authority, that *he that is dead, is freed from sin*; because he cannot in that state, which is without the body, sin any more; but he that writes idle books makes for himself another body, in which he always lives, and sins (after death) as fast and as foul, as ever he did in his life; which very consideration, deserves to be a sufficient antidote against this evil disease.

And here, because I would prevent a just censure by my free confession, I must remember, that I myself have, for many years together, languished of this very sickness; and it is no long time since I have recovered. But (blessed be God for it!) I have by his saving assistance suppressed my greatest follies, and those which escaped from me, are (I think) as innoxious, as most of that vein use to be; besides, they are interlined with many virtuous, and some pious mixtures. What I speak of them is truth; but let no man mistake it for an extenuation of faults, as if I intended an Apology for them, or myself, who am conscious of so much guilt in both, as can never be expiated without special sorrows, and that cleansing and precious effusion of my Almighty Redeemer: and if the world will be so charitable, as to grant my request, I do here most humbly and earnestly beg that none would read them.

But an idle or sensual subject is not all the poison in these pamphlets. Certain authors have been so irreverendly bold, as to dash Scriptures and the sacred Relatives of God with their impious conceits; and (which I cannot speak without grief of heart) some of those desperate adventurers may (I think) be reckoned amongst the principal or most learned writers of English verse.

Others of a later date, being corrupted (it may be) by that evil genius which came in with the public distractions, have stuffed their books with oaths, horrid execrations, and a most gross and studied filthiness. But the hurt that ensues by the publication of pieces so notoriously ill, lies heavily upon the stationer's account, who ought

in conscience to refuse them, when they are put into his hands. No
loss is so doleful as that gain, that will endamage the soul; he that
prints lewdness and impieties is that mad man in the Proverbs, who
casteth firebrands, arrows and death.

The suppression of this pleasing and prevailing evil lies not
altogether in the power of the Magistrate; for it will fly abroad in
manuscripts, when it fails of entertainment at the press. The true
remedy lies wholly in their bosoms, who are the gifted persons, by a
wise exchange of vain and vicious subjects, for divine themes and 120
celestial praise. The performance is easy, and were it the most dif-
ficult in the world, the reward is so glorious, that it infinitely tran-
scends it: for *they that turn many to righteousness, shall shine like the
stars for ever and ever*: whence follows this undeniable inference, that
the corrupting of many, being a contrary work, the recompense must
be so too; and then I know nothing reserved for them, but the black-
ness of darkness for ever; from which (O God!) deliver all penitent
and reformed spirits!

The first, that with any effectual success attempted a diversion of
this foul and overflowing stream, was the blessed man, Mr. George 130
Herbert, whose holy life and verse gained many pious converts (of
whom I am the least) and gave the first check to a most flourishing
and admired *wit* of his time. After him followed diverse,—*Sed non
passibus aequis*; they had more of fashion than force. And the reason
of their so vast distance from him, besides differing spirits and quali-
fications (for his measure was eminent) I suspect to be, because they
aimed more at verse than perfection; as may be easily gathered by
their frequent impressions, and numerous pages. Hence sprang
those wide, those weak, and lean conceptions, which in the most
inclinable reader will scarce give any nourishment or help to de- 140
votion; for not flowing from a true, practic piety, it was impossible
they should effect those things abroad, which they never had ac-
quaintance with at home; being only the productions of a common
spirit, and the obvious ebullitions of that light humour, which takes
the pen in hand, out of no other consideration, than to be seen in
print. It is true indeed, that to give up our thoughts to pious themes
and contemplations (if it be done for piety's sake) is a great step
towards perfection; because it will refine and dispose to devotion and
sanctity. And further, it will procure for us (so easily communicable
is that loving spirit) some small prelibation of those heavenly re- 150
freshments, which descend but seldom, and then very sparingly,
upon men of an ordinary or indifferent holiness; but he that desires

to excel in this kind of hagiography, or holy writing, must strive (by all means) for perfection and true holiness, that *a door may be opened to him in heaven*, Rev. 4: 1, and then he will be able to write (with Hierotheus and holy Herbert) *A true Hymn*.

To effect this in some measure, I have begged leave to communicate this my poor talent to the Church, under the protection and conduct of her glorious Head: who (if he will vouchsafe to own it, and go along with it) can make it as useful now in the public as it 160 hath been to me in private. In the perusal of it, you will (peradventure) observe some passages, whose history or reason may seem something remote; but were they brought nearer, and plainly exposed to your view (though that perhaps might quiet your curiosity), yet would it not conduce much to your greater advantage. And therefore I must desire you to accept of them in that latitude, which is already allowed them. By the last poems in the book (were not that mistake here prevented) you would judge all to be fatherless, and the edition posthume; for (indeed) *I was nigh unto death*, and am still at no great distance from it; which was the necessary reason for that 170 solemn and accomplished dress, you will now find this impression in.

But *the God of the spirits of all flesh* hath granted me a further use of mine, than I did look for in the body; and when I expected, and had (by his assistance) prepared for a message of death, then did he answer me with life; I hope to his glory, and my great advantage: that I may flourish not with leaf only, but with some fruit also; which hope and earnest desire of his poor creature, I humbly beseech him to perfect and fulfil for his dear Son's sake, unto whom, with him and the most holy and loving Spirit, be ascribed by angels, by men, and 180 by all his works, all glory, and wisdom, and dominion, in this the temporal and in the Eternal Being. *Amen.*

Newton by Usk, near
Sketh-rock, Septem. 30. 1654.

O Lord, the hope of Israel, all they that forsake thee shall be ashamed; and they that depart from thee, shall be written in the earth, because they have forsaken the Lord, the fountain of living waters.

Heal me, O Lord, and I shall be healed; save me, and I shall be saved, for thou art my health, and my great deliverer.   190

I said in the cutting off of my days, I shall go to the gates of the grave; I have deprived myself of the residue of my years.

I said, I shall not see the Lord, even the Lord in the land of the living: I shall behold man no more with the inhabitants of the world.

O Lord! by thee doth man live, and from thee is the life of my spirit: therefore wilt thou recover me, and make me to live.

Thou hast in love to my soul delivered it from the pit of corruption; for thou hast cast all my sins behind thy back.

For thy name's sake hast thou put off thine anger; for thy praise hast thou refrained from me, that I should not be cut off.   200

For the grave cannot praise thee, death cannot celebrate thee: they that go down into the pit, cannot hope for thy truth.

The living, the living, he shall praise thee, as I do this day: the father to the children shall make known thy truth.

O Lord! thou hast been merciful, thou hast brought back my life from corruption: thou hast redeemed me from my sin.

They that follow after lying vanities, forsake their own mercy.

Therefore shall thy songs be with me, and my prayer unto the God of my life.

I will go unto the altar of my God, unto God, the joy of my youth; and in thy fear will I worship towards thy holy temple.   210

I will sacrifice unto thee with the voice of thanksgiving; I will pay that which I have vowed: salvation is of the Lord.

The Dedication

To my most merciful, my most
loving, and dearly loved Re-
deemer, the ever blessed,
the only Holy and
JUST ONE,

JESUS CHRIST,

The Son of the living

G O D,

And the sacred

Virgin Mary.

I

My God! thou that didst die for me,
These thy death's fruits I offer thee;
Death that to me was life and light,
But dark and deep pangs to thy sight.
Some drops of thy all-quick'ning blood
Fell on my heart; those made it bud
And put forth thus, though Lord, before
The ground was cursed, and void of store.
Indeed I had some here to hire
Which long resisted thy desire,   10
That stoned thy servants, and did move
To have thee murthered for thy love;
But Lord, I have expelled them, and so bent,
Beg, thou wouldst take thy tenant's rent.

II

Dear Lord, 'tis finished! and now he
That copied it, presents it thee.
'Twas thine first, and to thee returns,
From thee it shined, though here it burns;
If the sun rise on rocks, is't right,
To call it their inherent light?   20
No, nor can I say, this is mine,
For, dearest Jesus, 'tis all thine.
As thy clothes (when thou with clothes wert clad)
Both light from thee, and virtue had,
And now (as then within this place)
Thou to poor rags dost still give grace.
This is the earnest thy love sheds,
The *Candle* shining on some heads,
Till at thy charges they shall be,
Clothed all with immortality.   30

My dear Redeemer, the world's light,
And life too, and my heart's delight!
For all thy mercies and thy truth
Showed to me in my sinful youth,
For my sad failings and my wild
Murmurings at thee, when most mild:

For all my secret faults, and each
Frequent relapse and wilful breach,
For all designs meant against thee,
And ev'ry published vanity   40
Which thou divinely hast forgiven,
While thy blood washed me white as heaven:
I nothing have to give to thee,
But this thy own gift, given to me;
Refuse it not! for now thy *Token*
Can tell thee where a heart is broken.

Revel. Cap. 1. ver. 5, 6, 7

Unto him that loved us, and washed us from our sins in his own blood.
And hath made us Kings and Priests unto God and his Father; to him
be glory and dominion, for ever and ever. Amen.
Behold, he cometh with clouds, and every eye shall see him, and they
also which pierced him; and all kinreds of the earth shall wail because of
him: even so. Amen.

¶

Vain wits and eyes
Leave, and be wise:
Abuse not, shun not holy fire,
But with true tears wash off your mire.
Tears and these flames will soon grow kind,
And mix an eye-salve for the blind.
Tears cleanse and supple without fail,
And fire will purge your callous veil.
Then comes the light! which when you spy,
And see your nakedness thereby,   10
Praise him, who dealt his gifts so free
In tears to you, in fire to me.

SILEX SCINTILLANS

Ascension-day

Lord Jesus! with what sweetness and delights,
Sure, holy hopes, high joys and quick'ning flights
Dost thou feed thine! O thou! the hand that lifts
To him, who gives all good and perfect gifts.
Thy glorious, bright Ascension (though removed
So many Ages from me) is so proved
And by thy Spirit sealed to me, that I
Feel me a sharer in thy victory.
      I soar and rise
      Up to the skies,   10
          Leaving the world their day,
      And in my flight,
      For the true light
          Go seeking all the way;
I greet thy sepulchre, salute thy grave,
That blest inclosure, where the angels gave
The first glad tidings of thy early light,
And resurrection from the earth and night.
I see that morning in thy Convert's tears,
Fresh as the dew, which but this dawning wears!   20
I smell her spices, and her ointment yields
As rich a scent as the now primrosed fields:
The day-star smiles, and light with thee deceased,
Now shines in all the chambers of the East.
What stirs, what posting intercourse and mirth
Of saints and angels glorify the earth?
What sighs, what whispers, busy stops and stays,
Private and holy talk fill all the ways?
They pass as at the last great day, and run
In their white robes to seek the risen Sun;   30
I see them, hear them, mark their haste, and move
Amongst them, with them, winged with faith and love.
Thy forty days more secret commerce here,
After thy death and funeral, so clear
And indisputable shows to my sight
As the Sun doth, which to those days gave light.

I walk the fields of Bethany which shine
All now as fresh as Eden, and as fine.
Such was the bright world, on the first seventh day,
Before man brought forth sin, and sin decay;   40
When like a virgin clad in *flowers* and *green*
The pure earth sat, and the fair woods had seen
No frost, but flourished in that youthful vest,
With which their great Creator had them dressed:
When Heav'n above them shined like molten glass,
While all the planets did unclouded pass;
And springs, like dissolved pearls their streams did pour,
Ne'er marred with floods, nor angered with a shower.
With these fair thoughts I move in this fair place,
And the last steps of my mild Master trace;   50
I see him leading out his chosen train,
All sad with tears, which like warm summer-rain
In silent drops steal from their holy eyes,
Fixed lately on the Cross, now on the skies.
And now (eternal Jesus!) thou dost heave
Thy blessèd hands to bless these thou dost leave;
The cloud doth now receive thee, and their sight
Having lost thee, behold two men in white!
Two and no more: *what two attest, is true,*
Was thine own answer to the stubborn Jew.   60
Come then thou faithful witness! come dear Lord
Upon the clouds again to judge this world!

Ascension Hymn

                Dust and clay
                Man's ancient wear!
                Here you must stay,
                But I elsewhere;
Souls sojourn here, but may not rest;
Who will ascend, must be undressed.

                And yet some
                That know to die
                Before death come,
                Walk to the sky   10
Even in this life; but all such can
Leave behind them the old Man.

     If a star
     Should leave the sphere,
     She must first mar
     Her flaming wear,
And after fall, for in her dress
Of glory, she cannot transgress.

     Man of old
     Within the line   20
     Of Eden could
     Like the sun shine
All naked, innocent and bright,
And intimate with Heav'n, as light;

     But since he
     That brightness soiled,
     His garments be
     All dark and spoiled,
And here are left as nothing worth,
Till the Refiner's fire breaks forth.   30

     Then comes he!
     Whose mighty light
     Made his clothes be
     Like Heav'n, all bright;
The Fuller, whose pure blood did flow
To make stained man more white than snow.

     He alone
     And none else can
     Bring bone to bone
     And rebuild man,   40
And by his all-subduing might
Make clay ascend more quick than light.

¶

They are all gone into the world of light!
   And I alone sit ling'ring here;
Their very memory is fair and bright,
    And my sad thoughts doth clear.

It glows and glitters in my cloudy breast
    Like stars upon some gloomy grove,
Or those faint beams in which this hill is dressed,
        After the sun's remove.

I see them walking in an air of glory,
    Whose light doth trample on my days: 10
My days, which are at best but dull and hoary,
        Mere glimmering and decays.

O holy hope! and high humility,
    High as the Heavens above!
These are your walks, and you have showed them me
        To kindle my cold love.

Dear, beauteous death! the jewel of the Just,
    Shining nowhere, but in the dark;
What mysteries do lie beyond thy dust;
        Could man outlook that mark!   20

He that hath found some fledged bird's nest may know
    At first sight, if the bird be flown;
But what fair well, or grove he sings in now,
        That is to him unknown.

And yet, as angels in some brighter dreams
    Call to the soul, when man doth sleep:
So some strange thoughts transcend our wonted themes,
        And into glory peep.

If a star were confined into a tomb
    Her captive flames must needs burn there;   30
But when the hand that locked her up gives room,
        She'll shine through all the sphere.

O Father of eternal life, and all
    Created glories under thee!
Resume thy spirit from this world of thrall
        Into true liberty.

Either disperse these mists, which blot and fill
    My perspective (still) as they pass,
Or else remove me hence unto that hill,
    Where I shall need no glass.   40

White Sunday

Welcome white day! a thousand suns,
Though seen at once, were black to thee;
For after their light, darkness comes,
But thine shines to eternity.

Those flames which on the Apostles rushed
At this great feast, and in a tire
Of cloven tongues their heads all brushed,
And crowned them with prophetic fire:

Can these new lights be like to those,
These lights of Serpents like the Dove?   10
Thou hadst no *gall*, ev'n for thy foes,
And thy two wings were *grief* and *love*.

Though then some boast that fire each day,
And on Christ's coat pin all their shreds;
Not sparing openly to say,
His candle shines upon their heads:

Yet while some rays of that great light
Shine here below within thy Book,
They never shall so blind my sight
But I will know which way to look.   20

For though thou dost that great light lock,
And by this lesser commerce keep:
Yet by these glances of the flock
I can discern wolves from the sheep.

Not, but that I have wishes too,
And pray, *These last may be as first,*
Or better; but thou long ago
Hast said, *These last should be the worst.*

Besides, thy method with thy own,
Thy own dear people pens our times,   30
Our stories are in theirs set down
And penalties spread to our crimes.

Again, if worst and worst implies
A state that no redress admits,
Then from thy Cross unto these days
The *rule* without *exception* fits.

And yet, as in night's gloomy page
One silent star may interline:
So in this last and lewdest age,
Thy ancient love on some may shine.   40

For, though we hourly breathe decays,
And our best *note* and highest *ease*
Is but mere changing of the *keys*,
And a *consumption* that doth please;

Yet thou the great eternal Rock
Whose height above all ages shines,
Art still the same, and canst unlock
Thy waters to a soul that pines.

Since then thou art the same this day
And ever, as thou wert of old,   50
And nothing doth thy love allay
But our hearts' dead and sinful cold:

As thou long since wert pleased to buy
Our drowned estate, taking the Curse
Upon thyself, so to destroy
The knots we tied upon thy purse,

So let thy grace now make the way
Even for thy love; for by that means
We, who are nothing but foul clay,
Shall be fine gold, which thou didst cleanse.   60

O come! refine us with thy fire!
Refine us! we are at a loss.
Let not thy stars for Balaam's hire
Dissolve into the common dross!

The Proffer

Be still black parasites,
          Flutter no more;
Were it still winter, as it was before,
          You'd make no flights;
But now the dew and Sun have warmed my bowers,
     You fly and flock to suck the flowers.

But you would honey make:
          These buds will wither,
And what you now extract, in harder weather
          Will serve to take;   10
Wise husband will (you say) there wants prevent,
     Who do not so, too late repent.

O pois'nous, subtle fowls!
          The flies of hell
That buzz in every ear, and blow on souls
          Until they smell
And rot, descend not here, nor think to stay,
     I've read, who 'twas, drove you away.

Think you these longing eyes,
          Though sick and spent,
And almost famished, ever will consent   20
          To leave those skies,
That glass of souls and spirits, where well dressed
     They shine in white (like stars) and rest.

Shall my short hour, my inch,
  My one poor sand,
And crumb of life, now ready to disband,
  Revolt and flinch,
And having borne the burthen all the day,
  Now cast at night my crown away?   30

  No, No; I am not he,
    Go seek elsewhere.
I skill not your fine tinsel and false hair,
    Your sorcery
And smooth seducements: I'll not stuff my story
  With your Commonwealth and glory.

  There are, that will sow tares
    And scatter death
Amongst the quick, selling their souls and breath
    For any wares;   40
But when thy Master comes, they'll find and see
  There's a reward for them and thee.

  Then keep the ancient way!
    Spit out their phlegm
And fill thy breast with home; think on thy dream:
    A calm, bright day!
A land of flowers and spices! the word given,
  If these be fair, O what is Heaven!

Cock-crowing

Father of lights! what sunny seed,
What glance of day hast thou confined
Into this bird? To all the breed
This busy ray thou hast assigned;
    Their magnetism works all night,
    And dreams of Paradise and light.

Their eyes watch for the morning hue,
Their little grain expelling night
So shines and sings, as if it knew
The path unto the house of light.   10
       It seems their candle, howe'er done,
       Was tinned and lighted at the sun.

If such a tincture, such a touch,
So firm a longing can impower
Shall thy own image think it much
To watch for thy appearing hour?
       If a mere blast so fill the sail,
       Shall not the breath of God prevail?

O thou immortal light and heat!
Whose hand so shines through all this frame,   20
That by the beauty of the seat,
We plainly see, who made the same,
       Seeing thy seed abides in me,
       Dwell thou in it, and I in thee.

To sleep without thee, is to die;
Yea, 'tis a death partakes of hell:
For where thou dost not close the eye
It never opens, I can tell.
       In such a dark, Egyptian border,
       The shades of death dwell and disorder.   30

If joys, and hopes, and earnest throes,
And hearts, whose pulse beats still for light
Are given to birds; who, but thee, knows
A love-sick soul's exalted flight?
       Can souls be tracked by any eye
       But his, who gave them wings to fly?

Only this veil which thou hast broke,
And must be broken yet in me,
This veil, I say, is all the cloak
And cloud which shadows thee from me.   40
       This veil thy full-eyed love denies,
       And only gleams and fractions spies.

O take it off! make no delay,
But brush me with thy light, that I
May shine unto a perfect day,
And warm me at thy glorious Eye!
    O take it off! or till it flee,
    Though with no lily, stay with me!

The Star

Whatever 'tis, whose beauty here below
Attracts thee thus and makes thee stream and flow,
    And wind and curl, and wink and smile,
    Shifting thy gait and guile:

Though thy close commerce nought at all imbars
My present search, for eagles eye not stars,
    And still the lesser by the best
    And highest good is blest:

Yet, seeing all things that subsist and be,
Have their commissions from Divinity,   10
    And teach us duty, I will see
    What man may learn from thee.

First, I am sure, the subject so respected
Is well disposed, for bodies once infected,
    Depraved or dead, can have with thee
    No hold, nor sympathy.

Next, there's in it a restless, pure desire
And longing for thy bright and vital fire,
    Desire that never will be quenched,
    Nor can be writhed, nor wrenched.   20

These are the magnets which so strongly move
And work all night upon thy light and love,
    As beauteous shapes, we know not why,
    Command and guide the eye.

For where desire, celestial, pure desire
Hath taken root, and grows, and doth not tire,
    There God a commerce states, and sheds
      His secret on their heads.

This is the heart he craves; and whoso will
But give it him, and grudge not; he shall feel   30
    That God is true, as herbs unseen
      Put on their youth and green.

The Palm-tree

Dear friend sit down, and bear awhile this shade
As I have yours long since; this plant, you see
So pressed and bowed, before sin did degrade
Both you and it, had equal liberty

With other trees: but now shut from the breath
And air of Eden, like a malcontent
It thrives nowhere. This makes these weights (like death
And sin) hang at him; for the more he's bent

The more he grows. Celestial natures still
Aspire for home; this Solomon of old   10
By flowers and carvings and mysterious skill
Of wings, and cherubims, and palms foretold.

This is the life which hid above with Christ
In God, doth always (hidden) multiply,
And spring, and grow, a tree ne'er to be priced,
A tree, whose fruit is immortality.

Here spirits that have run their race and fought
And won the fight, and have not feared the frowns
Nor loved the smiles of greatness, but have wrought
Their master's will, meet to receive their crowns.   20

Here is the patience of the saints: this tree
Is watered by their tears, as flowers are fed
With dew by night; but One you cannot see
Sits here and numbers all the tears they shed.

Here is their faith too, which if you will keep
When we two part, I will a journey make
To pluck a garland hence, while you do sleep,
And weave it for your head against you wake.

Joy

Be dumb, coarse measures, jar no more; to me
There is no discord, but your harmony.
False, juggling sounds; a groan well dressed, where care
Moves in disguise, and sighs afflict the air:
Sorrows in white; griefs tuned; a sugared dosis
Of wormwood, and a Death's-head crowned with Roses.
He weighs not your forced accents, who can have
A lesson played him by a wind or wave.
Such numbers tell their days, whose spirits be
Lulled by those charmers to a lethargy.   10
    But as for thee, whose faults long since require
More eyes than stars; whose breath, could it aspire
To equal winds, would prove too short: thou hast
Another mirth, a mirth though overcast
With clouds and rain, yet full as calm and fine
As those *clear heights* which above tempests shine.
           Therefore while the various showers
           Kill and cure the tender flowers,
           While the winds refresh the year
           Now with clouds, now making clear,   20
           Be sure under pains of death
           To ply both thine eyes and breath.
               As leafs in bowers
               Whisper their hours,
               And hermit-wells
               Drop in their cells:
           So in sighs and unseen tears
           Pass thy solitary years,
And going hence, leave written on some tree,
Sighs make joy sure, and shaking fastens thee.   30

The Favour

O thy bright looks! thy glance of love
Shown, and but shown me from above!
Rare looks! that can dispense such joy
As without wooing wins the coy,
And makes him mourn, and pine and die
Like a starved eaglet, for thine eye.
Some kind herbs here, though low and far,
Watch for, and know their loving star.
O let no star compare with thee!
Nor any herb out-duty me!   10
So shall my nights and mornings be
Thy time to shine, and mine to see.

The Garland

Thou, who dost flow and flourish here below,
To whom a falling star and nine-days' glory,
Or some frail beauty makes the bravest show,
Hark, and make use of this ensuing story.

    When first my youthful, sinful age
        Grew master of my ways,
    Appointing error for my page,
        And darkness for my days;
    I flung away, and with full cry
        Of wild affections, rid   10
    In post for pleasures, bent to try
        All gamesters that would bid.
    I played with fire, did counsel spurn,
        Made life my common stake;
    But never thought that fire would burn,
        Or that a soul could ache.
    Glorious deceptions, gilded mists,
        False joys, phantastic flights,
    Pieces of sackcloth with silk-lists,
        These were my prime delights.   20
    I sought choice bowers, haunted the spring,

Culled flowers and made me posies:
Gave my fond humours their full wing,
    And crowned my head with roses.
But at the height of this career
    I met with a dead man,
Who noting well my vain abear,
    Thus unto me began:
Desist fond fool, be not undone,
    What thou hast cut today   30
Will fade at night, and with this sun
    Quite vanish and decay.

Flowers gathered in this world, die here; if thou
Wouldst have a wreath that fades not, let them grow,
And grow for thee; who spares them here, shall find
A garland, where comes neither rain, nor wind.

Love-sick

Jesus, my life! how shall I truly love thee?
O that thy Spirit would so strongly move me,
That thou wert pleased to shed thy grace so far
As to make man all pure love, flesh a star!
A star that would ne'er set, but ever rise,
So rise and run, as to out-run these skies,
These narrow skies (narrow to me) that bar,
So bar me in, that I am still at war,
At constant war with them. O come and rend,
Or bow the heavens! Lord bow them and descend,   10
And at thy presence make these mountains flow,
These mountains of cold ice in me! Thou art
Refining fire, O then refine my heart,
My foul, foul heart! Thou art immortal heat,
Heat motion gives; then warm it, till it beat,
So beat for thee, till thou in mercy hear,
So hear that thou must open: open to
A sinful wretch, a wretch that caused thy woe,
Thy woe, who caused his weal; so far his weal
That thou forgott'st thine own, for thou didst seal   20
Mine with thy blood, thy blood which makes thee mine,
Mine ever, ever; and me ever thine.

Trinity Sunday

O holy, blessed, glorious three,
Eternal witnesses that be
In heaven, one God in trinity!

As here on earth (when men withstood)
The Spirit, Water, and the Blood,
Made my Lord's Incarnation good:

So let the *antitypes* in me
Elected, bought and sealed for free,
Be owned, saved, *sainted* by you three!

Psalm 104

Up, O my soul, and bless the Lord. O God,
   My God, how great, how very great art thou!
Honour and majesty have their abode
    With thee, and crown thy brow.

Thou cloth'st thyself with light, as with a robe,
   And the high, glorious heav'ns thy mighty hand
Doth spread like curtains round about this globe
    Of air, and sea, and land.

The beams of thy bright chambers thou dost lay
   In the deep waters, which no eye can find;   10
The clouds thy chariots are, and thy pathway
    The wings of the swift wind.

In thy celestial, gladsome messages
   Dispatched to holy souls, sick with desire
And love of thee, each willing angel is
    Thy minister in fire.

Thy arm unmovable forever laid
    And founded the firm earth; then with the deep
As with a veil thou hidst it, thy floods played
    Above the mountains steep.   20

At thy rebuke they fled, at the known voice
    Of their Lord's thunder they retired apace:
Some up the mountains passed by secret ways,
    Some downwards to their place.

For thou to them a bound hast set, a bound
    Which (though but sand) keeps in and curbs whole seas:
There all their fury, foam and hideous sound
    Must languish and decrease.

And as thy care bounds these, so thy rich love
    Doth broach the earth, and lesser brooks lets forth,   30
Which run from hills to valleys, and improve
    Their pleasure and their worth.

These to the beasts of every field give drink;
    There the wild asses swallow the cool spring:
And birds amongst the branches on their brink
    Their dwellings have and sing.

Thou from thy upper springs above, from those
    Chambers of rain, where Heav'n's large bottles lie,
Dost water the parched hills, whose breaches close
    Healed by the showers from high.   40

Grass for the cattle, and herbs for man's use
    Thou mak'st to grow; these (blest by thee) the earth
Brings forth, with wine, oil, bread: all which infuse
    To man's heart strength and mirth.

Thou giv'st the trees their greenness, ev'n to those
    Cedars in Lebanon, in whose thick boughs
The birds their nests build; though the stork doth choose
    The fir-trees for her house.

To the wild goats the high hills serve for folds,
    The rocks give conies a retiring place: 50
Above them the cool moon her known course holds,
    And the sun runs his race.

Thou makest darkness, and then comes the night;
    In whose thick shades and silence each wild beast
Creeps forth, and pinched for food, with scent and sight
    Hunts in an eager quest.

The lion's whelps impatient of delay
    Roar in the covert of the woods, and seek
Their meat from thee, who dost appoint the prey
    And feed'st them all the week.   60

This past, the sun shines on the earth, and they
    Retire into their dens; man goes abroad
Unto his work, and at the close of day
    Returns home with his load.

O Lord my God, how many and how rare
    Are thy great works! In wisdom hast thou made
Them all, and this the earth, and every blade
    Of grass we tread, declare.

So doth the deep and wide sea, wherein are
    Innumerable, creeping things both small   70
And great: there ships go, and the shipmen's fear,
    The comely spacious whale.

These all upon thee wait, that thou mayst feed
    Them in due season: what thou giv'st, they take;
Thy bounteous open hand helps them at need,
    And plenteous meals they make.

When thou dost hide thy face (thy face which keeps
    All things in being) they consume and mourn:
When thou withdraw'st their breath, their vigour sleeps,
    And they to dust return.   80

Thou send'st thy spirit forth, and they revive,
    The frozen earth's dead face thou dost renew.
Thus thou thy glory through the world dost drive,
    And to thy works art true.

Thine eyes behold the earth, and the whole stage
    Is moved and trembles, the hills melt and smoke
With thy least touch: lightnings and winds that rage
    At thy rebuke are broke.

Therefore as long as thou wilt give me breath
    I will in songs to thy great name employ   90
That gift of thine, and to my day of death
    Thou shalt be all my joy.

I'll *spice* my thoughts with thee, and from thy word
    Gather true comforts; but the wicked liver
Shall be consumed. O my soul, bless thy Lord!
    Yea, bless thou him for ever!

The Bird

Hither thou com'st: the busy wind all night
Blew through thy lodging, where thy own warm wing
Thy pillow was. Many a sullen storm
(For which course man seems much the fitter born)
    Rained on thy bed
    And harmless head.

And now as fresh and cheerful as the light
Thy little heart in early hymns doth sing
Unto that *Providence*, whose unseen arm
Curbed them, and clothed thee well and warm.   10
    All things that be, praise him; and had
    Their lesson taught them, when first made.

So hills and valleys into singing break,
And though poor stones have neither speech nor tongue,
While active winds and streams both run and speak,
Yet stones are deep in admiration.
Thus praise and prayer here beneath the sun
Make lesser mornings, when the great are done.

For each inclosèd spirit is a star
　　Inlight'ning his own little sphere,　　　　　　　　20
Whose light, though fetched and borrowèd from far,
　　Both mornings makes, and evenings there.

But as these birds of light make a land glad,
Chirping their solemn matins on each tree:
So in the shades of night some dark fowls be,
Whose heavy notes make all that hear them, sad.

　　The turtle then in palm-trees mourns,
　　　　While owls and satyrs howl;
　　The pleasant land to brimstone turns
　　　　And all her streams grow foul.　　　　　　　30

Brightness and mirth, and love and faith, all fly,
Till the day-spring breaks forth again from high.

The Timber

Sure thou didst flourish once! and many springs,
Many bright mornings, much dew, many showers
Passed o'er thy head: many light *hearts* and *wings*
Which now are dead, lodged in thy living bowers.

And still a new succession sings and flies;
Fresh groves grow up, and their green branches shoot
Towards the old and still enduring skies,
While the low *violet* thrives at their root.

But thou beneath the sad and heavy *line*
Of death, dost waste all senseless, cold and dark;　　　　10
Where not so much as dreams of light may shine,
Nor any thought of greenness, leaf or bark.

And yet (as if some deep hate and dissent,
Bred in thy growth betwixt high winds and thee,
Were still alive) thou dost great storms resent
Before they come, and know'st how near they be.

Else all at rest thou liest, and the fierce breath
Of tempests can no more disturb thy ease;
But this thy strange resentment after death
Means only those, who broke (in life) thy peace.   20

So murthered man, when lovely life is done,
And his blood freezed, keeps in the centre still
Some secret sense, which makes the dead blood run
At his approach, that did the body kill.

And is there any murth'rer worse than sin?
Or any storms more foul than a lewd life?
Or what *resentient* can work more within,
Than true remorse, when with past sins at strife?

He that hath left life's vain joys and vain care,
And truly hates to be detained on earth,   30
Hath got an house where many mansions are,
And keeps his soul unto eternal mirth.

But though thus dead unto the world, and ceased
From sin, he walks a narrow, private way;
Yet grief and old wounds make him sore displeased,
And all his life a rainy, weeping day.

For though he should forsake the world, and live
As mere a stranger, as men long since dead,
Yet joy itself will make a right soul grieve
To think, he should be so long vainly led.   40

But as shades set off light, so tears and grief
(Though of themselves but a sad blubbered story)
By showing the sin great, show the relief
Far greater, and so speak my Saviour's glory.

If my way lies through deserts and wild woods,
Where all the land with scorching heat is cursed,
Better, the pools should flow with rain and floods
To fill my bottle, than I die with thirst.

Blest showers they are, and streams sent from above
Begetting *virgins* where they use to flow;   50
And trees of life no other waters love,
These upper springs and none else make them grow.

But these chaste fountains flow not till we die;
Some drops may fall before, but a clear spring
And ever running, till we leave to fling
Dirt in her way, will keep above the sky.

Rom. Cap. 6. ver. 7
He that is dead is freed from sin.

The Jews

When the fair year
Of your deliverer comes,
And that long frost which now benumbs
Your hearts shall thaw; when angels here
Shall yet to man appear,
And familiarly confer
Beneath the oak and juniper:
When the bright *Dove*
Which now these many, many springs
Hath kept above,   10
Shall with spread wings
Descend, and living waters flow
To make dry dust, and dead trees grow;

O then that I
Might live, and see the olive bear
Her proper branches! which now lie
Scattered each where,
And without root and sap decay
Cast by the husbandman away.
And sure it is not far!   20
For as your fast and foul decays
Forerunning the bright morning-star,
Did sadly note his healing rays

Would shine elsewhere, since you were blind,
And would be cross, when God was kind:
     So by all signs
Our fullness too is now come in,
And the same Sun which here declines
And sets, will few hours hence begin
To rise on you again, and look   30
Towards old Mamre and Eshcol's brook.
     For surely he
Who loved the world so, as to give
His only Son to make it free,
Whose spirit too doth mourn and grieve
To see man lost, will for old love
From your dark hearts this veil remove.

Faith sojourned first on earth in you,
You were the dear and chosen stock:
The Arm of God, glorious and true,   40
Was first revealed to be your rock.

You were the *eldest* child, and when
Your stony hearts despisèd love,
The *youngest*, ev'n the Gentiles then
Were cheered, your jealousy to move.

Thus, righteous Father! dost thou deal
With brutish men; thy gifts go round
By turns, and timely, and so heal
The lost son by the newly found.

Begging (II)

O, do not go! thou know'st, I'll die!
My *Spring* and *Fall* are in thy book!
Or, if thou goest, do not deny
To lend me, though from far, one look!

My sins long since have made thee strange,
A very stranger unto me;
No morning-meetings since this change,
Nor evening-walks have I with thee.

Why is my God thus slow and cold,
When I am most, most sick and sad?   10
Well fare those blessèd days of old
When thou didst hear the *weeping lad*!

O do not thou do as I did,
Do not despise a love-sick heart!
What though some clouds defiance bid
Thy Sun must shine in every part.

Though I have spoiled, O spoil not thou!
Hate not thine own dear gift and token!
Poor birds sing best, and prettiest show,
When their nest is fall'n and broken.   20

Dear Lord! restore thy ancient peace,
Thy quick'ning friendship, man's bright wealth!
And if thou wilt not give me ease
From sickness, give my spirit health!

Palm Sunday

Come, drop your branches, strow the way,
          Plants of the day!
Whom sufferings make most green and gay.

The King of grief, the man of sorrow
Weeping still, like the wet morrow,
Your shades and freshness comes to borrow.

Put on, put on your best array;
Let the joyed road make holy-day,
And flowers that into fields do stray,
Or secret groves, keep the highway.   10

Trees, flowers and herbs, birds, beasts and stones,
That since man fell, expect with groans
To see the Lamb, which all at ones,
Lift up your heads and leave your moans!

      For here comes he
      Whose death will be
Man's life, and your full liberty.

Hark! how the children shrill and high
    Hosanna cry,
Their joys provoke the distant sky,   20
Where thrones and seraphins reply,
And their own angels shine and sing
        In a bright ring:
        Such young, sweet mirth
        Makes heaven and earth
Join in a joyful symphony.

The harmless, young and happy ass,
Seen long before this came to pass,
Is in these joys an high partaker
Ordained, and made to bear his Maker.   30

Dear feast of palms, of flowers and dew!
Whose fruitful dawn sheds hopes and lights;
Thy bright solemnities did shew
The third glad day through two sad nights.

I'll get me up before the sun,
I'll cut me boughs off many a tree,
And all alone full early run
To gather flowers to welcome thee.

Then like the *palm*, though wrong, I'll bear,
I will be still a child, still meek   40
As the poor ass, which the proud jeer,
And only my dear Jesus seek.

If I lose all, and must endure
The proverbed griefs of holy Job,
I care not, so I may secure
But one *green branch* and a *white robe*.

Jesus Weeping (I)

S. Luke 19. ver. 41

Blessed, unhappy city! dearly loved
But still unkind! art this day nothing moved?
    Art senseless still? O can'st thou sleep
    When God himself for thee doth weep!
    Stiff-neckèd Jews! your fathers' breed
    That served the calf, not *Abr'am's* seed,
    Had not the babes *Hosanna* cried,
    The stones had spoke, what you denied.

Dear Jesus weep on! pour this latter
Soul-quick'ning rain, this living water   10
    On their dead hearts; but (O my fears!)
    They will drink blood, that despise tears.
    My dear, bright Lord! my Morning-star!
    Shed this live-dew on fields which far
    From hence long for it! shed it there,
    Where the starved earth groans for one tear!

This land, though with thy heart's blest extract fed,
Will nothing yield but thorns to wound thy head.

The Daughter of Herodias

St. Matth. chap. 14. ver. 6 etc.

Vain, sinful art! who first did fit
Thy lewd loathed *motions* unto *sounds*,
And made grave *music* like wild *wit*
Err in loose airs beyond her bounds?

What fires hath he heaped on his head?
Since to his sins (as needs it must)
His *art* adds still (though he be dead)
New fresh accounts of blood and lust.

Leave then young sorceress; the *ice*
Will those coy spirits cast asleep,   10
Which teach thee now to please his eyes
Who doth thy loathsome mother keep.

But thou hast pleased so well, he swears,
And gratifies thy sin with vows:
His shameless lust in public wears,
And to thy soft arts strongly bows.

Skilful enchantress and true bred!
Who out of evil can bring forth good?
Thy mother's nets in thee were spread,
She tempts to *incest*, thou to *blood*.   20

Jesus Weeping (II)

St. John, chap. 11. ver. 35

My dear, Almighty Lord! why dost thou weep?
Why dost thou groan and groan again,
　　　And with such deep,
Repeated sighs thy kind heart pain,
Since the same sacred breath which thus
　　　　Doth mourn for us,
Can make man's dead and scattered bones
Unite, and raise up all that died, at once?

O holy groans! groans of the Dove!
O healing tears! the tears of love!   10
Dew of the dead! which makes dust move
And spring, how is't that you so sadly grieve,
　　　　Who can relieve?

Should not thy sighs refrain thy store
Of tears, and not provoke to more?
Since two afflictions may not reign
In one at one time, as some feign.
Those blasts, which o'er our heads here stray,
If showers then fall, will showers allay,
As those poor pilgrims oft have tried,   20
Who in this windy world abide.

Dear Lord! thou art all grief and love,
But which thou art most, none can prove.
Thou griev'st, man should himself undo,
And lov'st him, though he works thy woe.

'Twas not that vast, almighty measure
Which is required to make up life,
(Though purchased with thy heart's dear treasure)
   Did breed this strife
Of grief and pity in thy breast,   30
The throne where peace and power rest:
But 'twas thy love that (without leave)
Made thine eyes melt, and thy heart heave;
For though death cannot so undo
What thou hast done (but though man too
Should help to spoil) thou canst restore
All better far than 'twas before;
Yet, thou so full of pity art
(Pity which overflows thy heart!)
That, though the cure of all man's harm   40
Is nothing to thy glorious arm,
Yet canst not thou that free cure do,
But thou must sorrow for him too.

  Then farewell joys! for while I live,
My business here shall be to grieve:
A grief that shall outshine all joys
For mirth and life, yet without noise.
A grief, whose silent dew shall breed
Lilies and myrrh, where the cursed seed
Did sometimes rule. A grief so bright   50
'Twill make the land of darkness light;
And while too many sadly roam,
Shall send me (*swan-like*) singing home.

Psal. 73. ver. 25

*Whom have I in heaven but thee? and there is none upon earth that I
desire besides thee.*

Providence

Sacred and secret hand!
By whose assisting, swift command
The angel showed that holy well,
Which freed poor Hagar from her fears,
And turned to smiles the begging tears
Of young, distressèd Ishmael.

How in a mystic cloud
(Which doth thy strange sure mercies shroud)
Dost thou convey man food and money
Unseen by him, till they arrive   10
Just at his mouth, that thankless hive
Which kills thy bees, and eats thy honey!

If I thy servant be
(Whose service makes ev'n captives free)
A fish shall all my tribute pay,
The swift-winged raven shall bring me meat,
And I, like flowers shall still go neat,
As if I knew no month but May.

I will not fear what man,
With all his plots and power can;   20
Bags that wax old may plundered be,
But none can sequester or let
A state that with the sun doth set
And comes next morning fresh as he.

Poor birds this doctrine sing,
And herbs which on dry hills do spring
Or in the howling wilderness
Do know thy dewy morning-hours,
And watch all night for mists or showers,
Then drink and praise thy bounteousness.   30

May he for ever die
Who trusts not thee! but wretchedly
Hunts gold and wealth, and will not lend

Thy service, nor his soul one day:
May his crown, like his hopes, be clay,
And what he saves, may his foes spend!

    If all my portion here,
The measure given by thee each year
Were by my causeless enemies
Usurped; it never should me grieve   40
Who know, how well thou canst relieve,
Whose hands are open as thine eyes.

    Great King of love and truth!
Who would'st not hate my froward youth,
And wilt not leave me, when grown old;
Gladly will I, like Pontic sheep,
Unto their wormwood-diet keep
Since thou hast made thy Arm my fold.

The Knot

Bright Queen of Heaven! God's Virgin Spouse!
    The glad world's blessed maid!
Whose beauty tied life to thy house,
    And brought us saving aid.

Thou art the true Loves-knot; by thee
    God is made our ally,
And man's inferior essence he
    With his did dignify.

For coalescent by that band
    We are his body grown,   10
Nourished with favours from his hand
    Whom for our head we own.

And such a Knot, what arm dares loose,
    What life, what death can sever?
Which us in him, and him in us
    United keeps for ever.

The Ornament

The lucky world showed me one day
Her gorgeous mart and glittering store,
Where with proud haste the rich made way
To buy, the poor came to adore.

Serious they seemed and bought up all
The latest modes of pride and lust,
Although the first must surely fall,
And the last is most loathsome dust.

But while each gay, alluring wear
With idle hearts and busy looks   10
They viewed (for idleness hath there
Laid up all her archives and books)

Quite through their proud and pompous file
Blushing, and in meek weeds arrayed,
With native looks, which knew no guile,
Came the sheep-keeping Syrian maid.

Whom straight the shining row all faced,
Forced by her artless looks and dress,
While one cried out, We are disgraced
For she is bravest, you confess.   20

St. Mary Magdalen

Dear, beauteous Saint! more white than day,
When in his naked, pure array,
Fresher than morning-flowers which shew
As thou in tears dost, best in dew.
How art thou changed! how lively-fair,
Pleasing and innocent an air,
Not tutored by thy glass, but free,
Native and pure shines now in thee!
But since thy beauty doth still keep

Bloomy and fresh, why dost thou weep?   10
This dusky state of sighs and tears
Durst not look on those smiling years,
When Magdal-castle was thy seat,
Where all was sumptuous, rare and neat.
Why lies this *hair* despisèd now
Which once thy care and art did show?
Who then did dress the much loved toy,
In *spires*, *globes*, angry *curls* and coy,
Which with skilled negligence seemed shed
About thy curious, wild, young head?   20
Why is this rich, this pistic nard
Spilt, and the box quite broke and marred?
What pretty sullenness did haste
Thy easy hands to do this waste?
Why art thou humbled thus, and low
As earth, thy lovely head dost bow?
Dear *soul*! thou knew'st, flowers here on earth
At their Lord's foot-stool have their birth;
Therefore thy withered self in haste
Beneath his blest feet thou didst cast,   30
That at the root of this green tree
Thy great decays restored might be.
Thy curious vanities and rare;
Odorous ointments kept with care,
And dearly bought (when thou didst see
They could not cure, nor comfort thee)
Like a wise, early Penitent
Thou sadly didst to him present,
Whose interceding, meek and calm
Blood, is the world's all-healing *Balm*.   40
This, this Divine Restorative
Called forth thy tears, which ran in live
And hasty drops, as if they had
(Their Lord so near) sense to be glad.
Learn, *Ladies*, here the faithful cure
Makes beauty lasting, fresh and pure;
Learn Mary's art of tears, and then
Say, *You have got the day from men.*
Cheap, mighty Art! her Art of love,
Who loved much and much more could move;   50

Her Art! whose memory must last
Till truth through all the world be past,
Till his abused, despisèd flame
Return to Heaven, from whence it came,
And send a fire down, that shall bring
Destruction on his ruddy wing.

Her Art! whose pensive, weeping eyes,
Were once sin's loose and tempting spies,
But now are fixèd stars, whose light
Helps such dark stragglers to their sight.   60

Self-boasting Pharisee! how blind
A judge wert thou, and how unkind!
It was impossible, that thou
Who wert all false, should'st true grief know;
Is't just to judge her faithful tears
By that foul rheum thy false eye wears?

This woman (say'st thou) *is a sinner*:
And sate there none such at thy dinner?
Go leper, go; wash till thy flesh
Comes like a child's, spotless and fresh;   70
He is still leprous, that still paints:
Who saint themselves, they are no *saints*.

The Rainbow

Still young and fine! but what is still in view
We slight as old and soiled, though fresh and new.
How bright wert thou, when Shem's admiring eye
Thy burnished, flaming *Arch* did first descry!
When Terah, Nahor, Haran, Abram, Lot,
The youthful world's gray fathers in one knot,
Did with intentive looks watch every hour
For thy new light, and trembled at each shower!
When thou dost shine darkness looks white and fair,
Storms turn to music, clouds to smiles and air: 10
Rain gently spends his honey-drops, and pours

Balm on the cleft earth, milk on grass and flowers.
Bright pledge of peace and sunshine! the sure tie
Of thy Lord's hand, the object of his eye.
When I behold thee, though my light be dim,
Distant and low, I can in thine see him,
Who looks upon thee from his glorious throne
And minds the Covenant 'twixt *All* and *One*.
O foul, deceitful men! my God doth keep
His promise still, but we break ours and sleep.   20
After the *Fall*, the first sin was in *blood*,
And *drunkenness* quickly did succeed the flood;
But since Christ died (as if we did devise
To lose him too, as well as Paradise)
These two grand sins we join and act together,
Though blood and drunkenness make but foul, foul weather.
Water (though both Heaven's windows and the deep,
Full forty days o'er the drowned world did weep)
Could not reform us, and blood (in despite)
Yea God's own blood we tread upon and slight.   30
So those bad daughters, which God saved from fire,
While Sodom yet did smoke, lay with their sire.

Then peaceful, signal bow, but in a cloud
Still lodged, where all thy unseen arrows shroud,
I will on thee, as on a comet look,
A comet, the sad world's ill-boding book;
Thy light as luctual and stained with woes
I'll judge, where penal flames sit mixed and close.
For though some think, thou shin'st but to restrain
Bold storms, and simply dost attend on rain,   40
Yet I know well, and so our sins require,
Thou dost but court cold rain, till *rain* turns *fire*.

The Seed Growing Secretly

S. Mark 4. 26

If this world's friends might see but once
What some poor man may often feel,
Glory, and gold, and crowns and thrones
They would soon quit and learn to kneel.

My dew, my dew! my early love,
My soul's bright food, thy absence kills!
Hover not long, eternal Dove!
Life without thee is loose and spills.

Something I had, which long ago
Did learn to suck, and sip, and taste,   10
But now grown sickly, sad and slow,
Doth fret and wrangle, pine and waste.

O spread thy sacred wings and shake
One living drop! one drop life keeps!
If pious griefs Heaven's joys awake,
O fill his bottle! Thy child weeps!

Slowly and sadly doth he grow,
And soon as left, shrinks back to ill;
O feed that life, which makes him blow
And spread and open to thy will!   20

For thy eternal, living wells
None stained or withered shall come near:
A fresh, immortal *green* there dwells,
And spotless *white* is all the wear.

Dear, secret *greenness*! nursed below
Tempests and winds, and winter-nights,
Vex not, that but one sees thee grow,
That *One* made all these lesser lights.

If those bright joys he singly sheds
On thee, were all met in one crown,   30
Both sun and stars would hide their heads;
And moons, though full, would get them down.

Let glory be their bait, whose minds
Are all too high for a low cell:
Though hawks can prey through storms and winds,
The poor bee in her hive must dwell.

Glory, the crowd's cheap tinsel, still
To what most takes them, is a drudge;
And they too oft take good for ill,
And thriving vice for virtue judge.   40

What needs a conscience calm and bright
Within itself an outward test?
Who breaks his glass to take more light,
Makes way for storms into his rest.

Then bless thy secret growth, nor catch
At noise, but thrive unseen and dumb;
Keep clean, bear fruit, earn life and watch
Till the white-wingèd Reapers come!

¶

As time one day by me did pass
        Through a large dusky glass
        He held, I chanced to look
        And spied his curious book
Of past days, where sad Heav'n did shed
A mourning light upon the dead.

Many disordered lives I saw
        And foul records which thaw
        My kind eyes still, but in
        A fair, white page of thin   10
And ev'n, smooth lines, like the sun's rays,
Thy name was writ, and all thy days.

O bright and happy calendar!
        Where youth shines like a star
        All pearled with tears, and may
        Teach age, *The Holy way*;
Where through thick pangs, high agonies,
Faith into life breaks, and death dies.

As some meek *night-piece* which day quails,
   To candle-light unveils: 20
   So by one beamy line
   From thy bright lamp did shine,
In the same page thy humble grave
Set with green herbs, glad hopes and brave.

Here slept my thoughts' dear mark! which dust
   Seemed to devour, like rust;
   But dust (I did observe)
   By hiding doth preserve,
As we for long and sure recruits,
Candy with sugar our choice fruits.   30

O calm and sacred bed where lies
   In death's dark mysteries
   A beauty far more bright
   Than the noon's cloudless light
For whose dry dust green branches bud
And robes are bleached in the *Lamb's* blood.

Sleep happy ashes! (blessed sleep!)
   While hapless I still weep;
   Weep that I have out-lived
   My life, and unrelieved   40
Must (soul-less shadow!) so live on,
Though life be dead, and my joys gone.

¶

Fair and young light! my guide to holy
Grief and soul-curing melancholy;
Whom living here I did still shun
As sullen night-ravens do the sun,
And led by my own foolish fire
Wandered through darkness, dens and mire:
How am I now in love with all
That I termed then mere bonds and thrall,
And to thy name, which still I keep,

Like the surviving turtle, weep!   10
O bitter cursed delights of men!
Our souls' diseases first, and then
Our bodies'; poisons that entreat
With fatal sweetness, till we eat;
How artfully do you destroy,
That kill with smiles and seeming joy?
If all the subtleties of vice
Stood bare before unpracticed eyes,
And every act she doth commence
Had writ down its sad consequence,   20
Yet would not men grant their ill fate
Lodged in those false looks, till too late.
O holy, happy, healthy Heaven,
Where all is pure, where all is even,
Plain, harmless, faithful, fair and bright,
But what Earth breathes against thy light!
How blest had men been, had their *sire*
Lived still in league with thy chaste fire,
Nor made life through her long descents
A slave to lustful elements!   30
I did once read in an old book
Soiled with many a weeping look,
That the seeds of foul sorrows be
The finest things that are, to see.
So that famed fruit which made all die
Seemed fair unto the woman's eye.
If these supplanters in the shade
Of Paradise could make man fade,
How in this world should they deter
This world, their fellow-murtherer!   40
And why then grieve we to be sent
Home by our first fair punishment,
Without addition to our woes
And ling'ring wounds from weaker foes?
Since that doth quickly freedom win,
For he that's dead, is freed from sin.

O that I were wingèd and free
And quite undressed just now with thee,
Where freed souls dwell by living fountains

On everlasting, spicy mountains!   50
    Alas! my God! take home thy sheep;
    This world but laughs at those that weep.

The Stone

Josh. chap. 24. ver. 27

I have it now:
But where to act, that none shall know,
Where I shall have no cause to fear
        An eye or ear,
            What man will show?
If nights, and shades, and secret rooms,
            Silent as tombs,
Will nor conceal nor assent to
My dark designs, what shall I do?
Man I can bribe, and woman will   10
Consent to any gainful ill,
But these dumb creatures are so true,
No gold nor gifts can them subdue.
Hedges have ears, said the old *sooth*,
And ev'ry bush is something's booth;
This cautious fools mistake, and fear
Nothing but man, when ambushed there.

        But I (alas!)
Was shown one day in a strange glass
That busy commerce kept between   20
God and his Creatures, though unseen.

        They hear, see, speak,
And into loud discoveries break,
As loud as blood. Not that God needs
Intelligence, whose spirit feeds
All things with life, before whose eyes,
Hell and all hearts stark naked lies.
But he that judgeth as he hears,
He that accuseth none, so steers

His righteous course, that though he knows   30
All that man doth, conceals or shows,
Yet will not he by his own light
(Though both all-seeing and all right)
Condemn men; but will try them by
A process, which ev'n man's own eye
Must needs acknowledge to be just.
        Hence sand and dust
Are shaked for witnesses, and stones
Which some think dead, shall all at once
With one attesting voice detect   40
Those secret sins we least suspect.
For know, wild men, that when you err
Each thing turns Scribe and Register,
And in obedience to his Lord,
Doth your most private sins record.

        The *Law* delivered to the Jews,
Who promised much, but did refuse
Performance, will for that same deed
Against them by a *stone* proceed;
Whose substance, though 'tis hard enough,   50
Will prove their hearts more stiff and tough.
But now, since God on himself took
What all mankind could never brook,
If any (for he all invites)
His easy yoke rejects or slights,
The *Gospel* then (for 'tis his word
And not himself shall judge the world)
Will by loose *dust* that man arraign,
As one than dust more vile and vain.

The Dwelling-place

S. John, chap. 1. ver. 38, 39

What happy, secret fountain,
    Fair shade, or mountain,
Whose undiscovered virgin glory
Boasts it this day, though not in story,

Was then thy dwelling? did some cloud
Fixed to a tent, descend and shroud
My distressed Lord? or did a star
Beckoned by thee, though high and far,
In sparkling smiles haste gladly down
To lodge light, and increase her own?   10
My dear, dear God! I do not know
What lodged thee then, nor where, nor how;
But I am sure, thou dost now come
Oft to a narrow, homely room,
Where thou too hast but the least part,
My God, I mean *my sinful heart.*

The Men of War

S. Luke, chap. 23. ver. 11

If any have an ear
Saith holy John, *then let him hear.*
He that into captivity
Leads others, shall a captive be.
Who with the sword doth others kill,
A sword shall his blood likewise spill.
Here is the patience of the saints,
And the true faith, which never faints.

Were not thy word (dear Lord!) my light,
How would I run to endless night,   10
And persecuting thee and thine,
Enact for *saints* myself and mine.
But now enlightened thus by thee,
I dare not think such villainy;
Nor for a temporal self-end
Successful wickedness commend.
For in this bright, instructing verse
Thy saints are not the conquerors;
But patient, meek, and overcome
Like thee, when set at naught and dumb.   20
Armies thou hast in Heaven, which fight,
And follow thee all clothed in white,

But here on earth (though thou hast need)
Thou wouldst no legions, but wouldst bleed.
The sword wherewith thou dost command
Is in thy mouth, not in thy hand,
And all thy saints do overcome
By thy blood, and their martyrdom.
But seeing soldiers long ago
Did spit on thee, and smote thee too;   30
Crowned thee with thorns, and bowed the knee,
But in contempt, as still we see,
I'll marvel not at ought they do,
Because they used my Saviour so;
Since of my *Lord* they had their will,
The servant must not take it ill.

   Dear Jesus give me patience here,
And faith to see my crown as near
And almost reached, because 'tis sure
If I hold fast and slight the *lure*.   40
Give me humility and peace,
Contented thoughts, innoxious ease,
A sweet, revengeless, quiet mind,
And to my greatest haters kind.
Give me, my God! a heart as mild
And plain, as when I was a child;
That when *thy throne is set*, and all
These *conquerors* before it fall,
I may be found (preserved by thee)
Amongst that chosen company,   50
Who by no blood (here) overcame
But the blood of the *blessed Lamb*.

The Ass

St. Matt. 21

Thou! who didst place me in this busy street
Of flesh and blood, where two ways meet:
The *One* of goodness, peace and life,
The *other* of death, sin and strife;

Where frail visibles rule the mind,
And present things find men most kind:
Where obscure cares the *mean* defeat,
And splendid vice destroys the *great*;
As thou didst set no law for me,
But that of perfect liberty,   10
Which neither tires, nor doth corrode,
But is a *pillow*, not a *load*:
So give me grace ever to rest,
And build on it, because the best;
Teach both mine eyes and feet to move
Within those bounds set by thy love;
Grant I may soft and lowly be,
And mind those things I cannot see;
Tie me to faith, though above reason,
Who question power, they speak treason: 20
Let me thy Ass be only wise
To carry, not search mysteries;
Who carries thee, is by thee led,
Who argues, follows his own head.
To check bad motions, keep me still
Amongst the dead, where thriving ill
Without his brags and conquests lies,
And truth (oppressed here) gets the prize.
At all times, whatsoe'er I do,
Let me not fail to question, who   30
Shares in the *act*, and puts me to't?
And if not thou, let not me do't.
Above all, make me love the poor,
Those burthens to the rich man's door,
Let me admire those, and be kind
To low estates, and a low mind.
If the world offers to me ought,
That by thy book must not be sought,
Or though it should be lawful, may
Prove not expedient for thy way;   40
To shun that peril, let thy grace
Prevail with me to shun the place.
Let me be wise to please thee still,
And let men call me what they will.
  When thus thy mild, instructing hand

Finds thy poor *foal* at thy command,
When he from wild is become wise,
And slights that most, which men most prize;
When all things here to thistles turn
Pricking his lips, till he doth mourn   50
And hang the head, sighing for those
Pastures of life, where the Lamb goes:
O then, just then! break or untie
These bonds, this sad captivity,
This leaden state, which men miscall
Being and life, but is dead thrall.
And when (O God!) the Ass is free,
In a state known to none but thee;
O let him by his *Lord* be led,
To living springs, and there be fed   60
Where light, joy, health and perfect peace
Shut out all pain and each disease;
Where death and frailty are forgotten,
And bones rejoice, which once were broken!

The Hidden Treasure

S. Matt. 13. 44

What can the man do that succeeds the King?
Even what was done before, and no new thing.
Who shows me but one grain of sincere light?
False stars and fire-drakes, the deceits of night
Set forth to fool and foil thee, do not boast;
Such coal-flames show but kitchen-rooms at most.
And those I saw searched through; yea those and all
That these three thousand years time did let fall
To blind the eyes of lookers-back, and I
Now all is done, find all is vanity.   10
Those secret searches, which afflict the wise,
Paths that are hidden from the *vulture's* eyes
I saw at distance, and where grows that fruit
Which others only grope for and dispute.
    The world's loved wisdom (for the world's friends think
There is none else), did not the dreadful brink

And precipice it leads to, bid me fly,
None could with more advantage use, than I.
   Man's favourite sins, those tainting appetites
Which nature breeds, and some fine clay invites,   20
With all their soft, kind arts and easy strains
Which strongly operate, though without pains,
Did not a greater beauty rule mine eyes,
None would more dote on, nor so soon entice.
But since these sweets are sour and poisoned here
Where the impure seeds flourish all the year,
And private tapers will but help to stray
Ev'n those, who *by them* would find out the day,
I'll seal my eyes up, and to thy commands
Submit my wild heart, and restrain my hands;   30
I will do nothing, nothing know, nor see
But what thou bidst, and showst, and teachest me.
Look what thou gav'st; all that I do restore
But for one thing, though purchased once before.

Child-hood

I cannot reach it; and my striving eye
Dazzles at it, as at eternity.
      Were now that Chronicle alive,
Those white designs which children drive,
And the thoughts of each harmless hour,
With their content too in my pow'r,
Quickly would I make my path even,
And by mere playing go to Heaven.
      Why should men love
A Wolf, more than a Lamb or Dove?   10
Or choose hell-fire and brimstone streams
Before bright stars, and God's own beams?
Who kisseth thorns, will hurt his face,
But flowers do both refresh and grace,
And sweetly living (*fie on men!*)
Are when dead, medicinal then.
If seeing much should make staid eyes,
And long experience should make wise;

Since all that age doth teach, is ill,
Why should I not love child-hood still?   20
Why if I see a rock or shelf,
Shall I from thence cast down myself,
Or by complying with the world,
From the same precipice be hurled?
Those observations are but foul
Which make me wise to lose my soul.

And yet the *practice* worldlings call
Business and weighty action all,
Checking the poor child for his play,
But gravely cast themselves away.   30

    Dear, harmless age! the short, swift span,
Where weeping virtue parts with man;
Where love without lust dwells, and bends
What way we please, without self-ends.

An age of mysteries! which he
Must live twice, that would God's face see;
Which *angels* guard, and with it play,
Angels! which foul men drive away.

How do I study now, and scan
Thee, more than e'er I studied man,   40
And only see through a long night
Thy edges, and thy bordering light!
O for thy Centre and mid-day!
For sure that is the *narrow way*.

The Night

John 3. 2

    Through that pure *Virgin-shrine*,
That sacred veil drawn o'er thy glorious noon
That men might look and live as glow-worms shine,
        And face the moon:
    Wise Nicodemus saw such light
    As made him know his God by night.

Most blest believer he!
Who in that land of darkness and blind eyes
Thy long expected healing wings could see,
          When thou didst rise,   10
          And what can never more be done,
          Did at mid-night speak with the Sun!

          O who will tell me, where
He found thee at that dead and silent hour!
What hallowed solitary ground did bear
          So rare a flower,
          Within whose sacred leafs did lie
          The fullness of the Deity.

          No mercy-seat of gold,
No dead and dusty *cherub*, nor carved stone,   20
But his own living works did my Lord hold
          And lodge alone;
          Where *trees* and *herbs* did watch and peep
          And wonder, while the Jews did sleep.

          Dear night! this world's defeat;
The stop to busy fools; care's check and curb;
The day of spirits; my soul's calm retreat
          Which none disturb!
          Christ's progress, and his prayer time;
          The hours to which high Heaven doth chime.   30

          God's silent, searching flight:
When my Lord's head is filled with dew, and all
His locks are wet with the clear drops of night;
          His still, soft call;
          His knocking time; the soul's dumb watch,
          When spirits their fair kinred catch.

          Were all my loud, evil days
Calm and unhaunted as is thy dark tent,
Whose peace but by some *angel's* wing or voice
          Is seldom rent;   40
          Then I in Heaven all the long year
          Would keep, and never wander here.

But living where the sun
Doth all things wake, and where all mix and tire
Themselves and others, I consent and run
    To ev'ry mire,
    And by this world's ill-guiding light,
    Err more than I can do by night.

    There is in God (some say)
A deep, but dazzling darkness; as men here   50
Say it is late and dusky, because they
    See not all clear;
    O for that night! where I in him
    Might live invisible and dim.

Abel's Blood

Sad, purple well! whose bubbling eye
Did first against a murth'rer cry;
Whose streams still vocal, still complain
    Of bloody Cain,
And now at evening are as red
As in the morning when first shed.
    If single thou
(Though single voices are but low)
Could'st such a shrill and long cry rear
As speaks still in thy maker's ear,   10
What thunders shall those men arraign
Who cannot count those they have slain,
Who bathe not in a shallow flood,
But in a deep, wide sea of blood?
A sea, whose loud waves cannot sleep,
But *deep* still calleth upon *deep*:
Whose urgent *sound* like unto that
Of many waters, beateth at
The everlasting doors above,
Where souls behind the altar move,   20
And with one strong, incessant cry
Inquire *How long?* of the most high.
    Almighty Judge!

At whose just laws no just men grudge;
Whose blessed, sweet commands do pour
Comforts and joys, and hopes each hour
On those that keep them; O accept
Of his vowed heart, whom thou hast kept
From bloody men! and grant, I may
That sworn memorial duly pay   30
To thy bright arm, which was my light
And leader through thick death and night!
                    Aye, may that flood,
That proudly spilt and despised blood,
Speechless and calm, as infants sleep!
Or if it watch, forgive and weep
For those that spilt it! May no cries
From the low earth to high Heaven rise,
But what (like his, whose blood peace brings)
Shall (when they rise) *speak better things*,   40
Than Abel's doth! may Abel be
Still single heard, while these agree
With his mild blood in voice and will,
Who prayed for those that did him kill!

Righteousness

Fair, solitary path! whose blessed shades
The old, white prophets planted first and dressed:
Leaving for us (whose goodness quickly fades)
A shelter all the way, and bowers to rest.

Who is the man that walks in thee? who loves
Heav'n's secret solitude, those fair abodes
Where turtles build, and careless sparrows move
Without tomorrow's evils and future loads?

Who hath the upright heart, the single eye,
The clean, pure hand, which never meddled pitch?   10
Who sees *Invisibles*, and doth comply
With hidden treasures that make truly rich?

He that doth seek and love
　　The things above,
Whose spirit ever poor, is meek and low;
　　Who simple still and wise,
　　Still homewards flies,
Quick to advance, and to retreat most slow.

　　Whose acts, words and pretence
　　Have all one sense,   20
One aim and end; who walks not by his sight:
　　Whose eyes are both put out,
　　And goes about
Guided by faith, not by exterior light.

　　Who spills no blood, nor spreads
　　Thorns in the beds
Of the distressed, hasting their overthrow;
　　Making the time they had
　　Bitter and sad
Like *chronic* pains, which surely kill, though slow.   30

　　Who knows earth nothing hath
　　Worth love or wrath,
But in his *hope* and *Rock* is ever glad.
　　Who seeks and follows peace,
　　When with the ease
And health of conscience it is to be had.

　　Who bears his cross with joy
　　And doth employ
His heart and tongue in prayers for his foes;
　　Who lends, not to be paid,   40
　　And gives full aid
Without that bribe which usurers impose.

　　Who never looks on man
　　Fearful and wan,
But firmly trusts in God; the great man's measure
　　Though high and haughty must
　　Be ta'en in dust,
But the good man is God's peculiar treasure.

Who doth thus, and doth not
            These good deeds blot   50
With bad, or with neglect; and heaps not wrath
            By secret filth, nor feeds
                Some snake, or weeds,
Cheating himself; that man walks in this path.

Anguish

My God and King! to thee
            I bow my knee,
I bow my troubled soul, and greet
With my foul heart thy holy feet.
Cast it, or tread it! It shall do
Even what thou wilt, and praise thee too.

My God, could I weep blood,
            Gladly I would;
Or if thou wilt give me that art,
Which through the eyes pours out the heart,   10
I will exhaust it all, and make
Myself all tears, a weeping lake.

O! 'tis an easy thing
            To write and sing;
But to write true, unfeignèd verse
Is very hard! O God, disperse
These weights, and give my spirit leave
To act as well as to conceive!

O my God, hear my cry;
            Or let me die!—   20

Tears

O when my God, my glory brings
            His white and holy train,
Unto those clear and living *springs*,
            Where comes no *stain*!

Where all is *light*, and *flowers*, and *fruit*,
            And *joy*, and *rest*,
Make me amongst them ('tis my suit!)
            The last one, and the least.

And when they all are fed, and have
            Drunk of thy living stream,   10
Bid thy poor Ass (with tears I crave!)
            Drink after them.

Thy love claims highest thanks, my sin
            The lowest pitch:
But if he pays, who *loves much*, then
            Thou hast made beggars rich.

Jacob's Pillow and Pillar

I see the Temple in thy Pillar reared,
And that dread glory, which thy children feared,
In mild, clear visions, without a frown,
Unto thy solitary self is shown.
'Tis number makes a schism: throngs are rude,
And God himself died by the multitude.
This made him put on clouds, and fire and smoke,
Hence he in thunder to thy offspring spoke;
The small, still voice, at some low cottage knocks,
But a strong wind must break thy lofty rocks.   10

        The first true worship of the world's great King
From private and selected hearts did spring,
But he most willing to save all mankind,
Enlarged that light, and to the bad was kind.
Hence Catholic or Universal came
A most fair notion, but a very name.
For this rich Pearl, like some more common stone,
When once made public, is esteemed by none.
Man slights his Maker, when familiar grown,
And sets up laws, to pull his honour down.   20
This God foresaw: and when slain by the crowd
(Under that stately and mysterious cloud
Which his death scattered) he foretold the place,

And form to serve him in, should be true grace
And the meek heart, not in a Mount, nor at
Jerusalem, with blood of beasts and fat.
A heart is that dread place, that awful cell,
That secret Ark, where the mild Dove doth dwell
When the proud waters rage: when heathens rule
By God's permission, and man turns a mule.   30
This little Goshen, in the midst of night
And Satan's seat, in all her coasts hath light,
Yea Bethel shall have tithes (saith Israel's stone)
And vows and visions, though her foes cry, None.
Thus is the solemn temple sunk again
Into a Pillar, and concealed from men.
And glory be to his eternal Name!
Who is contented, that this holy flame
Shall lodge in such a narrow pit, till he
With his strong arm turns our captivity.   40

     But blessèd Jacob, though thy sad distress
Was just the same with ours, and nothing less;
For thou a brother, and blood-thirsty too
Didst fly, whose children wrought thy children's woe:
Yet thou in all thy solitude and grief,
On stones didst sleep and found'st but cold relief;
Thou from the Day-star a long way didst stand
And all that distance was Law and command.
But we a healing Sun by day and night,
Have our sure Guardian, and our leading light;   50
What thou didst hope for and believe, we find
And feel a friend most ready, sure and kind.
Thy pillow was but type and shade at best,
But we the substance have, and on him rest.

The Agreement

I wrote it down. But one that saw
And envied that record, did since
Such a mist over my mind draw,
It quite forgot that purposed glimpse.
     I read it sadly oft, but still
     Simply believed, 'twas not my quill;

At length, my life's kind angel came,
And with his bright and busy wing
Scatt'ring that cloud, showed me the flame
Which straight, like morning-stars did sing,   10
  And shine, and point me to a place,
  Which all the year sees the Sun's face.

O beamy book! O my mid-day
Exterminating fears and night!
The mount, whose white ascendents may
Be in conjunction with true light!
  My thoughts, when towards thee they move,
  Glitter and kindle with thy love.

Thou art the oil and the wine-house:
Thine are the present healing leaves,   20
Blown from the tree of life to us
By his breath whom my dead heart heaves.
  Each page of thine hath true life in't,
  And God's bright mind expressed in print.

Most modern books are blots on thee,
Their doctrine chaff and windy fits:
Darkened along, as their scribes be,
With those foul storms, when they were writ;
  While the man's zeal lays out and blends
  Only self-worship and self-ends.   30

Thou art the faithful, pearly rock,
The hive of beamy, living lights,
Ever the same, whose diffused stock
Entire still, wears out blackest nights.
  Thy lines are rays, the true Sun sheds;
  Thy leaves are healing wings he spreads.

For until thou didst comfort me,
I had not one poor word to say:
Thick busy clouds did multiply,
And said, I was no child of day;   40
  They said, my own hands did remove
  That candle given me from above.

O God! I know and do confess
My sins are great and still prevail,
Most heinous sins and numberless!
But thy *compassions* cannot fail.
    If thy sure mercies can be broken,
    Then all is true, my foes have spoken.

But while time runs, and after it
Eternity, which never ends,   50
Quite through them both, still infinite
Thy Covenant by Christ extends;
    No sins of frailty, nor of youth
    Can foil his merits, and thy truth.

And this I hourly find, for thou
Dost still renew, and purge and heal:
Thy care and love, which jointly flow
New cordials, new *cathartics* deal.
    But were I once cast off by thee
    I know (my God!) this would not be.   60

Wherefore with tears (tears by thee sent)
I beg, my faith may never fail!
And when in death my speech is spent,
O let that silence then prevail!
    O chase in that *cold calm* my foes,
    And hear my heart's last private throes!

So thou, who didst the work begin
(For *I till drawn came not to thee*)
Wilt finish it, and by no sin
Will thy free mercies hindered be.   70
    For which, O God, I only can
    Bless thee, and blame unthankful man.

The Day of Judgement

O day of life, of light, of love!
The only day dealt from above!
A day so fresh, so bright, so brave
'Twill show us each forgotten grave,
And make the dead, like flowers, arise
Youthful and fair to see new skies.
All other days, compared to thee,
Are but light's weak minority,
They are but veils and ciphers drawn
Like clouds, before thy glorious dawn.   10
O come, arise, shine, do not stay
        Dearly loved day!
The fields are long since white, and I
With earnest groans for freedom cry,
My fellow-creatures too say, *Come!*
And stones, though speechless, are not dumb.
When shall we hear that glorious voice
        Of life and joys?
That voice, which to each secret bed
        Of my Lord's dead,   20
Shall bring true day, and make dust see
The way to immortality.
When shall those first white pilgrims rise,
Whose holy, happy Histories
(Because they sleep so long) some men
Count but the blots of a vain pen?
        Dear Lord! make haste,
Sin every day commits more waste,
And thy old enemy, which knows
His time is short, more raging grows.   30
Nor moan I only (though profuse)
Thy Creatures' bondage and abuse;
But what is highest sin and shame,
The vile despite done to thy name;
The forgeries, which impious wit
And power force on Holy Writ,
With all detestable designs
That may dishonour those pure lines.

O God! though mercy be in thee
The greatest attribute we see,   40
And the most needful for our sins;
Yet, when thy mercy nothing wins
But mere disdain, let not man say
Thy arm doth sleep; but write this day
Thy judging one: Descend, descend!
Make all things new! and without end!

Psalm 65

Sion's true, glorious God! on thee
Praise waits in all humility.
All flesh shall unto thee repair,
To thee, O thou that hearest prayer!
But sinful words and works still spread
And overrun my heart and head;
Transgressions make me foul each day,
O purge them, purge them all away!

Happy is he! whom thou wilt choose
To serve thee in thy blessed house!   10
Who in thy holy Temple dwells,
And filled with joy, thy goodness tells!
King of Salvation! by strange things
And terrible, Thy Justice brings
Man to his duty. Thou alone
Art the world's hope, and but thee, none.
Sailors that float on flowing seas
Stand firm by thee, and have sure peace.
Thou still'st the loud waves, when most wild
And mak'st the raging people mild.   20
Thy arm did first the mountains lay
And girds their rocky heads this day.
The most remote, who know not thee,
At thy great works astonished be.

The *outgoings* of the *even* and *dawn*,
In *antiphones* sing to thy Name.
Thou visit'st the low earth, and then
Water'st it for the sons of men,
Thy upper river, which abounds

With fertile streams, makes rich all grounds, 30
And by thy mercies still supplied
The sower doth his bread provide.
Thou water'st every ridge of land
And settlest with thy secret hand
The furrows of it; then thy warm
And opening showers (restrained from harm)
Soften the mould, while all unseen
The blade grows up alive and green.
The year is with thy goodness crowned,
And all thy paths drop fatness round, 40
They drop upon the wilderness,
For thou dost even the deserts bless,
And hills full of springing pride,
Wear fresh adornments on each side.
The fruitful flocks fill every dale,
And purling corn doth clothe the vale;
They shout for joy, and jointly sing,
Glory to the eternal King!

The Throne

Revel. chap. 20. ver. 11

When with these eyes closed now by thee,
   But then restored,
The great and white throne I shall see
   Of my dread Lord:
And lowly kneeling (for the most
   Stiff then must kneel)
Shall look on him, at whose high cost
   (Unseen) such joys I feel.

Whatever arguments, or skill
   Wise heads shall use, 10
Tears only and my blushes still
   I will produce.
And should those speechless beggars fail,
   Which oft have won;
Then taught by thee, I will prevail,
   And say, *Thy will be done!*

Death

Though since thy first sad entrance by
        Just Abel's blood,
'Tis now six thousand years well nigh,
And still thy sov'reignty holds good:
Yet by none art thou understood.

We talk and name thee with much ease
        As a tried thing,
And everyone can slight his lease
As if it ended in a Spring,
Which shades and bowers doth rent-free bring.   10

To thy dark land these heedless go:
        But there was *One*,
Who searched it quite through to and fro,
And then returning, like the Sun,
Discovered all, that there is done.

And since his death, we throughly see
        All thy dark way;
Thy shades but thin and narrow be,
Which his first looks will quickly fray:
Mists make but triumphs for the day.   20

As harmless violets, which give
        Their virtues here
For salves and syrups, while they live,
Do after calmly disappear,
And neither grieve, repine, nor fear:

So die his servants; and as sure
        Shall they revive.
Then let not dust your eyes obscure,
But lift them up, where still alive,
Though fled from you, their spirits hive.   30

The Feast

O come away,
Make no delay,
   Come while my heart is clean and steady!
While Faith and Grace
Adorn the place,
   Making dust and ashes ready.

No bliss here lent
Is permanent,
   Such triumphs poor flesh cannot merit;
Short sips and sights   10
Endear delights,
   Who seeks for more, he would inherit.

Come then true bread,
Quick'ning the dead,
   Whose eater shall not, cannot die,
Come, antedate
On me that state
   Which brings poor dust the victory.

Aye victory
Which from thine eye   20
   Breaks as the day doth from the east,
When the spilt dew,
Like tears doth shew
   The sad world wept to be released.

Spring up, O wine,
And springing shine
   With some glad message from his heart,
Who did, when slain,
These means ordain
   For me to have in him a part.   30

Such a sure part
In his blest heart,
    The well, where living waters spring,
That with it fed
Poor dust though dead
    Shall rise again, and live and sing.

O drink and bread
Which strikes death dead,
    The food of man's immortal being!
Under veils here   40
Thou art my cheer,
    Present and sure without my seeing.

How dost thou fly
And search and pry
    Through all my parts, and like a quick
And knowing lamp
Hunt out each damp,
    Whose shadow makes me sad or sick?

O what high joys!
The turtle's voice   50
    And songs I hear! O quick'ning showers
Of my Lord's blood,
You make rocks bud
    And crown dry hills with wells and flowers!

For this true ease,
This healing peace,
    For this taste of living glory,
My soul and all,
Kneel down and fall
    And sing his sad victorious story.   60

O thorny crown
More soft than down!
    O painful Cross, my bed of rest!
O spear, the key
Opening the way!
    O thy worst state, my only best!

Oh! all thy griefs
Are my reliefs,
    And all my sins, thy sorrows were!
And what can I,   70
To this reply;
    What (O God!) but a silent tear?

Some toil and sow,
That wealth may flow,
    And dress this earth for next year's meat:
But let me heed,
Why thou didst bleed,
    And what in the next world to eat.

Revel. chap. 19. ver. 9
Blessed are they which are called unto the marriage supper of the Lamb!

The Obsequies

Since dying for me, thou didst crave no more
        Than common pay,
  Some few true tears, and those shed for
      My own ill way;
With a cheap, plain remembrance still
      Of thy sad death,
Because forgetfulness would kill
      Even life's own breath:
I were most foolish and unkind
      In my own sense,   10
  Should I not ever bear in mind,
If not thy mighty love, my own defence.
Therefore, those loose delights and lusts, which here
      Men call good cheer,
    I will close girt and tied
For mourning sack-cloth wear, all mortified.
Not but that mourners too, can have
      Rich weeds and shrouds;
For some wore *white* ev'n in thy grave,
And joy, like light, shines oft in clouds: 20

But thou, who didst man's whole life earn,
Dost so invite and woo me still,
That to be merry I want skill,
             And time to learn.
Besides, those kerchiefs sometimes shed
             To make me brave,
I cannot find, but where thy head
Was once laid for me in thy grave.
Thy grave! To which my thoughts shall move
Like bees in storms unto their hive,   30
That from the murd'ring world's false love
Thy death may keep my soul alive.

The Waterfall

With what deep murmurs through time's silent stealth
Doth thy transparent, cool and wat'ry wealth
          Here flowing fall,
          And chide, and call,
As if his liquid, loose retinue stayed
Ling'ring, and were of this steep place afraid,
          The common pass
          Where, clear as glass,
          All must descend
          Not to an end: 10
But quickened by this deep and rocky grave,
Rise to a longer course more bright and brave.

          Dear stream! dear bank, where often I
          Have sate, and pleased my pensive eye,
          Why, since each drop of thy quick store
          Runs thither, whence it flowed before,
          Should poor souls fear a shade or night,
          Who came (sure) from a sea of light?
          Or since those drops are all sent back
          So sure to thee, that none doth lack,   20
          Why should frail flesh doubt any more
          That what God takes, he'll not restore?

O useful element and clear!
My sacred wash and cleanser here,
My first consigner unto those
Fountains of life, where the Lamb goes!
What sublime truths, and wholesome themes,
Lodge in thy mystical, deep streams!
Such as dull man can never find
Unless that Spirit lead his mind,   30
Which first upon thy face did move,
And hatched all with his quick'ning love.
As this loud brook's incessant fall
In streaming rings restagnates all,
Which reach by course the bank, and then
Are no more seen, just so pass men.
O my invisible estate,
My glorious liberty, still late!
Thou art the channel my soul seeks,
Not this with cataracts and creeks.

Quickness

False life! a foil and no more, when
                    Wilt thou be gone?
Thou foul deception of all men
That would not have the true come on.

Thou art a moon-like toil; a blind
                    Self-posing state;
A dark contest of waves and wind;
A mere tempestuous debate.

Life is a fixed, discerning light,
                    A knowing joy;   10
No chance, or fit: but ever bright,
And calm and full, yet doth not cloy.

'Tis such a blissful thing, that still
                    Doth vivify,
And shine and smile, and hath the skill
To please without Eternity.

Thou art a toilsome mole, or less,
    A moving mist,
But life is, what none can express,
A quickness, which my God hath kissed.   20

The Wreath

Since I in storms used most to be
  And seldom yielded flowers,
How shall I get a wreath for thee
  From those rude, barren hours?

The softer dressings of the Spring,
  Or Summer's later store
I will not for thy temples bring,
  Which *thorns*, not *roses* wore.

But a twined wreath of *grief* and *praise*,
Praise soiled with tears, and tears again   10
Shining with joy, like dewy days,
This day I bring for all thy pain,
Thy causeless pain! and sad as death,
Which sadness breeds in the most vain,
(O not in vain!) now beg thy breath;
Thy quick'ning breath, which gladly bears
Through saddest clouds to that glad place,
Where cloudless choirs sing without tears,
Sing thy just praise, and see thy face.

The Queer

O tell me whence that joy doth spring
Whose diet is divine and fair,
Which wears heaven, like a bridal ring,
And tramples on doubts and despair?

Whose eastern traffic deals in bright
And boundless empyrean themes,
Mountains of spice, day-stars and light,
Green trees of life, and living streams?

Tell me, O tell who did thee bring
And here, without my knowledge, placed,   10
Till thou didst grow and get a wing,
A wing with eyes, and eyes that taste?

Sure, *holiness* the *magnet* is,
And *love* the *lure*, that woos thee down;
Which makes the high transcendent bliss
Of knowing thee, so rarely known.

The Book

Eternal God! maker of all
That have lived here, since the man's fall;
The Rock of ages! in whose shade
They live unseen, when here they fade.

Thou knew'st this *paper*, when it was
Mere *seed*, and after that but *grass*;
Before 'twas *dressed* or *spun*, and when
Made *linen*, who did *wear* it then:
What were their lives, their thoughts and deeds
Whether good *corn*, or fruitless *weeds*.   10

  Thou knew'st this *tree*, when a green *shade*
Covered it, since a *cover* made,
And where it flourished, grew and spread,
As if it never should be dead.

  Thou knew'st this harmless *beast*, when he
Did live and feed by thy decree
On each green thing; then slept (well fed)
Clothed with this *skin*, which now lies spread
A *covering* o'er this aged book,

Which makes me wisely weep and look   20
On my own dust; mere dust it is,
But not so dry and clean as this.
Thou knew'st and saw'st them all and though
Now scattered thus, dost know them so.

O knowing, glorious spirit! when
Thou shalt restore trees, beasts and men,
When thou shalt make all new again,
Destroying only death and pain,
Give him amongst thy works a place,
Who in them loved and sought thy face!   30

To the Holy Bible

O book! life's guide! how shall we part,
And thou so long seized of my heart!
Take this last kiss, and let me weep
True thanks to thee, before I sleep.

Thou wert the first put in my hand,
When yet I could not understand,
And daily didst my young eyes lead
To letters, till I learnt to read.
But as rash youths, when once grown strong
Fly from their nurses to the throng,   10
Where they new consorts choose, and stick
To those, till either hurt or sick:
So with that first light gained from thee
Ran I in chase of vanity,
Cried dross for gold, and never thought
My first cheap Book had all I sought.
Long reigned this vogue; and thou cast by
With meek, dumb looks didst woo mine eye,
And oft left open would'st convey
A sudden and most searching ray   20
Into my soul, with whose quick touch
Refining still, I struggled much.
By this mild art of love at length

Thou overcam'st my sinful strength,
And having brought me home, didst there
Show me that pearl I sought elsewhere.
Gladness, and peace, and hope, and love,
The secret favours of the Dove,
Her quick'ning kindness, smiles and kisses,
Exalted pleasures, crowning blisses,   30
Fruition, union, glory, life
Thou didst lead to, and still all strife.
Living, thou wert my soul's sure ease,
And dying mak'st me go in peace:
Thy next *effects* no tongue can tell;
Farewell O book of God! farewell!

> S. Luke, chap. 2. ver. 14
> *Glory be to God in the highest, and on*
> *Earth peace, good will towards men.*

L'Envoy

O the new world's new, quick'ning Sun!
Ever the same, and never done!
The seers of whose sacred light
Shall all be dressed in shining white,
And made conformable to his
Immortal shape, who wrought their bliss,
            Arise, arise!
And like old clothes fold up these skies,
This long worn veil: then shine and spread
Thy own bright self over each head,   10
And through thy creatures pierce and pass
Till all becomes thy cloudless glass,
Transparent as the purest day
And without blemish or decay,
Fixed by thy spirit to a state
For evermore immaculate.
A state fit for the sight of thy
Immediate, pure and unveiled eye,
A state agreeing with thy mind,

A state thy birth and death designed: 20
A state for which thy creatures all
Travail and groan, and look and call.
O seeing thou hast paid our score,
Why should the curse reign any more?
But since thy number is as yet
Unfinished, we shall gladly sit
Till all be ready, that the train
May fully fit thy glorious reign.
Only, let not our haters brag,
Thy seamless coat is grown a rag,   30
Or that thy truth was not here known,
Because we forced thy judgements down.
Dry up their arms, who vex thy spouse,
And take the glory of thy house
To deck their own; then give thy saints
That faithful zeal, which neither faints
Nor wildly burns, but meekly still
Dares own the truth, and show the ill.
Frustrate those cancerous, close arts
Which cause solution in all parts,   40
And strike them dumb, who for mere words
Wound thy belovèd, more than swords.
Dear Lord, do this! and then let grace
Descend, and hallow all the place.
Incline each hard heart to do good,
And cement us with thy son's blood,
That like true sheep, all in one fold
We may be fed, and one mind hold.
Give watchful spirits to our guides!
For sin (like water) hourly glides   50
By each man's door, and quickly will
Turn in, if not obstructed still.
Therefore write in their hearts thy law,
And let these long, sharp judgements awe
Their very thoughts, that by their clear
And holy lives, mercy may here
Sit regent yet, and blessings flow
As fast, as persecutions now.
So shall we know in war and peace
Thy service to be our sole ease,   60

With prostrate souls adoring thee,
Who turned our sad captivity!

S. Clemens apud Basil:
Ζῆ ὁ Θεὸς, καὶ ὁ κύριος Ἰησοῦς Χριστὸς,
καὶ τὸ πνεῦμα τὸ ἅγιον.

FINIS

Notes

Abbreviations

Geneva   The Geneva version of the Bible (1560)

KJ   The King James (Authorized) version of the Bible (1611)

OED   *The Oxford English Dictionary*

Martin   Vaughan's *Works* (2nd edn.), edited by L. C. Martin

Rudrum   Vaughan's *Complete Poems*, edited by Alan Rudrum

For other works identified in the notes by author or short title, a full reference is given in Further Reading.

Silex Scintillans (1650)
In this first edition all that precedes the opening poem, *Regeneration*, is the emblematic title-page, the Latin explanation of that emblem's meaning, and the 14-line *Dedication*. But in 1655, when the unsold sheets of 1650 were bound up with additional poems, Vaughan removed the emblematic title-page (along with the explanatory Latin poem) and replaced it with the printed title-page. He added a prose preface and a group of biblical texts, greatly expanded the dedication with an elaborate title and 32 additional lines, and also added the short poem 'Vain wits and eyes'. For these new prefatory materials, see pp. 95–104.

2 *The Author's Emblem.* l. 10. *Caro . . . Lapis.* Ezekiel 36: 26, 'I will take away the stony heart out of your flesh, and I will give you an heart of flesh.'

l. 13. *undantes Petras*: an allusion to Moses' bringing water out of the rock: Exodus 17: 6.

3 *The Dedication.* l. 8. *void of store*: empty of any produce.

ll. 9–11. The lines allude to the parable of the evil 'husbandmen'. Matthew 21: 33–41.

l. 14. *tenant's rent.* See Herbert, *Redemption*.

Regeneration. Compare Herbert's *The Pilgrimage* for stanza-form and a similar journey.

l. 1. *A ward, and still in bonds.* The first three stanzas narrate the speaker's troubles under the bondage of sin and the Old Testament Law; but the term *ward* indicates that he is in someone's care.

4 ll. 25–6. These lines appear to allegorize the doctrinal view of 'calling' and grace contained in the passage on 'predestination to life' in the

17th of the Articles of Religion of Vaughan's Church: 'Wherefore, they which be endued with so excellent a benefit of God be called according to God's purpose by his Spirit working in due season: they through Grace obey the calling . . . '

ll. 27–8. *Full East . . . Jacob's Bed.* Jacob made his journey 'into the land of the people of the east' (Genesis 29: 1). On his way 'he lighted upon a certain place, and tarried there all night, because the sun was set; and he took of the stones of that place, and put them for his pillows, and lay down in that place to sleep'. There he had the vision of the 'ladder' reaching to heaven and heard the voice of the Lord. See Genesis 28: 10–22.

l. 32. *friends of God.* 'In all ages entering into holy souls, she [Wisdom] maketh them friends of God, and Prophets' (Wisdom of Solomon 7: 27).

ll. 33–50. The state of grace is imaged through glancing allusions to the Song of Solomon 4: 12–15. 'A garden inclosed is my sister, my spouse; a spring shut up, a fountain sealed. Thy plants are an orchard of pomegranates, with pleasant fruits; camphire, with spikenard, Spikenard and saffron; calamus and cinnamon, with all trees of frankincense; myrrh and aloes, with all the chief spices: A fountain of gardens, a well of living waters, and streams from Lebanon.'

l. 41. *unthrift*: spendthrift. *vital*: life-giving.

5 l. 55. *divers stones.* I Peter 2: 5, 'Ye also, as lively stones, are built up a spiritual house, an holy priesthood, to offer up spiritual sacrifices, acceptable to God by Jesus Christ.'

l. 60. *Centre*: earth.

l. 70. *rushing wind.* 'And suddenly there came a sound from heaven as of a rushing mighty wind, and it filled all the house where they [the apostles] were sitting' (Acts 2: 2: the day of Pentecost).

l. 80. *Where I please.* 'The wind bloweth where it listeth, and thou hearest the sound thereof, but canst not tell whence it cometh, and whither it goeth: so is every one that is born of the Spirit' (John 3: 8).

6 The biblical verse at the end combines two versions of Song of Solomon 4: 16, the Genevan, 'Arise, O North, and come O South, and blow on my garden', and the King James, 'Awake, O north wind; and come, thou south; blow upon my garden.'

7 *Resurrection and Immortality*

Biblical motto. The heading from Hebrews follows Geneva, with minor differences.

l. 3. *Inspired*: breathed. *quick'ning*: life-giving.

l. 13. *Esteemed of*: estimated, regarded. *two whole elements*: water and earth.

8   l. 14. *mean, and span-extents*: contemptible, limited things extending only a hand's-breadth.

l. 21. *recruits*: fresh supplies, means of renewal. The whole of section 2 represents Vaughan's version of the 'Hermetic philosophy' of nature's constant power of renewal.

l. 26. *Incorporates*: becomes a body, takes form.

l. 33. *resolve*: dissolve into some other form.

l. 38. *deprave*: corrupt.

9   l. 51. *saw darkly in a glass*. 'For now we see through a glass darkly; but then face to face' (I Corinthians 13: 12).

l. 59. *To read some star, or min'ral*. The reference is to astrological studies, by which it was thought one could ascertain a relationship between the stars and certain earthly things, including human beings.

l. 68. See Deuteronomy 28: 66–7, 'and thou shalt fear day and night, and shalt have none assurance of thy life: In the morning thou shalt say, Would God it were even! and at even, thou shalt say, Would God it were morning!'

10 *Day of Judgement*. l. 13. *like a scroll*. 'And the heaven departed as a scroll when it is rolled together; and every mountain and island were moved out of their places' (Revelation 6: 14).

l. 21. *the clouds thy seat*. 'And I looked, and behold a white cloud, and upon the cloud one sat like unto the Son of man' (Revelation 14: 14).

l. 23. *The quick and dead*: a common biblical phrase concerning Judgement Day: see Acts 10: 42; II Timothy 4: 1; I Peter 4: 5; and the Apostles' Creed: '[. . . Jesus] shall come to judge the quick and the dead.' *quick*: alive. *small and great*. 'And I saw the dead, small and great, stand before God; and the books were opened' (Revelation 20: 12).

l. 32. *the man of sin*. See Romans 6: 6, 'Knowing this, that our old man is crucified with him, that the body of sin might be destroyed.' Also II Thessalonians 2: 3, 'for that day shall not come, except there come a falling away first, and that man of sin be revealed, the son of perdition.'

11 l. 41. *a HEART of flesh*. 'And I will give them one heart, and I will put a new spirit within you; and I will take the stony heart out of their flesh, and will give them an heart of flesh' (Ezekiel 11: 19).

The appended verse from I Peter is given in the Geneva version.

Religion. See Herbert's *Decay*.

l. 5. *juniper.* 'And as [Elijah] lay and slept under a juniper tree, behold, then an angel touched him, and said unto him, Arise and eat' (I Kings 19: 5).

l. 6. *myrtle's.* See Zechariah 1: 8–11 for the appearance of 'the angel of the Lord that stood among the myrtle trees'.

l. 7. *oak's.* 'And there came an angel of the Lord, and sat under an oak' (Judges 6: 11).

l. 8. *fountain's.* 'And the angel of the Lord found [Hagar] by a fountain of water in the wilderness' (Genesis 16: 7).

l. 9. *Jacob dreams and wrestles.* For Jacob's dream, see Genesis 28: 11–12. His wrestling with God is described in Genesis 32: 24–30.

l. 10. *Elias by a raven is fed.* 'And the ravens brought him bread and flesh in the morning, and bread and flesh in the evening; and he drank of the brook' (I Kings 17: 6).

l. 11. *Another time by th' Angel.* 'And he looked, and, behold, there was a cake baken on the coals, and a cruse of water at his head' (I Kings 19: 6).

ll. 13–16. *In Abr'ham's tent . . . shady even.* Abraham entertained three 'men' (interpreted as angels in disguise) at the time that Sarah's son was foretold. See Genesis 18: 1–8.

l. 17. *in fire.* 'And the angel of the Lord appeared unto him in a flame of fire out of the midst of a bush' (Exodus 3: 2). See also Leviticus 9: 24 and Deuteronomy 4: 12, 5: 4.

l. 18. *Whirlwinds.* 'Then the Lord answered Job out of the whirlwind' (Job 38: 1 and 40: 6). *clouds.* 'And the Lord came down in a cloud, and spake unto him [Moses]' (Numbers 11: 25). See also Exodus 24: 16, 'and the seventh day he called unto Moses out of the midst of the cloud.' *the soft voice.* 'And after the earthquake a fire; but the Lord was not in the fire: and after the fire a still small voice' (I Kings 19: 12).

l. 19. *admire*: am amazed, wonder.

l. 20. *conf'rence*: conversation, discourse.

12 l. 32. *Cordials*: invigorating drinks.

l. 37. *drilling*: flowing in a small stream, dripping.

l. 43. *puddle*: foul, polluted water.

l. 44. *physic*: medicine.

l. 45. *sink*: sewer, cesspool.

l. 46. *Samaritan's dead well.* See John 4: 5–15: the water from Jacob's well is 'dead' in comparison to the 'living water' Christ offers to the Samaritan woman.

l.50. *the springing rock*. See Exodus 17: 6. From the rock which Moses struck, water sprang forth for the Israelites in the desert. See St Paul's interpretation: 'for they drank of that spiritual Rock that followed them: and that Rock was Christ' (I Corinthians 10: 4).

l. 52. *water into wine*: as at the marriage-feast in Cana: John 2: 1–10. The final biblical verse is given in the Geneva version.

13 *The Search*. Vaughan's poem represents a subtle and ironic variation upon the ancient practice of meditating upon the life of Christ and using the imagination and the senses to re-create the scenes of his life and death as though one were 'really present' at the event. The point is that, for this searcher, these old methods do not work: nor need they work, for the 'Pilgrim-Sun' of the opening lines is also the 'Lord' of the closing biblical verse: constantly present.

l. 4. *ecstasy*: a mystical state of rapture wherein the body becomes incapable of sensation, while the soul contemplates divine things; a trance-like prophetic state.

ll. 15–17. *Temple . . . dust; town . . . ashes*: referring to the destruction of the temple at Jerusalem in AD 70, and the later destruction of the city itself.

l. 19. *beneath the pole*: under the pole-star, on the earth.

ll. 21–32. For Jesus' conversation with the Samaritan woman at Jacob's Well, see John 4: 5–14.

ll. 38–40. *Agony . . . bloody sweat*. For Christ's suffering in the Garden of Gethsemane, see Luke 22: 39–44.

14 l. 44. *Balsam*: a healing balm, medicinal oil.

ll. 45–7. *But, O his grave . . . monument*. Matthew 27: 57–60, 'When the even was come, there came a rich man of Arimathea, named Joseph, who also himself was Jesus' disciple: He went to Pilate, and begged the body of Jesus . . . he wrapped it in a clean linen cloth, And laid it in his own new tomb which he had hewn out in the rock.'

l. 48. *corner-stone*. Christ: Acts 4: 11, 'This is the stone which was set at nought of you builders, which is become the head of the corner.' Also I Peter 2: 6, 'Behold, I lay in Sion a chief corner stone, elect, precious: and he that believeth on him shall not be confounded.'

ll. 53–62. For Christ's sojourn and temptation in the wilderness, see Matthew 4: 1–11; Mark 1: 12–13; Luke 4: 1–13.

l. 64. *his bride*: the Church, the Bride of Christ. See Revelation 12: 6, 'And the woman fled into the wilderness, where she hath a place prepared of God.'

l. 74. See Herbert, *The Collar*, l. 35: 'Me thoughts I heard one calling, *Child*!'

15 l. 78. *Still*: ever, always.

l. 95. *another world*: the world within, not 'out of doors'.

Acts Cap. 17. happily. A variant spelling of *haply* ('perhaps'), but *happily* also meant 'by good fortune, successfully'.

Isaac's Marriage. Two leaves (B2, B3) of the 1650 *Silex* were reset for the 1655 edition, in order to allow some revisions in this poem—the only poem in *1650* so revised. The substantive variants are listed below.

Gen. Cap. 24. ver. 63. The KJ version, except that Vaughan chooses *pray* instead of *meditate*; *pray* is the reading of Geneva and is an alternative reading in the margin of KJ. *lift*: lifted. For the story of Isaac's marriage to Rebekah, see Genesis 24.

l. 2. *monstrous*: unnatural.

l. 4. *degenerate*: 'To become or be altered in nature or character (without implying debasement)' (*OED*).

16 l. 10. *constellation*: disposition, character—as determined by one's 'stars'.

ll. 11–12. The 1650 reading makes the point more clearly (and more bluntly): 'But being for a bride, sure, prayer was | Very strange stuff wherewith to court thy lass.'

l. 14. *dull*: 'coarse' (*1650*).

l. 16. *sev'ral*: different.

l. 19. 'When sin, by sinning oft, had not lost sense' (*1650*).

l. 21. *antic*. 'Absurd from fantastic incongruity; grotesque' (*OED*).

l. 23. *Retinue*: pronounced *retìnue*.

l. 28. *thy servant*. Abraham's 'eldest servant', sent to seek a wife for Isaac. See Genesis 24: 2–4.

ll. 35–6. 'But in a frighted, virgin-blush approached | Fresh as the morning, when 'tis newly coached' (*1650*).

l. 46. *fortunates*: makes fortunate.

17 l. 53: *Lahai-roi's well*. Vaughan provides here a marginal note: 'A well in the south country where Jacob dwelt, between Cadesh and Bered; Hebrew, the well of him that liveth and seeth me.' See Genesis 16: 13–14, 'And she [Hagar] called the name of the Lord that spake unto her, Thou God seest me: for she said, Have I also here looked after him that seeth me? Wherefore the well was called Beer-lahai-roi.'

l. 67. *timed*: matured, seasoned.

The British Church. The poem presents a marked contrast with Herbert's poem of the same title. Here, in accord with the traditional interpretation of the Song of Solomon, the Church as the bride of Christ laments the ravages of the English civil wars and the disruption of the established Church in the 1640s. Note that neither poet says 'English' or 'Church of England'. (The term 'Anglican' does not appear to be in common use in this era.) The phrase 'British Church' may derive from the ancient legend that British Christianity descended directly from Joseph of Arimathea, who came to Britain after Christ's death and established a centre of devotion at Glastonbury. Thus Vaughan's title implies a 'British' root for his Church, independent of Rome from the beginning. The Welsh, in particular, regarded their church as preserving the Christianity of the ancient Britons.

l. 4. *hills of myrrh and incense.* Song of Solomon 4: 6, 'Until the day break, and the shadows flee away, I will get me to the mountain of myrrh, and to the hill of frankincense.'

ll. 6–10. John 19: 23–4, 'Then the soldiers, when they had crucified Jesus, took his garments, and made four parts, to every soldier a part; and also his coat: now the coat was without seam, woven from the top throughout. They said therefore among themselves, Let us not rend it, but cast lots for it, whose it shall be.'

18 ll. 18–20. *And haste thee so . . . mounts of spices.* Song of Solomon 8: 14, 'Make haste, my beloved, and be thou like to a roe or to a young hart upon the mountains of spices.'

O rosa campi . . . aprorum. 'O rose of the field! O lily of the valleys! how have you now become the food of wild boars!' See Song of Solomon 2:1, 'I am the rose of Sharon, and the lily of the valleys.' Also Psalm 80: 13, 'The boar out of the wood doth waste it, and the wild beast of the field doth devour it.' The heading for Psalm 80 in the Geneva Bible interprets the psalm as 'A lamentable prayer to God to help the miseries of his Church'.

The Lamp. l. 2. *stars nod and sleep.* See Herbert, *Divinity*, l. 1: 'for fear the stars should sleep and nod'.

19 *Man's Fall and Recovery.* l. 1. *everlasting hills.* See Genesis 49: 26 (the dying words of Jacob to his sons), 'The blessings of thy father have prevailed above the blessings of my progenitors unto the utmost bound of the everlasting hills.'

l. 13. *sullen beam.* Conscience.

l. 16. *Jeshurun's king*: Moses. See Deuteronomy 33: 4–5.

ll. 18–20. *These swelled my fears . . . from the Law.* See Romans 7: 5, 7–8 for the effect of Old Testament Law in arousing consciousness of sin.

20 l. 32. *their Red Sea*. The Israelites laboured in their journey towards the Promised Land: they waded across the bed of the Red Sea (an image of the state of sin under the Old Testament Law). But now the speaker is washed in the blood of Christ.

Rom. Cap. 5. ver. 18. 1650 reads in error 'Cap. 18. ver. 19'. Vaughan gives the Geneva version of the verse, except that he substitutes 'righteousness' from KJ for 'justifying'.

The Shower. l. 9. *quick access*. See Herbert, *Prayer* (II), l. 1: 'Of what an easy quick access, | My blessed Lord, art thou!'

21 *Distraction*. l. 1. *crumbled dust*. See Herbert, *Church-monuments*, l. 22: 'crumbled into dust'; *The Temper* (I), l. 14: 'A crumb of dust'; and *Longing*, ll. 41–2: 'Thy pile of dust, wherein each crumb | Says, Come.'

l. 6. *a star, a pearl, or a rainbow*. See Herbert, *Mattens*, ll. 6–7: 'Silver, or gold, or precious stone, | Or star, or rainbow'.

l. 12. *Man is called and hurled*. See Herbert, *Doomsday*, ll. 27–8: 'Man is out of order hurled, | Parcelled out to all the world.'

l. 30. *Dust that would rise*. See Herbert, *Frailty*, ll. 15–16: 'That which was dust before, doth quickly rise, | And prick mine eyes.'

l. 34. *parcels*: parts, pieces.

22 *The Pursuit*. See Herbert, *The Pulley*.

l. 7. *commerce*: perhaps a reference to man's preoccupation with studying the stars.

l. 11. *the lost son*: the prodigal son of Luke 15: 16–19.

Mount of Olives (I). Just as Herbert has two poems entitled *Jordan*, urging poets to write sacred verse, so Vaughan has two poems on this theme, entitled *Mount of Olives*. As ll. 18–19 make plain, Vaughan is replacing Mount Helicon and the fountain of the pagan Muses with the 'hill' which Christ made his place for retirement and prayer.

l. 2. *My Saviour sate*. 'And as he sat upon the mount of Olives, the disciples came unto him privately' (Matthew 24: 3).

ll. 5–6. *wit*, | *Conceit*. Both terms here mean 'the faculty of conceiving, creating'.

l. 9. *Cotswold and Cooper's*. The Cotswolds were praised by Drayton, Jonson, Randolph, and others in *Annalia Dubrensia. Upon the yearly celebration of Mr. Robert Dover's Olympic Games upon Cotswold-Hills* (1636). Sir John Denham wrote *Cooper's Hill* (1642).

23 l. 16. *sheepward*: shepherd.

l. 21. *wept once*. Luke 19: 41, 'And when he was come near, he beheld the city [Jerusalem], and wept over it.' *walked whole nights on thee.*

Luke 21: 37, 'And in the daytime he was teaching in the temple; and at night he went out, and abode in the mount that is called the mount of Olives.'

ll. 22–4. Christ ascended into heaven from the Mount of Olives; see Acts 1: 9–12.

l. 26. *narrow footstool*. Isaiah 66: 1, 'Thus saith the Lord, the heaven is my throne, and the earth is my footstool.'

l. 28. *Unsearchable*. Romans 11: 33, 'how unsearchable are his judgments, and his ways past finding out!'

l. 29. *comprise*: comprehend.

l. 32. *chair*. See the last line of Herbert's *Pilgrimage*, 'And but a chair.'

The Incarnation and Passion. ll. 1–4. See Herbert, *The Bag*, ll. 7–12.

l. 6. *the morning-star*. Revelation 22: 16, 'I am the root and the offspring of David, and the bright and morning star.'

24 ll. 19–20. *for Love . . . than death*. Song of Solomon 8: 6, 'for love is strong as death.'

The Call. l. 11. *sands*: the sands of an hour-glass.

25 l. 29. *Those beasts were clean, that chewed the cud*. Leviticus 11: 3, 'Whatsoever parteth the hoof, and is cloven-footed, and cheweth the cud, among the beasts, that shall ye eat.'

'Thou that know'st for whom I mourn.' There are six untitled poems in *Silex 1650*, all headed by the symbol ¶. With one possible exception, they appear to commemorate Vaughan's younger brother, William, who died in July 1648, at about the age of 20.

26 l. 32. *close*: private, secret.

l. 36. *The wise man's madness, laughter*. Ecclesiastes 2: 2, 'I said of laughter, It is mad.'

l. 44. *And tares had choked the corn*. See the parable of the wheat and tares, Matthew 13: 24–30. *corn*: grain.

ll. 49–52. *silent tear . . . groan . . . arted string*. A striking recension of Herbertian words and themes: see *The Family*, ll. 17–20: 'Joys oft are there, and griefs as oft as joys; | But griefs without a noise: | Yet speak they louder than distempered fears. | What is so shrill as silent tears?' and *Sion*, ll. 21–4: 'But groans are quick and full of wings, | And all their motions upward be; | And ever as they mount, like larks they sing; | The note is sad, yet music for a King.'

l. 51. *airs*: melodies, music for voice or instruments.

l. 57. *know my end*. Psalm 39: 4, 'Lord, make me to know mine end, and the measure of my days, what it is; that I may know how frail I am.'

Vanity of Spirit. Ecclesiastes 1: 14, 'I have seen all the works that are done under the sun; and behold, all is vanity and vexation of spirit.'

27 l. 4. *brave*: grand, splendid.

ll. 9–14. *I summoned nature . . . Creatures.* Vaughan is describing here the first stage in the traditional mode of Augustinian meditation, which begins with meditation on the Creation. His account suggests a pursuit of the occult, alchemical researches regarded as scientific in his day.

ll. 15–24. *To search myself . . .* This is the second stage in the Augustinian mode of meditation: to find the 'traces' (*vestigia*) of God within the self, in the presence of the now defaced Image of God, man's soul, the 'piece of much antiquity' which the speaker here tries vainly to restore. He makes some progress, 'but this near done', he realizes that spiritual illumination in this life is transitory.

l. 17. *drills*: trickles, streams.

The Retreat. The title plays upon 'retreat' as backward movement and 'retreat' as an action of withdrawal from the world for religious devotion, or a place where seclusion occurs.

l. 4. *my second race.* Hebrews 12: 1, 'let us run with patience the race that is set before us.' The poem alludes throughout to the platonic doctrine of the soul's pre-existence.

28 l. 8. *my first love.* Revelation 2: 4, 'Nevertheless, I have somewhat against thee, because thou hast left thy first love.'

l. 18. *sev'ral*: separate.

l. 20. *shoots of everlastingness.* Owen Felltham calls the soul 'a shoot of everlastingness' in *Resolves*, i. 64 (1620).

l. 26. *city of palm trees.* Deuteronomy 34: 1–4, 'And Moses went up from the plains of Moab unto the mountain of Nebo, to the top of Pisgah, that is over against Jericho. And the Lord showed him . . . the plain of the valley of Jericho, the city of palm trees.' Here an image of the Heavenly City.

ll. 27–8. *soul . . . is drunk, and staggers.* A parallel in Plato's *Phaedo* emphasizes the Christianized Platonism that inspires this poem: 'Were we not saying [asks Socrates] that the soul too is then dragged by the body into the region of the changeable, and wanders and is confused; the world spins round her, and she is like a drunkard, when she touches change? . . . But when returning into herself she reflects, then she passes into the other world, the region of purity, and eternity, and immortality, and unchangeableness, which are her kindred.' *Dialogues of Plato*, trans. by B. Jowett (3rd edn., 5 vols., Oxford University Press, 1892), ii. 222.

'Come, come, what do I here?' l. 2. *he is gone*. William, his brother; see 'Thou that know'st for whom I mourn'.

29 *Midnight*. l. 4. *Baruch* 3: 34, 'The stars shined in their watches, and rejoiced: when he calleth them, they say, Here we be; and so with cheerfulness they showed light unto him that made them.'

30 l. 19. *aye*: ever, always.

ll. 22–3. *Shine on this blood* | *And water in one beam*. I John 5: 6–8, 'This is he that came by water and blood, even Jesus Christ, not by water only, but by water and blood. . . . And there are three that bear witness in earth, the spirit, and the water, and the blood: and these three agree in one.'

Content. l. 1. *brave*: splendid, fine, fashionable.

l. 4. *piece*: article of (fine) clothing.

l. 6. *wardrobes*: stock of clothing (with overtones of finery).

31 l. 17. *points*. A *point* is 'a tagged lace or cord, of twisted yarn, silk, or leather, for attaching the hose to the doublet, lacing a bodice, and fastening various parts where buttons are now used' (*OED*).

l. 18. *story*: probably in the sense of a work of visual art that tells a 'story'.

l. 23. *cross to*: in opposition to.

'Joy of my life! while left me here'. l. 1. *Joy of my life!* Probably his brother, as in the other untitled poems of *1650*; possibly his first wife, the date of whose death is uncertain.

32 l. 17. *Saints*. Vaughan is using the term in the reformed, Protestant sense: the chosen of God, or persons of extraordinary holiness of life.

l. 25. *pillar-fires*. The Lord in a pillar of fire led the Israelites by night through the wilderness: Exodus 13: 21.

ll. 27–8. *They are that City's shining spires* | *We travel to*. For a description of the city of God or the heavenly Jerusalem, see Revelation 21.

ll. 29–31. *A swordlike gleam . . . First Out*. Genesis 3: 24, 'So he drove out the man: and he placed at the east of the garden of Eden cherubims, and a flaming sword which turned every way, to keep the way of the tree of life.'

The Storm. See Herbert's poem by this title, also in three stanzas, with similar two-foot line.

l. 1. *use*: moral application; but see different implications of *use* in l. 23.

l. 11. *discuss*: debate.

33 l. 17. *round*: surround.

l. 21. *Recluse*. As usual, Vaughan's typographical emphasis suggests special meanings: the *recluse* (hermit devoted to religious life) is his inner self, secluded within the body; but *OED* also records the obsolete meaning of *recluse* as a 'reservoir for water'.

ll. 21–4. See Herbert's *The Storm*, 'If as the winds and waters here below | Do fly and flow, | My sighs and tears as busy were above . . . | Poets have wronged poor storms: such days are best; | They purge the air without, within the breast' (ll. 1–3, 17–18).

l. 23. *to thy use*: for thy purpose.

The Morning-watch. *watch*: devotional observance, prayer.

l. 1. *O joys! Infinite sweetness!* See Herbert, *The H. Scriptures* (I), l. 1: 'O book! infinite sweetness!'

l. 10. *quick*: alive, lively.

l. 16. *hurled*: whirled.

ll. 18–19. *Prayer is | The world in tune*. See Herbert, *Prayer* (I), l. 8: 'A kind of tune, which all things hear and fear'.

l. 22. *Echo is heav'n's bliss*. Prayer produces a distant response that intimates heavenly bliss.

34 *The Evening-watch*. l. 2. *the day-star*. Christ. II Peter 1: 19, 'Until the day dawn, and the day-star arise in your hearts'. Also Revelation 22: 16, 'I am the root and the offspring of David, and the bright and morning star.'

l. 8. *Writ in his book*. Revelation 20: 12, 'And I saw the dead, small and great, stand before God; and the books were opened: and another book was opened, which is the book of life: and the dead were judged out of those things which were written in the books, according to their works.'

l. 14. *blinds*: things which conceal the design.

l. 16. *prime*. The first hour of the day in the ancient 'hours' of the Church; also the spring; the time of full strength and vigour.

'Silence, and stealth of days!' Once again, about his brother William's death.

l. 3. *Twelve hundred hours*. Since William died about 14 July 1648, this poem must have been composed around 1 September 1648.

l. 9. *sun*: the lamp of l. 7: the memory of his brother.

35 l. 19. *snuff*: burnt wick or candle-end.

l. 29. *one Pearl*. Matthew 13: 45–6, 'Again, the kingdom of heaven is like unto a merchant man, seeking goodly pearls: who when he had found one pearl of great price, went and sold all that he had, and bought it.' Vaughan's 'pearl' seems to be the presence of Christ within; or it may be the Bible.

Church Service. ll. 4–6. *interceding . . . stones.* Romans 8: 26, 'For we know not what we should pray for as we ought: but the Spirit itself maketh intercession for us with groanings which cannot be uttered.'

36 l. 24. *sighs and groans.* See Herbert's poem with these words as title.

Burial. l. 1. *the first fruits.* I Corinthians 15: 20, 'But now is Christ risen from the dead, and become the firstfruits of them that slept.'

l. 5. *wages of my sin.* Romans 6: 23, 'For the wages of sin is death; but the gift of God is eternal life through Jesus Christ our Lord.'

l. 10. *sometimes*: at one time.

37 ll. 39–40. *come . . . quickly.* See Revelation 22: 20.

38 *Cheerfulness.* ll. 22–4. *And to . . . here below.* See Herbert, *Doomsday.* ll. 29–30: 'Lord, thy broken consort raise, | And the music shall be praise.'

l. 23. *consort*: music created by several voices or instruments.

'Sure, there's a tie of bodies!' ll. 5–6. The italicized words suggest the technical vocabulary of the Hermetic 'science' which underlies this poem. *centred*: fixed to the earth in death. *contaction*: contact, touching.

l. 7. *these*: 'beams and action'—capacity for contact.

l. 9. *Absents . . . sense.* Note the word-play. *Absents*: things distant from one another. *within the line.* Perhaps with allusion to the phrase 'line of life': 'the thread fabled to be spun by the Fates, determining the duration of a person's life' (*OED*). *conspire*: breathe together, work together. *sense*: physical sense-perception.

l. 13. *kind*: closely related.

39 l. 17. *Lazarus was carried out of town*: inferred from the fact that his tomb was in a cave (John 11: 38).

l. 18. *foe's.* May be either singular or plural possessive.

l. 21. *Death's-head*: a skull kept as a reminder of mortality.

The Passion. l. 1. *O my chief good!* See Herbert, *Good Friday,* l. 1.

l. 4. *forced by the rod.* Christ was buffeted by hands and struck by a reed, but, as Rudrum points out, Vaughan's use of 'rod' evokes Moses' smiting the rock in the wilderness, and bringing forth water; the incident was interpreted as a 'type' of the Crucifixion.

40 l. 15. *Most blessed Vine!* John 15: 5, 'I am the vine, ye are the branches.'

ll. 15–18. *Most . . . as blood.* See Herbert, *The Agony*, ll. 17–18: 'Love is that liquor sweet and most divine, | Which my God feels as blood; but I, as wine.'

ll. 19–20. *How wert thou pressed | To be my feast!* See Herbert, *The Bunch of Grapes*, ll. 27–8: 'Who of the law's sour juice sweet wine did make, | Ev'n God himself, being pressèd for my sake.'

l. 28. *When none would own thee*: an allusion to Peter's denial: Matthew 26: 69–75.

l. 40. *Father forgive.* See Luke 23: 34.

41   l. 51. *two small mites.* For the story of the widow's mites, see Mark 12: 42–4.

'And do they so?' The scriptural text is Beza's Latin translation: 'For created things, watching with upraised head, await the revelation of the sons of God.'

l. 2. *influence*: astrological influence.

l. 3. *expect*: wait for; also, look forward to.

l. 4. *And groan too?* Romans 8: 22, 'For we know that the whole creation groaneth.'

ll. 9–14. *Go, go . . . to sing!* See Herbert, *Affliction* (I), ll. 55–60.

l. 16. *my date*: the day of his death.

42   ll. 39–40. *Sure, thou wilt joy.* See Herbert, *The Star*, l. 29.

The Relapse. ll. 9–12. Another combination of Herbertian words and themes: see Herbert, *Discipline*, ll. 1–4: 'Throw away thy rod, | Throw away thy wrath: | O my God | Take the gentle path'; and *The Thanksgiving*, l. 34: 'But mend mine own without delays.'

ll. 13–14. See Exodus 10: 22, 'and there was a thick darkness in all the land of Egypt three days.' Also Herbert, *Sighs and Groans*. ll. 14–15: 'I have deserved that an Egyptian night | Should thicken all my powers.'

43   l. 15. *mist.* As so often, Vaughan's italic indicates a biblical allusion: Acts 13: 11, the curse of Paul upon the false prophet, 'And now, behold, the hand of the Lord is upon thee, and thou shalt be blind, not seeing the sun for a season. And immediately there fell on him a mist and a darkness.' Also II Peter 2: 17, speaking of false prophets, 'These are wells without water, clouds that are carried with a tempest; to whom the mist of darkness is reserved for ever.'

l. 18. *yew*: the graveyard tree.

l. 22. *scores*: debts.

l. 23. *challenge*: lay claim to, demand.

ll. 23–4. *challenge . . . day*. See Herbert, *Confession*, l. 28: 'I challenge here the brightest day.'

l. 25. *lily-shades*. Again, Vaughan's italic hints at a biblical allusion: the 'lily' or 'lilies' of the Song of Solomon 2: 1, 16, etc., or the 'lilies of the field' in Matthew 6: 28.

The Resolve. l. 1. *I have considered it; and find*. The same line as in Herbert, *The Reprisal*, l. 1.

l. 3. *mind*: have in mind.

l. 10. *catch at the place*. See Herbert, *Affliction* (I), l. 17: 'Therefore my sudden soul caught at the place, | And made her youth and fierceness seek thy face.'

l. 12. *case*: (1) exterior covering. (2) a chance occurrence, as in Latin *casus*, which also means falling down, or an adverse event.

l. 13. *parcelled*: divided into parts.

l. 17. *powers*. Probably the 'powers of the soul', memory, under-standing, and will.

l. 20. *span*. The italic seems to indicate a special sense: perhaps to 'span' (harness) horses? But the common sense of measuring with a hand's breadth is sufficient.

l. 21. *cry*: a term from hunting. The 'cry' is the yelping of hounds, or the pack of hounds: hence, any crowd.

44 ll. 23–4. See Herbert, *Affliction* (I), ll. 21–2: 'My days were strawed with flow'rs and happiness; | There was no month but May.'

l. 28. *Prize*. I Corinthians 9: 24, 'one receiveth the prize'. Also Philippians 3: 14, 'I press toward the mark for the prize of the high calling of God in Christ Jesus.'

The Match. l. 1. *Dear friend*. The opening words of Herbert's *Love Unknown*. The 'friend' here is Herbert; the poem is a direct response to the wish expressed in the last two stanzas of Herbert's *Obedience*: 'He that will pass his land, | As I have mine, may set his hand | And heart unto this Deed, when he hath read; | . . . How happy were my part, | If some kind man would thrust his heart | Into the lines.' Here *kind* means 'kindred, related in spirit,' as well as 'generous, charitable.'

l. 8. *Deed*. The legal term *Deed* is used three times in Herbert's *Obedience*, ll. 10, 33, 38.

l. 9. *duties*: in the old legal sense: debts or payments legally due.

ll. 10–11. *And if hereafter . . . claim their share*. See *Obedience*, ll. 11–12: 'If that hereafter Pleasure | Cavil, and claim her part and measure'.

l. 19. *lifes*: another legal term: a lease 'for two (or more) lives' is 'one which is to remain in force during the life of the longest liver of (two, three, etc.) specified persons' (*OED*). Herbert uses the same imagery in *Love Unknown*, ll. 4–5.

45 l. 28. *house*. In this Herbertian context, the italicized word seems bound to evoke Herbert's *The Family*, where 'house' occurs twice (ll. 5, 21) and 'Humble Obedience near the door doth stand' (l. 13).

ll. 31–2. *Lord Jesu! . . . Upon a tree*. See Herbert, *Longing*, ll. 31–2: 'Lord Jesu, thou didst bow | Thy dying head upon the tree.'

ll. 40–2. *grain . . . tears . . . increase*: a complex of biblical allusions: Matthew 13: 31–2, the parable of the 'grain of mustard seed'; Psalm 126: 5, 'They that sow in tears shall reap in joy'; I Corinthians 3: 7, 'So then neither is he that planteth anything, neither he that watereth; but God that giveth the increase.'

Rules and Lessons. The stanza-form and epigrammatic manner are modelled on Herbert's *Church-porch*; but, whereas Herbert has composed a series of 77 stanzas (a 'perfect' number) leading up to the 'Church', Vaughan has composed a series of 24 stanzas giving directions for daily conduct of a religious life from sunrise to sunrise, and has placed them exactly in the centre of the *1650* volume.

ll. 9–10. *the manna . . . sun-rising*. Exodus 16: 21, 'And they gathered it every morning, every man according to his eating: and when the sun waxed hot, it melted.'

l. 11. *prevent*: anticipate. Wisdom of Solomon 16: 28, 'we must prevent the sun, to give thee thanks.'

l. 16. *I AM*. Exodus 3: 14, 'and God said unto Moses, I AM THAT I AM: and he said, Thus shalt thou say unto the children of Israel, I AM hath sent me unto you.'

46 ll. 19–22. *let him not go . . . shine*. See Genesis 32: 24–30, where Jacob wrestles with the angel, particularly verse 26: 'And he said, Let me go, for the day breaketh. And he [Jacob] said, I will not let thee go, except thou bless me.'

ll. 23–4. *Pour . . . heav'n*. When Jacob had finished his dream of the ladder he awoke and consecrated the spot: Genesis 28: 18, 'And Jacob rose up early in the morning, and took the stone that he had put for his pillows, and set it up for a pillar, and poured oil upon the top of it.'

l. 27. *Shroud in*: lie hid within.

l. 28. *their star, the stone, and hidden food*. Revelation 22: 16, 'I am the root and offspring of David, and the bright and morning star.' Also Revelation 2: 17, 'To him that overcometh will I give to eat of the hidden manna, and will give him a white stone, and in the stone a new name written, which no man knoweth saving he that receiveth it.'

l. 32. *temper*: equanimity, balanced disposition.

l. 36. *choose the better part*. See Christ's admonition about temporal and spiritual activity, Luke 10: 41–2, 'Martha, Martha, thou art careful and troubled about many things: But one thing is needful: and Mary hath chosen that good part, which shall not be taken away from her.'

l. 45. *Judas Jew*. See Herbert, *Self-condemnation*, ll. 17–18: 'For he hath sold for money his dear Lord, | And is a Judas-Jew.'

ll. 50–2. *Sure trot . . . lag behind*. See Herbert, *Constancy*, ll. 9–10: 'Who rides his sure and even trot, | While the world now rides by, now lags behind.' *dust it on*. hurry on (raise a dust).

47   ll. 63–4. See Matthew 25: 31–46, especially verses 34–6: 'Then shall the King say unto them on his right hand, Come, ye blessed of my Father, inherit the kingdom prepared for you from the foundation of the world: For I was an hungered, and ye gave me meat: I was thirsty, and ye gave me drink: I was a stranger, and ye took me in: Naked, and ye clothed me.'

l. 64. *fence*: ward off, protect against.

ll. 65–6. *Though . . . day*. Ecclesiastes 11: 1, 'Cast thy bread upon the waters: for thou shalt find it after many days.'

l. 66. *fraughts*: shiploads, freight.

l. 71. *unbitted*: unbridled, unrestrained.

l. 75. *voids*: issues, empties out.

48   l. 108. *span*: the measure of an extended hand.

l. 110. *trim thy lamp, buy oil*. See the parable of the virgins, Matthew 25: 1–13, 'Then shall the kingdom of heaven be likened unto ten virgins, which took their lamps, and went forth to meet the bridegroom. . . . the wise took oil in their vessels with their lamps.'

l. 125. *conversation*: society, company.

l. 126. See Herbert, *Church-monuments*, ll. 2–3: 'Here I intomb my flesh, that it betimes | May take acquaintance of this heap of dust.'

49   l. 132. *That bush where God is, shall not burn*. Exodus 3: 2, 'And the angel of the Lord appeared unto him [Moses] in a flame of fire out of the midst of a bush: and he looked, and, behold, the bush burned with fire, and the bush was not consumed.'

ll. 139–40. The same biblical verses are quoted in Herbert's *Divinity*, ll. 17–18; see Matthew 22: 37–9; 26: 41; Luke 6: 31.

Corruption. l. 9. *till*: the act of tilling or ploughing. (But *sweat* and *till* may also be read as verbs.)

l. 10. *a thorn, or weed*. Genesis 3: 17–19, 'cursed is the ground for thy sake; in sorrow shalt thou eat of it all the days of thy life; Thorns also and thistles shall it bring forth to thee . . . In the sweat of thy face shalt thou eat bread.'

l. 14. *felled. 1650* reads *fel*. This seems to be a misprint for *fel'd*, in parallel with *foyl'd*.

50   l. 25. *leiger*: 'resident in the capacity of ambassador' (*OED*: 'ledger').

ll. 25–8. *each bush . . . view them*. See Herbert, *Decay*, ll. 6–7: 'One might have sought and found thee presently | At some fair oak, or bush, or cave, or well.'

l. 30. *freezeth on*. See Herbert, *Employment* (II), l. 29.

ll. 33–4. *thy bow . . . cloud*: the rainbow of the Covenant: Genesis 9: 13.

l. 36. *Centre*: the earth.

l. 37. *thick darkness*. A frequent biblical phrase: see Exodus 10: 22 (the plagues of Egypt), and especially Joel 2: 1–2, the prophecy of the day of Judgement: 'Blow ye the trumpet in Zion . . . for the day of the Lord cometh, for it is nigh at hand; A day of darkness and of gloominess, a day of clouds and of thick darkness.'

l. 38. *hatcheth o'er*: closes over, forms a 'hatch' over. Perhaps also with the suggestion of bringing to maturity a hidden process.

ll. 39–40. See Revelation 14: 15, 'And another angel came out of the temple, crying with a loud voice to him that sat on the cloud, Thrust in thy sickle, and reap: for the time is come for thee to reap; for the harvest of the earth is ripe.'

H. Scriptures. l. 5. *the hidden stone, the manna*. See note to *Rules and Lessons*, l. 28.

l. 6. *elixir*: a preparation by which alchemists tried to change base metals into gold. Also 'a supposed drug or essence with the property of indefinitely prolonging life' (*OED*).

l. 8. *characters*: letters of the alphabet.

51   ll. 9–10. *O that . . . thee!* See Herbert, *The Altar*, ll. 5–12.

l. 12. *the Law and stones*. The Mosaic law was recorded on 'tables of stone, written with the finger of God' (Exodus 31: 18).

l. 13. *my faults are thine*. See Herbert, *Judgement*, l. 15: 'There thou shalt find my faults are thine.'

Unprofitableness. Luke 17: 10, 'when ye shall have done all those things which are commanded you, say, We are unprofitable servants:

we have done that which was our duty to do'; and Matthew 25: 30, 'And cast ye the unprofitable servant into outer darkness.'

l. 1. *How rich . . . are!* See Herbert, *The Flower*, ll. 1–2: 'How fresh, O Lord, how sweet and clean | Are thy returns!' The whole poem echoes themes and phrases from Herbert's *The Flower* and *The Glance*, with a closing echo of Herbert's *The Odour*.

l. 4. *share*: shear.

52 *Christ's Nativity.* l. 7. *hark . . . rings.* See Herbert, *Man's Medley*, ll. 1–2: 'Hark, how the birds do sing, | And woods do ring.'

l. 9. *consort*: harmonious combination of voices or instruments.

ll. 11–12. *Man . . . sacrifice.* See Herbert, *Providence*, ll. 13–14: 'Man is the world's high priest: he doth present | The sacrifice for all.'

l. 29. *mystic birth*: the spiritual renewal of the speaker himself.

ll. 31–3. *How kind . . . joy.* Luke 15: 7, 'likewise joy shall be in heaven over one sinner that repenteth, more than over ninety and nine just persons, which need no repentance.'

53 l. 45. *passions mind*: remember his sufferings.

ll. 45–8. These lines, and all of Part II, reflect Vaughan's bitter opposition to the act passed by Parliament on 23 December 1644, abolishing the observance of Good Friday and Christmas, along with other traditional holy days.

The Check. l. 10. *kind*: naturally related.

l. 11. *dear flesh.* See Herbert, *Church-monuments*, l. 17: 'Dear flesh, while I do pray'.

l. 23. *mind it not*: pay no attention, take no heed.

54 l. 25. *fore-runners.* See Herbert's poem by this title.

ll. 39–40. *these thy days . . . thy own good*: an allusion to Luke 19: 42, 'If thou hadst known, even thou, at least in this thy day, the things which belong unto thy peace!'

l. 47. *The day . . . observation.* Luke 17: 20, 'The Kingdom of God cometh not with observation.'

55 *Disorder and Frailty.* l. 16. *threaten*: attempt to achieve, seem about to achieve.

ll. 20–1. *grow and stretch.* See Herbert, *The Discharge*, l. 5: 'And in thy lookings stretch and grow'; and *The Flower*, ll. 29–30: 'But while I grow in a straight line, | Still upwards bent.' The whole of Vaughan's stanza 2 echoes words and themes from *The Flower*.

l. 31. *exhalation*: a body of vapour, a meteor: see Herbert's use of a similar image in *The Answer*, ll. 8–12.

56 l. 46. *yes. 1650* reads *is*, apparently a colloquial form of *yis* (*yes*).

ll. 46–8. *give wings . . . thou art*. See Herbert, *Whitsunday*, ll. 1–4.

l. 48. *tire*: attire, specifically, a head-dress.

The biblical motto blends the Genevan and the KJ versions.

Idle Verse. l. 4. *on the score*: in debt.

l. 5. *amidst my youth and night*. See Herbert, *The Glance*, l. 2.

l. 7. *my only light*. See Herbert, *The Flower*, l. 39.

l. 9. *fits*. Besides spasms, or attacks of disease, there is a sense of *fit* as part of a poem, a canto.

57 l. 13. *purls*. Vaughan's italic indicates a complex pun:(1) whirling rills of water; (2) in the context of 'dress and trim' (l. 10), the loops of decorative edging used for fine garments ('robes', l. 14); (3) perhaps also, in view of 'bowls', a kind of liquor 'made by infusing . . . bitter herbs in ale or beer' (*OED*).

l. 16. *Sick with a scarf, or glove*. See Herbert, *Love* (I), ll. 13–14: 'only a scarf or glove | Doth warm our hands, and make them write of love.'

l. 18. *Simpered and shined*. See Herbert, *The Search*, l. 14.

l. 19. *cypress*: a tree planted in churchyards. *bays*: the laurel used to crown poets.

l. 20. *yew*: another churchyard tree.

l. 23. *nightingales . . . spring*. See Herbert, *Jordan* (I), l. 13: 'I envy no man's nightingale or spring.'

Son–days. The whole poem is done in the Elizabethan mode of the definition-poem (a rapid sequence of analogies)—used by Southwell and Sidney, and by Herbert, in *Sin* (I), *Prayer* (I), and the first stanza of his own poem *Sunday*.

l. 9. *The pulleys*. See Herbert, *The Pulley*.

ll. 11–12. *God's . . . day*. Genesis 3: 8, 'And they heard the voice of the Lord God walking in the garden in the cool of the day.'

l. 13. *Jubilee*. The jubilee year was celebrated every fifty years by the Jews as a time of restitution and emancipation. See Leviticus 25: 8–13.

58 *Repentance*. ll. 7–9. *little gate* | *And narrow way . . . passage*. See Herbert, *H. Baptism* (II), ll. 1–3; Matthew 7: 14.

l. 17. *not sorting to my end*: not suiting my purpose.

59 l. 32. *outvie my score*: exceed my list (of sins).

l. 41. *signature*. This technical term is explained by Vaughan in his treatise on *Hermetical Physic*: 'That thou mayst have some knowledge of those materials or ingredients which are requisite and proper to make such specifical medicaments, thou must diligently read the books of the Hermetists, *De signaturis rerum*, that is to say, Of those impressions and characters which God hath communicated to, and marked (as I may say) all his Creatures with.' (Martin, p. 583).

l. 44. *told*: counted.

l. 53. *Cut me not off for my transgressions.* See Herbert, *Repentance*, l. 15.

ll. 65–6. *The heavens . . . thy sight.* Job 25: 4–5, 'How then can man be justified with God? or how can he be clean that is born of a woman? Behold even to the moon, and it shineth not; yea, the stars are not pure in his sight.'

ll. 67–8. *How then . . . charge with folly?* Job 4: 17–18, 'Shall mortal man be more just than God? shall a man be more pure than his maker? Behold, he put no trust in his servants; and his angels he charged with folly.'

60 l. 70. *Figs . . . weed!* Luke 6: 44, 'For of thorns men do not gather figs, nor of a bramble bush gather they grapes.'

ll. 71–2. *I am the gourd of sin . . . tomorrow.* See Jonah 4: 6–10. A gourd grew over Jonah to give shade and it withered the next day by God's will.

ll. 75–6. *Profaneness . . . Defects and darkness in my breast.* See Herbert, *Aaron*, ll. 6–7.

ll. 79–80. *Only in him . . . well dressed.* See Herbert, *Aaron*, l. 15.

l. 81. *quits all score*: pays the debt, balances the books.

l. 82. *the boxes of his poor.* See Herbert, *Praise* (III), l. 28.

The Burial of an Infant, l. 11. *Expecting*: waiting.

61 *Faith*. l. 5. *raying*: emitting, sending forth.

l. 6. *his spouse*: the Church.

l. 9. *co-heirs.* Romans 8: 16–17, 'The Spirit itself beareth witness with our spirit, that we are the children of God: and if children, then heirs; heirs of God, and joint-heirs with Christ.'

l. 10. *Of bond, or free.* Galatians 3: 28, 'There is neither Jew nor Greek, there is neither bond nor free, there is neither male nor female: for ye are all one in Christ Jesus.'

l. 21. *Sun of righteousness.* Malachi 4: 2, 'But unto you that fear my name shall the Sun of righteousness arise with healing in his wings.'

ll. 31–2. *figured in . . . rites.* See Hebrews 9: St Paul's account of how the Hebrew ceremonies formed a 'figure' of imperfect 'gifts and sacrifices . . . imposed on them until the time of reformation'.

l. 37. *spans up*: reaches (as by a span or arch); encompasses.

62 *The Dawning*. Matthew 24: 36, 42, 'But of that day and hour knoweth no man, no, not the angels of heaven, but my Father only . . . Watch therefore, for ye know not what hour your Lord doth come.'

l. 2. *The Bridegroom's coming*. Matthew 25: 6, 'And at midnight there was a cry made, Behold, the bridegroom cometh.'

l. 24. *That morning-star*. Revelation 22: 16, 'I am the root and the offspring of David, and the bright and morning star.'

l. 29. *puddle*: foul, dirty water.

63 *Admission*. l. 1. *How shrill are silent tears*. See Herbert, *The Family*, l. 20: 'What is so shrill as silent tears?' *got head*: gained power.

l. 2. *bowels*: feelings (centre of compassion).

l. 3. *when my stock lay dead*. See Herbert, *Grace*, l. 1: 'My stock lies dead.'

l. 9. *wink*: close the eyes.

l. 10. *thy beggar*. See Herbert, *Gratefulness*, ll. 3–4: 'See how thy beggar works on thee | By art.'

l. 13. *Bowels of love!* See Colossians 3: 12, 'bowels of mercies'; I John 3: 17, 'bowels of compassion'; and Herbert, *Longing*, l. 19: 'Bowels of pity, hear!'

ll. 13–14, *rate . . . price*. See Herbert, *The Pearl*, l. 35: 'And at what rate and price I have thy love.'

64 l. 17. *infants . . . suck thee*. See Herbert, *Longing*, l. 17: 'Their infants, them; and they suck thee | More free.'

ll. 29–32. *O hear! . . . blood*. See Herbert, *Church-lock and key*, ll. 9–12.

Praise. See Herbert, *Praise* (II) for the model of Vaughan's first thirty-two lines here. The second part of Herbert's *An Offering*, which follows *Praise* (II) in *The Temple*, has a stanza-form similar to ll. 33–56 of this poem.

l. 1. *King . . . life!* See Herbert, *Praise* (II), l. 1: 'King of Glory, King of Peace.'

ll. 9–10. *Wherefore . . . thee*. See Herbert, *Praise* (II), ll. 9–10: 'Wherefore with my utmost art | I will sing thee.'

l. 13. *Day . . . day*. See Herbert, *Praise* (II), l. 17: 'Sev'n whole days, not one in seven.'

65 l. 19. *seal and bracelet*. Song of Solomon 8: 6, 'Set me as a seal upon thine heart, as a seal upon thine arm.'

l. 46. *board*: Communion table.

l. 49. *to his pow'r*: as he is able.

66 *Dressing*: preparation for taking Communion.

ll. 2–3. *that feed'st . . . shadows flee.* Song of Solomon 2: 16–17, 'My beloved is mine, and I am his: he feedeth among the lilies. Until the day break, and the shadows flee away, turn, my beloved.'

ll. 3–4. *touch with one coal | My frozen heart.* See Isaiah 6: 6–7, where a seraph touches the lips of the prophet with a 'live coal'.

ll. 4–5. *key . . . rooms.* See Herbert, *The H. Communion*, ll. 21–2: 'And hath the privy key, | Op'ning the soul's most subtle rooms.'

l. 6. *thy clear fire.* Malachi 3: 2, 'For he is like a refiner's fire.'

l. 12. *even . . . win.* Psalm 8: 2,'Out of the mouth of babes and sucklings hast thou ordained strength because of thine enemies.'

ll. 19–20. *thy private . . . sign.* II Corinthians 1: 21–2, 'Now he which stablisheth us with you in Christ, and hath anointed us, is God; who hath also sealed us, and given the earnest of the Spirit in our hearts.' *earnest*: pledge, foretaste.

67 l. 30. *resent*: 'to feel (something) as a cause of depression or sorrow; to feel deeply or sharply' (*OED*).

ll. 35–42. The more extreme Protestants chose to sit rather than kneel while receiving the Communion, in order to avoid the tradition of Roman Catholicism.

Easter-day. See Herbert's *The Dawning* for Vaughan's model here.

l. 8. *two deaths*: temporal and spiritual deaths.

l. 16. *Whose spittle . . . blind.* See Mark 8: 22–5 and John 9: 1–7 for the story of how Christ healed the blind man by putting spit, or spit (spittle) mixed with clay, upon his eyes.

68 *The Holy Communion.* l. 1. *Welcome . . . life!* See Herbert, *The Banquet*, ll. 1–2: 'Welcome sweet and sacred cheer, | Welcome dear.'

l. 4. *quickened*: revived, enlivened. *dry stubble.* Job 13: 25, 'And wilt thou pursue the dry stubble?'

ll. 6–8. *at first . . . date.* See Genesis 1: 1–3.

69 ll. 21–2. *But . . . last breath.* Matthew 27: 45, 50–1, 'Now from the sixth hour there was darkness over all the land unto the ninth hour. . . . Jesus, when he had cried again with a loud voice, yielded up the ghost. And, behold, the veil of the temple was rent in twain from the top to the bottom.'

l. 33. *paid the price.* I Corinthians 6: 20, 'for ye are bought with a price.'

ll. 35–6. *take | Us by the hand.* See Herbert, *Easter*, l. 3; *Lent*, l. 41; *Love* (III), l. 11.

ll. 49–50. *O rose . . . valley.* See Song of Solomon 2: 1.

70 *Psalm 121*. A very free adaptation in the ballad metre used by Herbert for his version of Psalm 23—which occurs in roughly the same position, near the close of *The Church*.

l. 19. *my pillar and my cloud*. See Exodus 13: 21; the allusion is added by Vaughan.

Affliction. The poem seems to imitate the irregular verse-form of Herbert's *The Collar*, with a similar effect of greater regularity in the last four lines.

l. 2. *physic*: medicine.

l. 3. *accessions*: attacks of bad health.

l. 4. *Elixir*: both in the alchemical sense of a transforming substance that turns a base metal to gold, and in the medicinal sense of a drug to cure disease or to prolong life.

71 ll. 19–20. *the famous fan . . . disturbs*: a winnowing fan. See Matthew 3: 12, 'Whose fan is in his hand, and he will thoroughly purge his floor, and gather his wheat into the garner; but he will burn up the chaff with unquenchable fire.'

l. 29. *plays all the game*. See Herbert, *Misery*, l. 3.

l. 35. *key*: tune.

ll. 37–40. *Tuning his breast . . . musical*. See Herbert, *The Temper* (I), ll. 22–4: 'Stretch or contract me, thy poor debtor: | This is but tuning of my breast, | To make the music better.'

The Tempest. l. 1. *How is man parcelled out!* See Herbert, *Doomsday*, ll. 27–8: 'Man is out of order hurled, | Parcelled out to all the world.'

72 ll. 5–16. The italicized passage is a poetical 'emblem' from which the following commentary arises.

l. 30. *Issachar*. Genesis 49: 14, 'Issachar is a strong ass couching down between two burdens.'

l. 32. *all three*. A marginal note in *1650* explains: 'Light, motion, heat.'

l. 35. *subtlety*: fineness of texture.

l. 36. *kinred*: old form of *kindred*.

l. 37. *keys . . . ascents*: as in music.

l. 39. *Sleeps at the ladder's foot*. See Genesis 28: 12, Jacob's ladder.

73 l. 45. *Yet hugs he still his dirt*. See Herbert, *Misery*, l. 46: 'Give him his dirt to wallow in all night.'

l. 49. *Life's but a blast, he knows it*. See Herbert, *Misery*, ll. 5–6: 'Man is but grass, | He knows it.'

ll. 49–52. *what? . . . law?* See Herbert, *The Collar*, ll. 3, 13–15, 21–5.

l. 53. *O foolish man! . . . sight?* See Herbert, *Misery*, l. 49: 'Oh foolish man! where are thine eyes?'

l. 55. *thick darkness.* See note on l. 37 of *Corruption. thy bread, a stone.* Matthew 7: 9, 'Or what man is there of you, whom if his son ask bread, will he give him a stone?'

ll. 58–60. *flints . . . steel . . . flint to dust.* A reminder of the emblem which opened the volume of 1650.

74 *Retirement.* l. 14. *Have . . . way.* See Herbert, *Affliction* (I) l. 20: 'I had my wish and way.'

l. 22. *love-twist.* See Herbert, *The Pearl*, l. 38: 'thy silk twist let down from heav'n to me'.

ll. 36–8. *I have a house . . . dwell.* Psalm 26: 8, 'Lord, I have loved the habitation of thy house, and the place where thine honour dwelleth.'

l. 40. *I make all new.* Revelation 21: 5, 'And he that sat upon the throne said, Behold, I make all things new.'

75 ll. 45–8. *faithful school . . . true descent.* See Herbert, *Church-monuments*, ll. 6–9, 17–18.

ll. 51–2. *dust . . . eyes, and blind thee still.* See Herbert, *Love* (II), ll. 9–10, 'Our eyes shall see thee, which before saw dust; | Dust blown by wit, till that they both were blind.'

Love and Discipline. l. 3. *My lot is fall'n.* See Psalm 16: 6 (*BCP*), 'The lot is fallen unto me in a fair ground' (Rudrum).

ll. 5–6. *Some tares . . . sow'st.* See the parable of the wheat and tares. Matthew 13: 24–30.

ll. 17–18. *So thrive I . . . green ears.* See Herbert, *Hope*, ll. 5–6: 'With that I gave a vial full of tears: | But he a few green ears.'

76 *The Pilgrimage.* l. 3. *accidents*: events, incidents.

l. 5. *Jacob-like . . . place.* See Genesis 28: 11.

ll. 23–4. *bread . . . live.* Matthew 4: 4, 'Man shall not live by bread alone, but by every word that proceedeth out of the mouth of God.'

ll. 25–8. *O feed me then! . . . Mount.* I Kings 19: 8, 'And he [Elijah] arose, and did eat and drink, and went in the strength of that meat forty days and forty nights unto Horeb the mount of God.'

77 *The Law and the Gospel.* l. 1. *on Sinai pitch.* Exodus 19: 2, 'For they were departed from Rephidim, and were come to the desert of Sinai, and had pitched in the wilderness; and there Israel camped before the mount.'

l. 2. *And shine . . . fiery Law.* Deuteronomy 33: 2, 'And he [Moses] said, The Lord came from Sinai, and rose up from Seir unto them; he shined forth from mount Paran . . . from his right hand went a fiery law for them.'

ll. 2–10. *Law . . . inclined.* For the details, see Exodus 19: 16 and 20: 18–21.

ll. 4–5. *thy weeds . . . for light.* Exodus 24: 17, 'And the sight of the glory of the Lord was like devouring fire on the top of the mount in the eyes of the children of Israel.' *weeds*: garments.

78 *The World.*

l. 8. *doting lover . . . quaintest strain.* See Herbert, *Dullness*, l. 5: 'The wanton lover in a curious strain'. *quaintest*: most ingenious.

l. 14. *pore*: 'ruin one's sight by close reading or over-study' (*OED*).

79 ll. 23–5. *Yet digged . . . clutch his prey.* See Herbert, *Confession*, ll. 13–16: 'they, | Like moles within us, heave, and cast about: | And till they foot and clutch their prey, | They never cool.'

ll. 44–5. *And poor . . . victory.* See Herbert, *The Church Militant*, l. 190: 'While Truth sat by, counting his [Sin's] victories.'

ll. 46–7. *Yet some . . . sing and weep.* Revelation 7: 14, 17, 'These are they which came out of great tribulation, and have washed their robes, and made them white in the blood of the Lamb . . . and God shall wipe away all tears from their eyes'; Revelation 15: 3, 'And they sing the song of Moses the servant of God, and the song of the Lamb.'

80 ll. 59–60. *Bridegroom . . . bride*: alluding both to the Song of Solomon and the 'marriage' of Revelation 19: 7–9.

The Mutiny. Stanza 1. The imagery of 'straw' and 'brick' is based on the labours of the Israelites in Egypt: Exodus 5.

l. 6. *start*: cause to break away.

l. 10. *coil*: tumult.

ll. 11–12. *who made . . . waves.* See Herbert, *Providence*, ll. 47–8: 'Thou hast made poor sand | Check the proud sea, ev'n when it swells and gathers.'

l. 18. *Babel-weight.* See Genesis 11: 1–9, for the tower of Babel.

ll. 22–3. *May look . . . faith.* Hebrews 12: 2, 'Looking unto Jesus the author and finisher of our faith'.

81 ll. 30–1. *than through . . . serpents.* Refers to the forty years of Exodus. For the serpents, see Numbers 21: 6.

l. 38. *bruised reed.* See Isaiah 42: 3 and Matthew 12: 20.

ll. 39–40. *seized | Of*: 'to be the legal possessor of ' (*OED*).

82 *The Constellation.* l. 14. *clue*: a ball of thread or yarn.

l. 16. *slips his span*: wastes, idles away his time or life.

l. 21. *Music and mirth*. See Herbert, *The Pearl*, l. 24.

ll. 27–8. *effects . . . much more*: with allusion to the astrological theory of the close relation between stars and plants.

l. 31. *though . . . star*. I Corinthians 15: 41, 'one star differeth from another star in glory.'

l. 33. *Since . . . names*. Psalm 147: 4, 'He telleth the number of the stars; he calleth them all by their names.'

l. 36. *in your courses fought*. Judges 5: 20, 'the stars in their courses fought against Sisera.'

ll. 37–44. A bitter attack on those reformers whose reliance on biblical authority and 'zeal' had, as Vaughan sees it, caused the civil wars of the 1640s and the destruction of the established Church of England (their 'mother'). The 'father' may well be Charles I, executed on 30 Jan. 1649.

83 l. 43. *Lamb . . . dragon's voice*. Revelation 13: 11, 'And I beheld another beast coming up out of the earth; and he had two horns like a lamb, and he spake as a dragon.'

ll. 59–60. *repair these rents . . . all agree*. I Corinthians 1: 10, 'Now I beseech you, brethren, by the name of our Lord Jesus Christ, that ye all speak the same thing, and that there be no divisions among you; but that ye be perfectly joined together in the same mind and in the same judgment.' See also I John 4.

The Shepherds. l. 1. *lives*. Sometimes emended to *livers*, for metrical reasons.

ll. 5–6. *How . . . true light*. See Luke 2: 8–9.

ll. 9–11. *first and blessed swains . . . promise*. Abraham and his family were shepherds when he was promised a chosen progeny in Genesis 12: 2–3.

84 l. 17. *Salem*: Jerusalem.

l. 21. *cots*: cottages.

l. 23. *cedar . . . gold*: used to build the temple at Jerusalem: II Chronicles 2–4.

l. 30. *rack*: manger (though Vaughan's italic may indicate a glance at *rack* as an instrument of torture, i.e. Christ's sufferings).

ll. 49–50. *kings and prophets . . . missed*. See Matthew 13–17.

l. 53. *to*: compared to.

85 *Misery*. l. 5. *The wind . . . fist*. Proverbs 30: 4, 'who hath gathered the wind in his fists?'

l. 6. *blow still . . . list.* John 3: 8, 'the wind bloweth where it listeth.' *where it list*: where it wishes.

l. 23. *fig-leafs.* See Genesis 3: 7.

l. 36. *Would make a court . . . dwell.* See Herbert, *The Glimpse*, l. 30: 'Who by thy coming may be made a court.'

ll. 38–40. *spirit grieves . . . dust.* See Herbert's poem on the text 'Ephes. 4. 30. Grieve not the Holy Spirit', ll. 1–10, 16.

86 l. 41. *devest*: literally, unclothe: an old form of *divest*.

ll. 57–8. *I school . . . cell.* See Herbert, *Mortification*, ll. 20–2: 'Getting a house and home, where he may move | Within the circle of his breath, | Schooling his eyes.'

l. 66. *snudge*: nestle, be snug and secure. See Herbert, *Giddiness*, l. 11: 'snudge in quiet'.

l. 74. *travel, fight or die.* See Herbert, *Nature*, ll. 1–2: 'Full of rebellion, I would die, | Or fight, or travel.'

ll. 77–81. *flames . . . work and wind . . . fierce soul bustles . . . wilded by a peevish heart.* A complex of Herbertian echoes: see *Jordan* (II), ll. 13–15; *The Collar*, l. 33; and *Sion*, l. 13.

87 l. 87. *tempers*: transient feelings.

l. 96. *To look . . . pain.* See Herbert, *The Glance*, l. 21: 'When thou shalt look us out of pain'.

l. 114. *mend and make.* See Herbert, *Love* (II), l. 14.

88 *The Sap.* The poem's theme is the spiritual nourishment gained from taking the Communion; hence it echoes many of Herbert's eucharistic poems and passages, and bears an especially close relation to Herbert's *Peace*, which closes with words that suggest the service of Communion.

ll. 7–8. *Thy root . . . meat.* See Herbert, *Peace*, ll. 16–18: 'Peace at the root must dwell. | But when I digged, I saw a worm devour | What showed so well.'

l. 11. *an hill of myrrh.* Song of Solomon 4: 6, 'Until the day break, and the shadows flee away, I will get me to the mountain of myrrh, and to the hill of frankincense.'

l. 13. *Prince of Salem.* Christ. See Genesis 14: 18, 'And Melchizedek king of Salem brought forth bread and wine'—a passage interpreted as foreshadowing the elements of the Communion. In Hebrews 6: 20 and 7: 1–2 Melchizedek is interpreted as a 'type' of Jesus, who was 'made an high priest for ever after the order of Melchisedec'.

l. 22. *two . . . due.* See Herbert, *Business*, l. 22: 'And two deaths had been thy fee.' Death of the body and condemnation of the soul.

ll. 25–6. *strange love . . . sacred blood*. See Herbert, *Obedience*, ll. 26–7: 'thy death and blood | Showed a strange love to all our good.' Also Donne, *Holy Sonnet* XI (Grierson's order), l. 9: 'Oh let me then his strange love still admire.'

ll. 26–9. *his sacred blood . . . cordial . . . decay*. See Herbert, *The Sacrifice*, ll. 158–9: 'Which shows my blood to be the only way | And cordial left to repair man's decay.'

ll. 29–31. *who but truly tastes it . . . secret life and virtue*. See Herbert, *Peace*, ll. 33–6: 'For they that taste it do rehearse, | That virtue lies therein, | A secret virtue bringing peace and mirth | By flight of sin.' *virtue*: inherent power.

89 l. 40. *A powerful, rare dew*: repentance, tears.

l. 45. *one who drank it thus*. An allusion to Herbert, as the following Herbertian echoes indicate: see *The H. Communion*, where the first poem under this title deals with the action of grace, and the second celebrates the 'ease' with which the soul here communicates with heaven; also *The Invitation*, stanza 4, concerned with 'joy', and *The Banquet*, which celebrates the 'sweet and sacred cheer' of the Communion and its power of raising the soul to 'the sky'.

Mount of Olives (II). See notes on preceding poem by this title.

l. 1. *When first . . . thy joys*: reminiscent of the opening line of Herbert's *Jordan* (II): 'When first my lines of heav'nly joys made mention'.

ll. 1–8: reminiscent of the opening line and stanza of Herbert's *The Glance*: 'When first thy sweet and gracious eye | Vouchsafed . . . | To look upon me . . . | I felt a sugared strange delight . . . | Bedew, embalm, and overrun my heart.'

l. 4. *sweets*: fragrances (which 'perfume' the whole being, as in Herbert's *The Odour*).

ll. 12–22: reminiscent of Herbert's *The Flower*, in theme and occasional wording.

l. 14. *And was blown through by ev'ry storm and wind*: almost identical with l. 36 of Herbert's *Affliction* (I).

l. 17. *paisage*: landscape (Vaughan's italic indicates both a foreign word and perhaps also a technical term in painting).

90 *Man*: a striking contrast, in theme and mood, with Herbert's poem *Man*.

ll. 12–14. *The birds . . . fine*. Matthew 6: 26, 28–9, 'Behold the fowls of the air: for they sow not, neither do they reap, nor gather into barns; yet your heavenly Father feedeth them . . . And why take ye thought for raiment? Consider the lilies of the field, how they grow; they toil not, neither do they spin: And yet I say unto you, that even Solomon in all his glory was not arrayed like one of these.'

l. 23. *wit*: intelligence. *stones*: loadstones—used as magnetic compasses.

91 'I walked the other day'. Another poem on the death of his brother William.

l. 1. *to spend my hour*: his usual hour of meditation.

l. 4. *a gallant flower*. The same phrase occurs in l. 14 of Herbert's *Peace*.

ll. 5–6. *ruffled . . . bower . . . curious store*. See Herbert, *Affliction* (V), ll. 21–2: 'While blust'ring winds destroy the wanton bowers, | And ruffle all their curious knots and store.' *curious store*: fine abundance.

ll. 19–21. *I saw . . . unseen*. See Herbert, *The Flower*, ll. 8–14.

92 l. 46. *frame*: construction: (1) human body; (2) universe.

l. 49. *Thy steps*. The *vestigia*, the signs of God's presence and power that may be found by meditating on the creation.

93 l. 59. *light, joy, leisure*. See Herbert, *Heaven*, l. 19: 'Light, joy, and leisure.'

l. 61. *hid in thee, show me his life again*. Colossians 3: 3, 'For ye are dead, and your life is hid with Christ in God.'

Begging (I). l. 1. *King of Mercy, King of Love*. See Herbert, *L'Envoy*, l. 1: 'King of Glory, King of Peace'. Also *Praise* (II), l. 1.

l. 2. *In whom . . . move*. Acts 17: 28, 'for in him we live, and move, and have our being.'

ll. 13–16. *O it is thy only Art . . . to thee*. See Herbert, *Nature*, ll. 4–6: 'O tame my heart; | It is thy highest art | To captivate strong-holds to thee.'

The verses from Jude follow KJ, with the substitution of *us* for *you*.

SILEX SCINTILLANS (1655)

97 *The Author's Preface*. l. 4. *idle words*. Matthew 12: 36, 'But I say unto you, That every idle word that men shall speak, they shall give account thereof in the day of judgment.'

l. 8. *parricides*: an allusion to Robert Greene's *Groatsworth of Wit* (1592): 'Ah Gentlemen, that live to read my broken and confused lines, look not I should (as I was wont) delight you with vain fantasies; but gather my follies all together, and as ye would deal with so many parricides, cast them into the fire.' *Brabeion*: a prize in athletic contests.

ll. 23–4. *Prudentius*. b. AD 348. *Symmachus*. b. *c.*AD 340; famous orator and defender of pagan religion.

98 ll. 57–8. *character . . . ivy-bush . . . persons of honour.* i.e., if the description ('character') of the author as a person of high rank or title ('honour') is no more than a mere advertisement, as an ivy-bush or a picture of it is placed outside a tavern to show that wine is sold there.

ll. 66–7. *idle word . . . no corrupt communication.* See Matthew 12: 36 and Ephesians 4: 29, 'Let no corrupt communication proceed out of your mouth, but that which is good to the use of edifying, that it may minister grace unto the hearers.'

l. 68–9. *mere design*: deliberate intent.

99 ll. 72–80. The passage is a free quotation from Owen Felltham, *Resolves* (1628), Century II, i, 'Of Idle Books'.

l. 81. *he that is dead*. Romans 6: 7.

l. 87. *prevent*: anticipate.

l. 104. *conceits*: conceptions, ingenious turns of thought.

l. 111. *stationer*: bookseller, publisher.

100 l. 115. *casteth firebrands*. Proverbs 26: 18.

ll. 123–4. *they that turn many*. Daniel 12: 3.

ll. 133–4. *non passibus aequis*. '[But] not with equal steps'. *Aeneid* 2. 724.

l. 137. *perfection*. Christian perfection, holiness of life.

l. 141. *practic*: pertaining to, shown in, practice or action.

l. 150. *prelibation*: foretaste.

101 l. 156. *Hierotheus*. 'A mythical first-century bishop of Athens, apparently invented by Dionysius the pseudo-Areopagite, who . . . speaks of Hierotheus as his teacher and as a writer of hymns' (Martin). *A true Hymn*. See Herbert's poem by that title.

l. 169. *nigh unto death*. See Paul's words concerning his companion Epaphroditus: 'For indeed he was sick nigh unto death: but God had mercy on him' (Philippians 2: 27).

l. 171. *accomplished dress*: completed appearance or presentation.

l. 173. *God . . . flesh*. Numbers 16: 22.

102 This *catena* (chain) of biblical verses follows an ancient tradition of creating a personal psalm out of an arrangement and adaptation of passages. The sequence runs as follows: Jeremiah 17: 13–14; Isaiah 38: 10–11, 16–17; 48: 9; 38: 18–19; Jonah 2: 6, 8: Psalms 42: 8; 43: 4; 5: 7; Jonah 2: 9.

103 *To my most merciful.* For section I, see notes to *The Dedication*, p. 174. ll. 23–4. The lines refer to the brightness of Christ's clothing at his Transfiguration (Matthew 17: 2) and to the *virtue* (healing power) of Christ demonstrated in the story of the woman who was healed by touching his clothes (Mark 5: 25–34).

l. 27. *earnest*: 'A foretaste, instalment, pledge, of anything afterwards to be received in greater abundance' (*OED*).

l. 28. *The Candle.* Job 29: 3, 'When his candle shined upon my head.'

104 l. 45. *Token*: probably a reference to the 'token of the covenant' in Genesis 9: 12–17.

105 *Ascension-day*: the Thursday forty days after Easter.

l. 4. *all good and perfect gifts.* James 1: 17, 'Every good gift and every perfect gift is from above.'

ll. 16–18. *where the angels . . . night.* At the empty tomb angels stood watch to announce the absence of the resurrected Lord. See Matthew 28: 1–7; Luke 24: 1–8.

l. 19. *thy Convert's tears. 1655* provides a footnote: 'St. Mary Magdalene.'

l. 21. *I smell her spices, and her ointment.* Mark 16: 1, 'And when the sabbath was past, Mary Magdalene, and Mary the mother of James, and Salome, had brought sweet spices, that they might come and anoint him.' Also Matthew 26: 12, 'For in that she hath poured this ointment on my body, she did it for my burial.'

l. 25. *posting*: swift.

l. 33. *commerce*: relations, activities: see Acts 1: 3, 'To whom [the apostles] also he shewed himself alive after his passion by many infallible proofs, being seen of them forty days, and speaking of the things pertaining to the Kingdom of God.'

106 l. 37. *the fields of Bethany.* Luke 24: 50–1, 'And he led them out as far as to Bethany, and he lifted up his hands, and blessed them. And it came to pass, while he blessed them, he was parted from them, and carried up into heaven.'

l. 43. *vest*: clothing, vesture.

l. 45. *Heaven . . . like molten glass.* Job 37: 18, 'Hast thou with him spread out the sky, which is strong, and as a molten looking glass?'

l. 51. *train*: followers.

ll. 57–8. *The cloud . . . behold two men in white.* Acts 1: 9–11, 'he was taken up; and a cloud received him out of their sight. And while they looked stedfastly toward heaven as he went up, behold, two men stood by them in white apparel.'

ll. 59–60. *Two and no more . . . stubborn Jew*. John 8: 17, 'It is also written in your law, that the testimony of two men is true.'

Ascension Hymn, ll. 7–11. *some . . . life*: the 'death' of mystical experience.

l. 12. *Leave . . . old Man*. Colossians 3: 9, 'ye have put off the old man with his deeds.'

107 l. 30. *the Refiner's fire*. Malachi 3: 2, 'But who may abide the day of his coming? . . . for he is like a refiner's fire, and like fullers' soap.'

ll. 33–5. *clothes . . . The Fuller*. Mark 9: 3, 'And his raiment became shining, exceeding white as snow; so as no fuller on earth can white them.' A *fuller* is one who *fulls* cloth, that is, cleans and whitens it.

l. 36. *more white than snow*. Isaiah 1: 18, 'though your sins be as scarlet, they shall be as white as snow.'

l. 39. *Bring bone to bone*. Ezekiel 37: 7, 'and the bones came together, bone to his bone.'

l. 41. *all-subduing might*. Philippians 3: 20–1, 'according to the working whereby he is able even to subdue all things unto himself.'

108 'They are all gone into the world of light!' l. 35. *Resume*: take back.

109 l. 38. *perspective*: telescope.

l. 40. *no glass*. I Corinthians 13: 12, 'For now we see through a glass, darkly; but then face to face.'

White Sunday: Whitsunday; the seventh Sunday after Easter— commemorating the descent of the Holy Spirit on the day of Pentecost: Acts 2: 1–4.

ll. 5–8. *Those flames . . . fire*. Acts 2: 3, 'And there appeared unto them cloven tongues like as of fire, and it sat upon each of them.'

l. 6. *tire*: head-dress.

ll. 9–16. *new lights . . . candle shines*. Vaughan is attacking the extreme sects of his day whose members claimed to have special illumination from God which justified new religious doctrines and practices.

l. 11. *gall*: with allusion to the vinegar 'mingled with gall' given as a drink to Christ just before his Crucifixion: Matthew 27: 34.

l. 16. *His candle shines*. Job 29: 3, 'When his candle shined upon my head, and when by his light I walked through darkness.'

l. 24. *discern wolves from the sheep*. Matthew 7: 15, 'Beware of false prophets, which come to you in sheep's clothing, but inwardly they are ravening wolves.'

110 l. 26. *These last may be as first*. Matthew 19: 30, 'But many that are first shall be last; and the last shall be first.'

l. 28. *These last should be the worst.* II Timothy 3: 13, 'But evil men and seducers shall wax worse and worse.'

ll. 29–31. *Thy method . . . set down.* See Herbert, *The Bunch of Grapes*, l. 11: 'Their story pens and sets us down', that is, God's way of dealing with the Israelites foretells the present times.

ll. 45–8. *great eternal Rock . . . soul that pines.* See Exodus 17: 6 and I Corinthians 10: 4, 'for they drank of that spiritual Rock that followed them: and that Rock was Christ.'

ll. 54–6. *Curse . . . purse.* See Herbert, *Prayer* (II), ll. 15–18: 'Wert fain to take our flesh and curse, | . . . That by destroying that which tied thy purse, | Thou mightst make sure for liberality!'

111 l. 63. *Balaam's hire.* See Numbers 22 for Balak's offers to 'promote' Balaam 'unto very great honour' if he will disobey God.

The Proffer. The poem appears to reject an offer of some appointment to an office in the government of the 'Commonwealth' (l. 36) established by Cromwell and his associates after the execution of Charles I in 1649.

l. 10. *to take*: i.e. to take as food.

l. 11. *Wise husband will (you say) there wants prevent. Good husband* was a common phrase for one who manages his household or business 'with skill and thrift' (*OED*). *there* refers to the time of 'harder weather' (l. 9). *prevent*: anticipate. The line is usually emended to read *husbands*, with *there* interpreted as *their*; but no emendation is needed.

l. 18. *I've read . . . away.* Exodus 8: 31, 'And the Lord did according to the word of Moses; and he removed the swarms of flies from Pharaoh, from his servants, and from his people: there remained not one.'

112 ll. 25–7. *Shall my short hour . . . crumb of life.* See Herbert, *Complaining*, ll. 16–18: 'Let not thy wrathful power | Afflict my hour, | My inch of life.'

l. 33. *skill not*: do not value.

ll. 37–42. *will sow tares . . . reward for them and thee.* See the parable of the wheat and tares, Matthew 13: 24–30, 37–42.

ll. 44–5. *Spit out . . . with home.* See Herbert, *The Church-porch*, l. 92: 'Spit out thy phlegm, and fill thy breast with glory.'

ll. 45–8. *think on thy dream . . . Heaven.* Patterned after the last four lines of Herbert's *The Size.* The similarity may serve as a reminder of a larger kinship between these two poems: both have eight stanzas; the stanza-forms are similar (though not identical); and the theme of both is renunciation of worldly prosperity.

Cock-crowing. Elizabeth Holmes (p. 37) has called attention to a passage in Thomas Vaughan's *Anima Magica Abscondita* (1650) which bears a close relation to this poem: 'For she [*Anima*] is guided in her operations by a *Spiritual Metaphysical Grain*, a Seed or Glance of *Light*, simple, and without any mixture, descending from the *first Father of Lights*. For though his *full-eyed* Love shines on nothing but *Man*, yet everything in the world is in some measure directed for his preservation by a *spice* or *touch* of the *first Intellect*' (Rudrum edn., p. 111).

l. 1. *Father of lights*. James 1: 17, 'Every good gift and every perfect gift is from above, and cometh down from the Father of lights.'

113 l. 12. *tinned*: kindled.

l. 13. *tincture*: a term from alchemy: a spiritual principle—the essence or soul of a thing.

l. 14. *impower*: bestow power on.

ll. 20–2. *Whose hand . . . who made the same*. Romans 1: 20, 'For the invisible things of him from the creation of the world are clearly seen, being understood by the things that are made, even his eternal power and Godhead.'

l. 29. *dark Egyptian border*. See Exodus 10: 21.

ll. 37–40. *Only this veil . . . thee from me*. II Corinthians 3: 14, 'But their minds were blinded: for until this day remaineth the same vail untaken away in the reading of the old testament; which vail is done away in Christ.' Also, Hebrews 10: 20, 'By a new and living way, which he hath consecrated for us, through the veil, that is to say, his flesh.'

l. 41. *full-eyed love*. The phrase occurs in Herbert's *The Glance*, l. 20; also in the above passage from Thomas Vaughan.

114 l. 48. *Though with no lily*. Song of Solomon 2: 16, 'My beloved is mine, and I am his: he feedeth among the lilies.'

The Star. The guiding concept of this poem is the Hermetic and astrological theory that a close and active inter-relationship ('commerce', ll. 5 and 27) exists between creatures on earth and the celestial bodies.

l. 3. *And wind . . . smile*. See Herbert, *The Star*, l. 26: 'Glitter, and curl, and wind as they.'

l. 5. *imbars*: impedes, prohibits.

l. 6. *eagles eye not stars*: because, according to tradition, they look toward the sun.

ll. 7–8. *And still the lesser . . . blest.* Hebrews 7: 7, 'And without all contradiction the less is blessed of the better.'

l. 13. *the subject*: whatever on earth attracts the star—the object of the star's streaming and flowing. *respected*: regarded, looked upon (with esteem and close attention).

l. 14. *well disposed*: healthy.

115 *The Palm-tree.* In this poem the soul (representing the 'inward speaking' of Christ) is addressing the body on the verge of death (as in Vaughan's *The Evening-watch*). The palm-tree had become a symbol of the Church, through the traditional interpretation of Song of Solomon 7: 7–8. The opening lines seem to allude to the physical church or churchyard, where the speaker's body will endure the 'shade' of death. But the chief reference is to the spiritual Church on earth and in heaven.

l. 1. *Dear friend sit down*: the opening words of Herbert's *Love Unknown*.

ll. 11–12. *By flowers . . . and palms foretold.* Details of Solomon's Temple: see I Kings 6: 23–35. Also Herbert, *Sion*, ll. 4–5.

ll. 13–14. *This is the life . . . God.* Colossians 3: 3, 'For ye are dead, and your life is hid with Christ in God.'

ll. 17–20. *Here spirits . . . won the fight . . . crowns.* II Timothy 4: 7–8, 'I have fought a good fight, I have finished my course, I have kept the faith: henceforth there is laid up for me a crown of righteousness'; Hebrews 12: 1, 'let us run with patience the race that is set before us'; I Corinthians 9: 24–5, 'Know ye not that they which run in a race run all, but one receiveth the prize? So run, that ye may obtain . . . Now they do it to obtain a corruptible crown; but we an incorruptible.'

116 ll. 21, 25. *Here is the patience of the saints . . . Here is their faith too.* Revelation 14: 12, 'Here is the patience of the saints: here are they that keep the commandments of God, and the faith of Jesus.' Also Revelation 13: 10, 'Here is the patience and the faith of the saints.'

l. 28. *against you wake*: in preparation for the Last Judgement.

Joy. l. 5. *dosis*: a prescribed quantity of medicine.

ll. 21–2. *pains of death . . . eyes and breath.* See Herbert, *The Banquet*, ll. 52–3: 'Hearken under pain of death, | Hands and breath.'

ll. 29–30. *leave written on some tree. . . fastens thee.* See Herbert, *Affliction* (V), l. 20: 'We are the trees, whom shaking fastens more.'

117 *The Favour.* l. 6. *starved eaglet.* See note on *The Star*, p. 208.

l. 7. *kind*: related to (the star).

The Garland. ll. 9–11. *I flung away . . . for pleasures.* See Herbert,

Christmas, ll. 1–3 (and note): 'All after pleasures as I rid one day, | My horse and I, both tired, body and mind, | With full cry of affections, quite astray.' Also Herbert, *The Pilgrimage*, ll. 31–2: 'so I flung away, | Yet heard a cry.'

l. 10. *affections*: passions, emotions. *rid*: rode.

l. 11. *In post*: in haste.

l. 19. *silk-lists*: silk borders or trimming.

118   l. 25. *career*: a term associated with horsemanship: 'a short gallop at full speed' (*OED*); see ll. 9–11.

l. 27. *abear*: behaviour (*OED*); perhaps also associated with the verb *aberr*: to go astray (?).

Love-sick. For the repetitive technique of this poem, compare Herbert's *A Wreath*.

ll. 9–11. *O come and rend . . . mountains flow*. Isaiah 64:1, 'Oh that thou wouldest rend the heavens, that thou wouldest come down, that the mountains might flow down at thy presence.'

ll. 12–13. *Thou art | Refining fire*. Malachi 3: 2, 'For he is like a refiner's fire.'

l. 17. *So hear that thou must open*. Matthew 7: 7, 'Knock, and it shall be opened unto you.'

119   *Trinity Sunday*. Patterned after Herbert's poem by this title.

l. 7. *antitypes*. *OED* defines an *antitype* as that which is shadowed forth or represented by the 'type' or symbol—Vaughan's own spirit and body (water and blood).

Psalm 104. A free paraphrase, greatly expanded; compare KJ version.

123   *The Bird*. l. 26. *heavy*: sad, melancholy.

l. 27. *turtle*: turtle-dove. See Song of Solomon 2: 12, 'the voice of the turtle'; and Isaiah 38: 14, 'I did mourn as a dove.'

l. 28. *satyrs*. 'In the English Bible the word is applied . . . to the hairy demons or monsters . . . supposed to inhabit deserts' (*OED*). See Isaiah 34: 14, 'The wild beasts of the desert shall also meet with the wild beasts of the island, and the satyr shall cry to his fellow; the screech owl also shall rest there.'

l. 29. *the pleasant land . . . turns*. Genesis 19: 24, 'The Lord rained upon Sodom and upon Gomorrah brimstone and fire.'

l. 32. *day-spring . . . from high*. Luke 1: 78, 'Through the tender mercy of our God; whereby the dayspring from on high hath visited us.'

The Timber. l. 15. *resent*: perceive, feel sharply (with overtones of the modern meaning?).

124 l. 19. *resentment*. See note on line 15.

l. 20. *Means*: refers to, signifies.

l. 27. *resentient*: 'that which causes a change of feeling'—Vaughan's use is the only example in the *OED*.

l. 31. *an house where many mansions are.* John 14: 2, 'In my Father's house are many mansions.' *mansions*: dwelling-places.

ll. 45–8. *If my way lies . . . thirst.* See the account of the thirst of Hagar and Ishmael in the wilderness: Genesis 21: 14–19, 'And God opened her eyes, and she saw a well of water; and she went, and filled the bottle with water, and gave the lad drink.'

125 ll. 51–2. *trees of life . . . make them grow.* See Revelation 22: 1–2.

The Jews. The poem is based on the tradition that the Jews would be converted shortly before the Last Judgement. To Vaughan (and many of his contemporaries) the troubled religious conditions of England seemed to point toward the Last Days.

l. 7. *Beneath the oak and juniper.* See notes for *Religion*, p. 177.

l. 12. *and living waters flow.* Jeremiah 17: 13, 'the Lord, the fountain of living waters.'

ll. 15–18. *the olive . . . decay.* Jeremiah 11: 16–17, 'The Lord called thy name, A green olive tree, fair, and of goodly fruit: with the noise of a great tumult he hath kindled fire upon it, and the branches of it are broken.'

l. 19. *the husbandman.* John 15: 1, 'I am the true vine, and my Father is the husbandman.'

l. 22. *the bright morning-star.* Christ. See Revelation 22: 16.

126 ll. 24–7. *blind . . . Our fullness . . . come in.* Romans 11: 25, 'that blindness in part is happened to Israel, until the fulness of the Gentiles be come in.'

l. 31. *Mamre.* Where Abraham dwelt: Genesis 13: 18. *Eschol's brook.* Place where the spies sent into Canaan cut down the 'cluster of grapes': Numbers 13: 23–4.

ll. 33–4. *Who loved . . . only Son.* See John 3: 16.

l. 37. *From . . . veil remove.* II Corinthians 3: 15–16, 'But even unto this day, when Moses is read, the vail is upon their heart. Nevertheless when it shall turn to the Lord, the vail shall be taken away.'

l. 49. *the lost son by the newly found.* See the parable of the Prodigal Son, Luke 15: 11–32—especially verse 32: 'It was meet that we should make merry, and be glad: for this thy brother was dead, and is alive again; and was lost, and is found.'

Begging (II). First published in Vaughan's *Flores Solitudinis* (1654).

l. 1. *O*. The reading of 1654: *1655* reads *I* ('Aye').

127 l. 12. *the weeping lad*. Ishmael. See Genesis 21: 17.

Palm Sunday. John 12: 12–13, 'On the next day much people that were come to the feast, when they heard that Jesus was coming to Jerusalem, Took branches of palm trees, and went forth to meet him, and cried, Hosanna: Blessed is the King of Israel that cometh in the name of the Lord.'

l. 3. *green and gay*. The phrase appears in Herbert's *The Search*, l. 10.

l. 4. *King of grief*. The phrase appears in Herbert's *The Thanksgiving*, l. 1. *man of sorrow*. See Isaiah 53: 3.

l. 12. *expect with groans*. Romans 8: 22, 'For we know that the whole creation groaneth.'

l. 13. *which all at ones*. *1655* reads *which all at once*, a reading that does not appear to make sense. The printer of *1655* may have been misled by Vaughan's division of *atones*, reaching back towards the root-meaning of the word: to make one, bring into concord, reconcile (*OED*, 'at one', 'atone').

128 l. 21. *thrones and seraphins*: the titles of two of the nine orders of angels.

l. 28. *Seen long before this came to pass*. Vaughan's note at this point in *1655* cites Zechariah 9: 9, 'Rejoice greatly, O daughter of Zion; shout, O daughter of Jerusalem: behold, thy King cometh unto thee: he is just, and having salvation; lowly, and riding upon an ass, and upon a colt the foal of an ass.'

ll. 35–6. *I'll get me up . . . off many a tree*. See Herbert, *Easter*, ll. 19–20, 'I got me flowers to straw thy way; | I got me boughs off many a tree.'

l. 39. *wrong*. Probably in the old sense of 'bent'.

l. 46. *green branch . . . white robe*. Revelation 7: 9, 'a great multitude, which no man could number . . . clothed with white robes, and palms in their hands.'

129 *Jesus Weeping* (I). Luke 19: 41, 'And when he was come near, he beheld the city, and wept over it.'

ll. 5–6. *your fathers' breed . . . not Abr'am's seed*: offspring of those who worshipped the golden calf (Exodus 32: 3–4), not the descendants of Abraham. *stiff-neckèd*. See Exodus 32: 9.

l. 8. *The stones had spoke*. Luke 19: 39–40, 'And some of the Pharisees

from among the multitude said unto him, Master, rebuke thy dis-
ciples. And he answered and said unto them, I tell you that, if these
should hold their peace, the stones would immediately cry out.'

l. 10. *living water*. See John 4: 10.

l. 17. *This land*: England, as well as Jerusalem and Judea.

The Daughter of Herodias. For the story of Salome's dancing and
asking for the head of John the Baptist, see Mark 6: 17–28 and
Matthew 14: 6–11.

130 l. 9. *young sorceress; the ice*. Vaughan adds a note here in *1655*: 'Her
name was Salome; in passing over a frozen river, the ice broke under
her, and chopped off her head.'

l. 11. *his*. Vaughan adds a note here in *1655*: 'Herod Antipas.'

l. 20. *She tempts to incest*. Herod had thrown John the Baptist into
prison because he denounced Herod's marriage to Herodias, the wife
of Herod's brother: 'For John had said unto Herod, It is not lawful for
thee to have thy brother's wife' (Mark 6: 18).

Jesus Weeping (II). John 11: 35, 'Jesus wept' (at the death of Lazarus).

l. 2. *groan and groan again*. John 11: 33, 38, 'When Jesus therefore saw
her weeping, and the Jews also weeping which came with her, he
groaned in the spirit, and was troubled . . . Jesus therefore again
groaning in himself cometh to the grave.'

l. 14. *refrain*: hold back.

l. 20. *tried*: known, experienced.

131 l. 32. *without leave*: without leaving off, without stopping.

l. 49. *Lilies and myrrh*. Song of Solomon 5: 13, 'his lips like lilies,
dropping sweet smelling myrrh.'

l. 53. *swan-like*. Swans were supposed to sing as death approached.

132 *Providence*. ll. 3–6. *holy well . . . Ishmael*: another reference to the
deliverance of Ishmael: Genesis 21: 14–19.

l. 15. *A fish shall all my tribute pay*. See the story of Peter and the
tribute money, Matthew 17: 25–7.

l. 16. *The swift-winged raven . . . meat*: as the ravens brought food to
Elijah: I Kings 17: 6.

l. 18. *I knew no month but May*. See Herbert, *Affliction* (I), l. 22:
'There was no month but May.'

l. 21. *Bags that wax old*. Luke 12: 33, 'provide yourselves bags which
wax not old, a treasure in the heavens that faileth not.'

133 l. 46. *Pontic sheep*. Pliny in his *Natural History* (xxvii. 28) mentions
Pontic wormwood because the cattle that are fattened on it are

without gall. Pontus was the Roman name for the region around the Black Sea.

The Knot. It is bold of Vaughan to publish such defiant praise of the Virgin in 1655, when even moderate Protestants regarded such devotion with suspicion, as encroaching on the prerogative of Christ.

134 *The Ornament.* l. 14. *weeds*: clothing, garments.

l. 16. *the sheep-keeping Syrian maid.* Rachel. See Genesis 29: 9, 17.

l. 20. *bravest*: the best dressed.

St. Mary Magdalen. Tradition identified the Mary of John 12: 3 with the unnamed 'sinner' (presumably a prostitute) of Luke 7: 36–50, 'And, behold, a woman in the city, which was a sinner, when she knew that Jesus sat at meat in the Pharisee's house, brought an alabaster box of ointment, and stood at his feet behind him weeping, and began to wash his feet with tears, and did wipe them with the hairs of her head, and kissed his feet, and anointed them with the ointment. Now when the Pharisee which had bidden him saw it, he spake within himself, saying, This man, if he were a prophet, would have known who and what manner of woman this is that toucheth him; for she is a sinner.'

135 l. 13. *Magdal-castle.* Tradition placed Mary's inheritance in the castle of Magdala, near Bethany.

l. 21. *pistic nard.* Translated as *spikenard* in John 12: 3, 'Then took Mary a pound of ointment of spikenard, very costly, and anointed the feet of Jesus, and wiped his feet with her hair.' *pistic* is derived from a Greek word possibly meaning 'genuine' or 'pure' (*OED*).

ll. 21–4. *Why is this . . . waste?* See the associated incident in Matthew 26: 6–8, 'Now when Jesus was in Bethany, in the house of Simon the leper, There came unto him a woman having an alabaster box of very precious ointment, and poured it on his head, as he sat at meat. But when his disciples saw it, they had indignation, saying, To what purpose is this waste?'

l. 27. *Dear soul! thou knew'st.* See Herbert, *Mary Magdalene*, l. 13: 'Dear soul, she knew.'

ll. 27–8. *on earth | At their Lord's footstool.* Matthew 5: 35, 'the earth; for it is his footstool.'

l. 37. *Penitent*: an allusion to the Penitents, the name of various congregations or orders in the medieval church.

l. 50. *Who loved much and much more could move.* Luke 7: 47, 'Wherefore I say unto thee, Her sins, which are many, are forgiven; for she loved much.'

136 l. 51. *Her Art! whose memory must last.* Matthew 26: 13, 'Verily, I say unto you, Wheresoever this gospel shall be preached in the whole

world, there shall also this, that this woman hath done, be told for a
memorial of her.'

l. 69. *Go leper*. Vaughan takes Simon the Pharisee, in Luke's account,
to be Simon the leper of Matthew 26: 6 and Mark 14: 3.

ll. 69–70. *till thy flesh | Comes like a child's*. See Naaman's cure from
leprosy in II Kings 5: 14, 'then went he down, and dipped himself
seven times in Jordan, according to the saying of the man of God: and
his flesh came again like unto the flesh of a little child, and he was
clean.'

l. 72. *Who saint themselves, they are no saints*. Since the epistles of St
Paul and the book of Revelation constantly refer to the 'chosen' body
of Christians as 'saints' (meaning 'holy ones'), some of the more
radical religious groups of Vaughan's day had taken to referring to
themselves as 'the saints'.

The Rainbow. l. 3. *Shem's*. Genesis 9: 18, 'And the sons of Noah, that
went forth of the ark, were Shem, and Ham, and Japheth.'

l. 5. *When . . . Lot*. Genesis 11: 27, 'Now these are the generations of
Terah: Terah begat Abraham, Nahor, and Haran, and Haran begat
Lot.'

l. 11. *Rain gently spends his honey-drops*. See the similar wording in
Herbert's *Providence*, ll. 117–18.

137 l. 14. *the object of his eye*. Vaughan's note at this point in *1655* refers to
Genesis 9: 16, 'And the bow shall be in the cloud; and I will look upon
it, that I may remember the everlasting covenant between God and
every living creature, of all flesh that is upon the earth.'

l. 21. *the first sin was in blood*. Cain's shedding of his 'brother's blood':
Genesis 4: 8–11.

l. 22. *drunkenness*: of Noah: Genesis 9: 21.

ll. 27–8. *though both . . . did weep*: the Flood: Genesis 7: 11–12.

ll. 31–2. *bad daughters . . . their sire*: Lot's daughters: Genesis 19:
30–8. For the 'smoke' of Sodom, see Genesis 19: 24–8.

l. 37. *luctual*: mourning, sorrowful.

l. 42. *till rain turns fire*. II Thessalonians 1: 7–8, 'when the Lord Jesus
shall be revealed from heaven with his mighty angels, In flaming fire
taking vengeance on them that know not God, and that obey not the
gospel of our Lord Jesus Christ.'

The Seed Growing Secretly. Mark 4: 26–7, 'So is the kingdom of God,
as if a man should cast seed into the ground; And should sleep, and
rise night and day, and the seed should spring and grow up, he
knoweth not how.'

138 ll. 13–14. *O spread thy sacred wings . . . drop.* Malachi 4: 2, 'But unto you that fear my name shall the Sun of righteousness arise with healing in his wings.'

l. 16. *O fill his bottle! Thy child weeps*: another allusion to Ishmael: Genesis 21: 14–19.

l. 19. *blow*: bloom.

ll. 25–6. *greenness . . . winter-nights.* Compare the second stanza of Herbert's *The Flower.*

l. 27. *Vex not*: be not disturbed.

l. 30. *in one crown.* Revelation 2: 10, 'be thou faithful unto death, and I will give thee a crown of life.'

l. 33. *bait*: food, along with modern sense.

139 ll. 45–6. *catch | At*: snatch at, attempt to lay hold of.

ll. 47–8. *bear fruit . . . Reapers.* Matthew 13: 39, 'the harvest is the end of the world; and the reapers are the angels.' Mark 4: 29, 'But when the fruit is brought forth, immediately he putteth in the sickle, because the harvest is come.'

'As time one day by me did pass'. This and the next poem are probably written in memory of Vaughan's first wife.

l. 4. *curious*: carefully prepared.

l. 9. *kind*: sympathetic, well-disposed; also, related.

l. 13. *calendar*: a list or register of documents or events (along with modern meaning).

l. 16. *The Holy way.* Vaughan's typographical emphasis suggests the title of a book—a guide to holy life.

140 l. 19. *night-piece*: 'a painting or picture representing a night scene' (*OED*). *quails*: spoils, overpowers.

l. 25. *mark*: goal, target.

l. 29. *recruits*: provisions for renewal of strength.

ll. 35–6. *For whose . . . green branches . . . are bleached.* Revelation 7: 9, 'lo, a great multitude . . . stood before the throne and before the Lamb, clothed with white robes, and palms in their hands.'

l. 36. *in the Lamb's blood.* Revelation 7: 13–14, 'What are these which are arrayed in white robes? . . . These are they which came out of great tribulation, and have washed their robes, and made them white in the blood of the Lamb.'

141 'Fair and young light!' l. 10. *the surviving turtle.* The turtle-dove: a symbol of conjugal affection and constancy.

l. 37. *supplanters*: those who dispossess or cause the downfall of others.

l. 46. *For he . . . sin*. See Romans 6: 7.

142 l. 50. *spicy mountains*. Song of Solomon 8: 14, 'upon the mountains of spices'.

The Stone. Joshua 24: 27, 'And Joshua said unto all the people, Behold, this stone shall be a witness unto us; for it hath heard all the words of the Lord, which he spake unto us; it shall be therefore a witness unto you, lest ye deny your God.'

l. 24. *As loud as blood*. Genesis 4: 9–10, 'And the Lord said unto Cain, where is Abel thy brother? And he said, I know not: Am I my brother's keeper? And he said, What hast thou done? the voice of thy brother's blood crieth unto me from the ground.'

l. 28. *he that judgeth*. Vaughan's note at this point in *1655* cites John 5: 30, 45, 'I can of mine own self do nothing: as I hear, I judge: and my judgment is just; because I seek not mine own will, but the will of the Father which hath sent me. . . . Do not think that I will accuse you to the Father: there is one that accuseth you, even Moses, in whom ye trust.'

143 ll. 56–7. *his word | And not himself*. Vaughan's note at this point in *1655* cites John 12: 47–8, 'And if any man hear my words, and believe not, I judge him not: for I came not to judge the world, but to save the world. He that rejecteth me, and receiveth not my words, hath one that judgeth him: the word that I have spoken, the same shall judge him in the last day.'

The Dwelling-place. John 1: 38–9, 'Then Jesus turned, and saw them following, and saith unto them, What seek ye? They said unto him, Rabbi (which is to say, being interpreted, Master), where dwellest thou? He saith unto them, Come and see. They came and saw where he dwelt, and abode with him that day: for it was about the tenth hour.'

l. 4. *though not in story*: not told in any historical account.

144 l. 16. *My God, I mean*. See the last line of Herbert's *Misery*: 'My God, I mean myself.'

The Men of War. Luke 23: 11, 'And Herod with his men of war set him at nought, and mocked him, and arrayed him in a gorgeous robe, and sent him again to Pilate.'

l. 2. *saith holy John*. Vaughan's note at this point in *1655* cites Revelation 13: 10 (see also verse 9): 'If any man have an ear, let him hear. He that leadeth into captivity shall go into captivity: he that killeth with the sword must be killed with the sword. Here is the patience and the faith of the saints.'

l. 12. *Enact for saints.* See note on *St. Mary Magdalen*, p. 215.

l. 18. *conquerors.* Romans 8: 37, 'Nay, in all these things we are more than conquerors through him that loved us.'

ll. 21–2. *Armies thou hast . . . clothed in white.* Revelation 19: 14, 'And the armies which were in heaven followed him upon white horses, clothed in fine linen, white and clean.'

145   ll. 25–6. *The sword . . . in thy mouth.* Revelation 19: 15, 'And out of his mouth goeth a sharp sword that with it he should smite the nations.' Hebrews 4: 12, 'For the word of God is quick, and powerful, and sharper than any two-edged sword.'

ll. 27–8. *And all . . . martyrdom.* Revelation 12: 11, 'And they over-came him by the blood of the Lamb, and by the word of their testimony: and they loved not their lives unto the death.' See ll. 51–2.

ll. 29–31. *Soldiers . . . bowed the knee.* See Matthew 27: 29–30.

l. 42. *innoxious*: harmless, blameless.

l. 47. *thy throne is set.* Revelation 4: 2, 'behold, a throne was set in heaven, and one sat on the throne.'

146   *The Ass.* l. 6. *most kind.* (1) most akin, most like; (2) most favourable.

ll. 9–10. *no law . . . perfect liberty.* James 1: 25, 'But whoso looketh into the perfect law of liberty, and continueth therein, he being not a forgetful hearer, but a doer of the work, this man shall be blessed in his deed.'

ll. 39–40. *though . . . not expedient.* I Corinthians 10: 23, 'All things are lawful for me, but all things are not expedient.'

147   l. 64. *And bones rejoice, which once were broken!* Psalm 51: 8, 'Make me to hear joy and gladness; that the bones which thou hast broken may rejoice.'

The Hidden Treasure. Matthew 13: 44, 'Again, the kingdom of heaven is like unto treasure hid in a field; the which when a man hath found, he hideth, and for joy thereof goeth and selleth all that he hath, and buyeth that field.'

ll. 1–2. *the King . . . thing.* Vaughan's note at this point in *1655* cites Ecclesiastes 2: 12, 'And I turned myself to behold wisdom, and madness, and folly: for what can the man do that cometh after the king? even that which hath been already done.'

l. 4. *fire-drakes*: meteors, or will-o'-the-wisps.

l. 12. *Paths . . . the vulture's eyes.* Job 28: 7, 'There is a path which no fowl knoweth, and which the vulture's eye hath not seen.'

148 *Child-hood.* The hyphenated form of the title seems to stress the spiritual state which the speaker is striving to 'reach': to be one of the 'children of God', as in Romans 8: 16 or the passage cited below, note to ll. 35–7.

l. 7. *make my path even.* Matthew 3: 3, 'Prepare ye the way of the Lord, make his paths straight.'

ll. 14–16. *But flowers . . . medicinal then.* See Herbert, *Life*, ll. 13–15.

149 l. 27. *practice*: (1) 'usual, customary, or constant action'; (2) 'exercise of a profession or occupation'; (3) trickery, underhanded plotting (see *OED*).

ll. 35–7. *which he . . . God's face see . . . angels guard.* Matthew 18: 2–3, 10, 'And Jesus called a little child unto him, and set him in the midst of them, And said, Verily I say unto you, Except ye be converted and become as little children, ye shall not enter into the kingdom of heaven. . . . Take heed that ye despise not one of these little ones; for I say unto you, that in heaven their angels do always behold the face of my Father which is in heaven.'

l. 44. *the narrow way.* See Matthew 7: 14.

The Night. John 3: 2 (*1655* reads 'John 2. 3'), '[Nicodemus] came to Jesus by night, and said unto him, Rabbi, we know that thou art a teacher come from God: for no man can do these miracles that thou doest, except God be with him.'

ll. 1–2. *Virgin-shrine,* | *That sacred veil.* The body of Christ, 'the veil, that is to say, his flesh' (Hebrews 10: 20); the body derived from the Virgin Mary.

150 ll. 9–10. *healing wings . . . rise.* Malachi 4: 2, 'But unto you that fear my name shall the Sun of righteousness arise with healing in his wings.'

ll. 19–20. *No mercy-seat . . . nor carved stone.* Exodus 25: 17–22, 'And thou shalt make a mercy seat of pure gold . . . And thou shalt make two cherubims of gold . . . And the cherubims shall stretch forth their wings on high, covering the mercy seat with their wings . . . And there I will meet with thee, and I will commune with thee from above the mercy seat, from between the two cherubims which are upon the ark of the testimony.'

l. 29. *Christ's progress.* Vaughan's note at this point in *1655* cites Mark 1: 35, 'And in the morning, rising up a great while before day, he went out, and departed into a solitary place, and there prayed'; and Luke 21: 37, 'And in the day time he was teaching in the temple; and at night he went out, and abode in the mount that is called the mount of Olives.'

ll. 32–3. *When my Lord's head . . . drops of night.* Song of Solomon 5: 2, 'I sleep, but my heart waketh: it is the voice of my beloved that knocketh, saying, Open to me, my sister, my love, my dove, my undefiled: for my head is filled with dew, and my locks with the drops of the night.'

l. 34. *still, soft call.* Like the 'still small voice' heard by Elijah: I Kings 19: 12.

l. 35. *His knocking time.* See note on ll. 32–3; also Revelation 3: 20, 'Behold, I stand at the door, and knock.'

l. 36. *kinred*: old form of *kindred*.

151 l. 50. *A deep, but dazzling darkness*: a conception set forth by the writer of the fifth or sixth century (AD) known as Dionysius the Areopagite, or the 'pseudo-Dionysius'. His writings on the mystical approach to God had a great influence on medieval mystics and on the Spanish mystics of the sixteenth century.

Abel's Blood. l. 2. *first against a murth'rer cry.* Genesis 4: 10, 'the voice of thy brother's blood crieth unto me from the ground.'

l. 16. *deep still calleth upon deep.* See Psalm 42: 7.

l. 18. *many waters.* See Revelation 19: 6.

l. 22. *How long?* Revelation 6: 9–10, 'I saw under the altar the souls of them that were slain for the word of God, and for the testimony which they held: and they cried with a loud voice, saying, How long, O Lord, holy and true, dost thou not judge and avenge our blood on them that dwell on the earth?'

152 l. 33. *Aye. I* in 1655.

ll. 40–1. *speak better . . . Abel's doth.* Hebrews 12: 24, 'and to Jesus the mediator of the new covenant, and to the blood of sprinkling, that speaketh better things than that of Abel.'

l. 44. *Who prayed . . . kill.* Luke 23: 34, 'Father, forgive them; for they know not what they do.'

Righteousness. The theme and manner resemble Psalm 15, 'Lord who shall abide in thy tabernacle? who shall dwell in thy holy hill? He that walketh uprightly, and worketh righteousness, and speaketh the truth in his heart.' Compare also Herbert's *Constancy.*

l. 7. *turtles*: turtle-doves. *careless*: carefree.

l. 10. *meddled*: mixed with. See Ecclesiasticus 13: 1, 'He that toucheth pitch shall be defiled therewith.'

153 l. 19. *pretence*: expressed purpose.

l. 30. *pains*: an emendation: *1655* reads *prayers*.

l. 33. *his hope and Rock*. I Corinthians 10: 4, 'and that Rock was Christ.'

l. 48. *peculiar treasure*. Psalm 135: 4, 'For the Lord hath chosen Jacob unto himself, and Israel for his peculiar treasure.' Exodus 19: 5, 'If ye will obey my voice indeed, and keep my covenant, then ye shall be a peculiar treasure unto me above all people.'

155 *Tears*. l. 11. *thy poor Ass*. See *The Ass*, l. 21, 'me thy Ass'.

l. 14. *the lowest pitch*. The pitch of a falcon is the height of its flight before attacking its prey.

l. 15. *loves much*. See note on *St. Mary Magdalen*, l. 50.

Jacob's Pillow and Pillar. See Genesis 28: 11–22.

l. 1. *The Temple in thy Pillar reared*. Genesis 28: 18, 22, 'And Jacob rose up early in the morning, and took the stone that he had put for his pillows, and set it up for a pillar, and poured oil upon the top of it. . . . And [he said] this stone, which I have set for a pillar, shall be God's house.'

l. 3. *without a frown*. See Herbert, *To All Angels and Saints*, l. 2: 'the smooth face of God, without a frown'.

ll. 7–10. *This made him . . . lofty rocks*. Exodus 19: 16, 18, 'there were thunders and lightnings, and a thick cloud upon the mount . . . And mount Sinai was altogether on a smoke, because the Lord descended upon it in fire.' Also I Kings 19: 11–12, 'the Lord passed by, and a great and strong wind rent the mountains, and brake in pieces the rocks before the Lord; but the Lord was not in the wind: and after the wind an earthquake; but the Lord was not in the earthquake: And after the earthquake a fire; but the Lord was not in the fire: and after the fire a still small voice.'

ll. 22–3: an allusion to the 'darkness' that prevailed for the three hours preceding Christ's death: Matthew 27: 45–52.

ll. 23–6. *he foretold . . . nor at | Jerusalem*. John 4: 21, 23–4, 'the hour cometh, when ye shall neither in this mountain, nor yet at Jerusalem, worship the Father. . . . But the hour cometh, and now is, when true worshippers shall worship the Father in spirit and in truth: for the Father seeketh such to worship him. God is a Spirit: and they that worship him must worship him in spirit and in truth.'

156 l. 26. *with blood of beasts and fat*. See Ezekiel 44: 15.

l. 29. *proud waters*. See Psalm 124: 5.

ll. 31–2. *This little Goshen . . . hath light*. Goshen was the land where the Israelites lived while they were in Egypt. See Exodus 10: 22–3, 'And Moses stretched forth his hand toward heaven; and there was a thick darkness in all the land of Egypt three days . . . but all the children of Israel had light in their dwellings.'

l. 33. *Bethel shall have tithes (saith Israel's stone).* Genesis 28: 19–22, 'And he [Jacob] called the name of that place Beth-el ['house of God'] . . . And Jacob vowed a vow, saying . . . this stone, which I have set for a pillar, shall be God's house: and of all that thou shalt give me I will surely give the tenth unto thee.'

l. 40. *turns our captivity.* See Psalm 126: 1, 4.

ll. 43–4. *thou a brother . . . Didst fly*: Esau. Vaughan's note at this point in *1655* cites Obadiah 1: 11, but verse 10 makes the allusion clearer: 'For thy violence against thy brother Jacob shame shall cover thee, and thou shalt be cut off for ever.' Vaughan also cites here Amos 1: 11, 'Thus saith the Lord; For three transgressions of Edom, and for four, I will not turn away the punishment thereof; because he did pursue his brother with the sword, and did cast off all pity, and his anger did tear perpetually, and he kept his wrath for ever.'

l. 53. *type*: something in the Old Testament which prefigures an event, object, person, or doctrine in the New Testament.

157 *The Agreement.* l. 10. *Like morning-stars did sing.* Job 38: 7, 'When the morning stars sang together.'

l. 15. *ascendents*: those who ascend; with a play on the astrological meaning of *ascendent*: 'the point of the ecliptic, or degree of the Zodiac which at any moment . . . is just rising above the eastern horizon' (*OED*).

l. 36. *healing wings.* See Malachi 4: 2.

158 ll. 51–2. *still infinite | Thy Covenant by Christ extends.* See Hebrews 13: 20, 'the blood of the everlasting covenant', and Psalm 105: 8, 'He hath remembered his covenant for ever, the word which he commanded to a thousand generations.'

l. 58. *cathartics*: purgative medicines.

l. 68. *For I . . . to thee.* Vaughan's note at this point in *1655* cites John 6: 44, 65, 'No man can come to me, except the Father which hath sent me draw him: and I will raise him up at the last day. . . . Therefore said I unto you, that no man can come unto me, except it were given unto him of my Father.'

159 *The Day of Judgement.* l. 13. *The fields are long since white.* John 4: 35, 'Lift up your eyes, and look on the fields; for they are white already to harvest.'

ll. 29–30. *thy old enemy . . . more raging grows.* Revelation 12: 12, 'Woe to the inhabiters of the earth and of the sea! for the devil is come down unto you, having great wrath, because he knoweth that he hath but a short time.'

160 ll. 44. *Thy arm doth sleep*. Isaiah 51: 9, 'Awake, awake . . . O arm of the Lord.'

l. 46. *Make all things new*. Revelation 21: 5, 'And he that sat upon the throne said, Behold, I make all things new.'

Psalm 65. Another free paraphrase and expansion. Compare especially the third section with verses 9–13 of the KJ version.

161 l. 46. *purling*: rippling, undulating. *corn*: grain.

The Throne. Revelation 20: 11, 'And I saw a great white throne, and him that sat on it, from whose face the earth and the heaven fled away; and there was found no place for them.'

162 *Death*. l. 3. *six thousand years*: according to the widely-accepted chronology of Bishop Ussher.

ll. 12–13. *But there was One . . . to and fro*. I Peter 3: 18–20, 'For Christ also hath once suffered for sins, the just for the unjust, that he might bring us to God, being put to death in the flesh, but quickened by the Spirit: by which also he went and preached unto the spirits in prison; which sometime were disobedient.'

l. 15. *Discovered*: revealed.

l. 19. *fray*: disperse, frighten away.

l. 22. *virtues*: curative powers.

163 *The Feast*. ll. 1–2. *O come away, | Make no delay*. See the opening lines of Herbert's *Doomsday*.

l. 13. *true bread*. John 6: 32–3, 'Verily, verily, I say unto you, Moses gave you not that bread from heaven; but my Father giveth you the true bread from heaven. For the bread of God is he which cometh down from heaven, and giveth life unto the world.'

l. 19. *Aye. 1655* reads *I*.

164 l. 33. *The well, where living waters spring*. John 4: 14, 'but whosoever drinketh of the water that I shall give him shall never thirst; but the water that I shall give him shall be in him a well of water springing up into everlasting life.'

l. 50. *turtle's voice*. See Song of Solomon 2: 12.

165 *The Obsequies*. l. 19. *some wore white*. John 20: 12, 'two angels in white sitting, the one at the head, and the other at the feet, where the body of Jesus had lain.'

166 ll. 25–6. *Kerchiefs sometimes shed | To make me brave*. 'Those garments that were on one occasion shed to make me handsome.'

Vaughan is using *kerchief* in the sense of 'a covering for the breast, neck, or shoulders' (*OED*). *sometimes*: = *sometime*: 'at a certain time, on a particular occasion, in the past' (*OED*). The reference is to the grave-clothes left behind by Christ in his tomb: see Luke 24: 12 and John 20: 5–9.

167   *The Waterfall*. l. 26. *Fountains of Life, where the Lamb goes*. Revelation 7: 17, 'For the Lamb . . . shall feed them, and shall lead them unto living fountains of waters.'

ll. 30–2. *Unless that Spirit . . . quick'ning love*. See Genesis 1: 2.

l. 38. *My glorious liberty*. Romans 8: 21, 'the glorious liberty of the children of God'.

l. 40. *creeks*: inlets.

Quickness. The word means 'life, vitality'.

l. 1. *foil*. The word 'deception' (l. 3) indicates the meaning as a false or inferior gem, enhanced by foil to appear richer (see *OED*).

l. 5. *moon-like*: shifting, inconstant. *toil*: (1) labour, effort; (2) snare, trap.

l. 6. *self-posing*: self-puzzling.

l. 16. *without Eternity*. Even without the promise of immortality.

The Wreath. Compare the similar repetitive technique of Herbert's *A Wreath*.

The Queer. Title: Vaughan is using an old, apparently colloquial form of *quaerè* (see *OED*), a term that indicates the formal proposing of a question. The index of *1655* gives the title as *The Quere*.

169   l. 12. *A wing with eyes*. Revelation 4: 8, 'And the four beasts had each of them six wings about him; and they were full of eyes within.'

The Book. l. 12. *since a cover made*. Refers to the thin boards (covered with leather) used in binding books in Vaughan's day.

170   *To the Holy Bible*. l. 2. *seized of*: in possession of.

l. 15. *Cried dross for gold*: declared dross to be gold.

171   l. 26. *that pearl*. Matthew 13: 46, the 'pearl of great price'.

S. Luke chap. 2. ver. 14. Herbert closes *The Church* with this verse.

L'Envoy. Herbert closes *The Temple* with a shorter poem by this title, also in tetrameter couplets.

l. 4. *dressed in shining white*. Revelation 7: 9, 'lo, a great multitude, which no man could number . . . stood before the throne, and before the Lamb, clothed with white robes.'

l. 8. *like old clothes fold up these skies*. Hebrews 1: 10–12, 'the heavens are the works of thine hands: They shall perish; but thou remainest;

and they all shall wax old as doth a garment; And as a vesture shalt thou fold them up.'

172 ll. 21–2. *A state for which . . . and call.* See Romans 8: 19, 22.

l. 25. *Thy number*: the number of righteous souls saved: the 'train' (followers, retinue) of l. 27.

l. 30. *Thy seamless coat.* See John 19: 23.

l. 40. *solution*: dissolution.

173 l. 62. *turned our sad captivity.* See Psalm 126: 4.

Final motto. 'God lives, and the Lord Jesus Christ, and the Holy Spirit.' St Clement, quoted in *Liber de Spiritu Sancto* (chapter 29), by St Basil the Great.

Further Reading

EDITIONS

The Works of Henry Vaughan, ed. with commentary by L. C. Martin, second edn., revised and enlarged (Oxford: Clarendon Press, 1957). (First edn., 2 vols., 1914.)

The Complete Poetry of Henry Vaughan, ed. with notes by French Fogle (New York: Doubleday, 1964).

Henry Vaughan: The Complete Poems, ed. with notes by Alan Rudrum (Harmondsworth: Penguin Books, 1976; New Haven, Conn.: Yale University Press, 1981).

The Secular Poems of Henry Vaughan, ed. with notes and commentary by E. L. Marilla (Uppsala: Lundequistka Bokhandeln, 1958).

The Works of Thomas Vaughan, ed. with introduction and commentary by Alan Rudrum, with the assistance of Jennifer Drake-Brockman (Oxford: Clarendon Press, 1984).

GUIDES TO STUDY

Rudrum, Alan (ed.), *Essential Articles for the Study of Henry Vaughan* (Hamden, Conn.: Archon Books, 1987). Contains 21 essays.

Roberts, John R. (ed.), 'The Seventeenth-Century English Religious Lyric: A Selective Bibliography of Modern Criticism, 1952–1990,' in Roberts (ed.), *New Perspectives on the Seventeenth-Century English Religious Lyric* (Columbia, Mo.: University of Missouri Press, 1994), 269–321.

BIOGRAPHY

Hutchinson, F. E., *Henry Vaughan: A Life and Interpretation* (Oxford: Clarendon Press, 1947).

STUDIES

Calhoun, Thomas O., *Henry Vaughan: The Achievement of Silex Scintillans* (Newark, Del.: University of Delaware Press; London: Associated University Presses, 1981).

Clements, Arthur L., *Poetry of Contemplation* (Albany, N.Y.: State University of New York Press, 1990).

Durr, R. A., *On the Mystical Poetry of Henry Vaughan* (Cambridge, Mass.: Harvard University Press, 1962).

Friedenreich, Kenneth, *Henry Vaughan* (Boston: Twayne, 1978).

Garner, Ross, *Henry Vaughan: Experience and the Tradition* (Chicago:

University of Chicago Press, 1959). Also *The Unprofitable Servant in Henry Vaughan* (University of Nebraska Studies, NS 29; 1963).

Grant, Patrick, *The Transformation of Sin: Studies in Donne, Herbert, Vaughan, and Traherne* (Montreal: McGill–Queen's University Press; Amherst, Mass: University of Massachusetts Press, 1941).

Hammond, Gerald, 'Henry Vaughan's Verbal Subtlety: Word-play in *Silex Scintillans*', *Modern Language Review*, 79 (1984), 526–40.

Holmes, Elizabeth, *Henry Vaughan and the Hermetic Philosophy* (Oxford: Blackwell, 1932).

Lewalski, Barbara Kiefer, *Protestant Poetics and the Seventeenth-Century Religious Lyric* (Princeton, N.J.: Princeton University Press, 1979).

Low, Anthony, *Love's Architecture: Devotional Modes in Seventeenth-Century English Poetry* (New York: New York University Press, 1978).

Marcus, Leah Sinanoglu, *Childhood and Cultural Despair: A Theme and Variations in Seventeenth-Century Literature* (Pittsburgh: University of Pittsburgh Press, 1978).

Martz, Louis L., *The Paradise Within: Studies in Vaughan, Traherne, and Milton* (New Haven, Conn.: Yale University Press, 1964). Also 'Vaughan and Rembrandt: The Protestant Baroque', in *From Renaissance to Baroque: Essays on Literature and Art* (Columbia, Mo.: University of Missouri Press, 1991), 218–45.

Pettet, E. C., *Of Paradise and Light: A Study of Vaughan's Silex Scintillans* (Cambridge: Cambridge University Press, 1960).

Post, Jonathan F. S., *Henry Vaughan: The Unfolding Vision* (Princeton, N.J.: Princeton University Press, 1982).

——— (ed.), 'Special Issue on Henry Vaughan', *George Herbert Journal*, (1983–4).

Rudrum, Alan, *Henry Vaughan* (Writers of Wales; Cardiff: University of Wales Press, 1981).

Seelig, Sharon Cadman, *The Shadow of Eternity: Belief and Structure in Herbert, Vaughan, and Traherne* (Lexington, Ky.: University Press of Kentucky, 1981).

Simmonds, James D., *Masques of God: Form and Theme in the Poetry of Henry Vaughan* (Pittsburgh: University of Pittsburgh Press, 1972).